Mór Jókai, R. Nisbet Bain

Poor Plutocrats

Mór Jókai, R. Nisbet Bain

Poor Plutocrats

ISBN/EAN: 9783743330863

Manufactured in Europe, USA, Canada, Australia, Japa

Cover: Foto ©ninafisch / pixelio.de

Manufactured and distributed by brebook publishing software (www.brebook.com)

Mór Jókai, R. Nisbet Bain

Poor Plutocrats

WORKS OF MAURUS JÓKAI
HUNGARIAN EDITION

THE POOR PLUTOCRATS

Translated from the Hungarian

By

R. NISBET BAIN

NEW YORK
DOUBLEDAY, PAGE & COMPANY

COPYRIGHT, 1899, BY
DOUBLEDAY & McCLURE CO.

PREFACE

SZEGENY GAZDAGOK is, perhaps, the most widely known of all Maurus Jókai's masterpieces. It was first published at Budapest, in 1860, in four volumes, and has been repeatedly translated into German, while good Swedish, Danish, Dutch and Polish versions sufficiently testify to its popularity on the Continent. Essentially a tale of incident and adventure, it is one of the best novels of that inexhaustible type with which I am acquainted. It possesses in an eminent degree the quality of vividness which R. L. Stevenson prized so highly, and the ingenuity of its plot, the dramatic force of its episodes, and the startling unexpectedness of its *dénouement* are all in the Hungarian master's most characteristic style. I know of no more stirring incident in contemporary fiction than the terrible wrestling match between strong Juon the goatherd and the supple bandit Fatia Negra in the presence of two trembling, defenceless women, who can do nothing but look on, though their fate depends upon the issue of the struggle,—and we must go back to the pages of that unsurpassed master of the weird and thrilling Sheridan Le Fanu to find anything approaching the terror of poor Henrietta's awful midnight vigil in the deserted *csárda* upon the lonely heath when, at the very advent of her mysterious peril, she discovers, to her horror, that her sole companion and guardian, the brave old squire, cannot be aroused from his drugged slumbers.

There is naturally not so much scope for the display of Jókai's peculiar and delightful humour, in a novel of incident like the present tale as there is in that fine novel of manners: "A Hungarian Nabob." Yet even in "Szegény Gazdagok," many of the minor characters (e.g., the parasite Margari, the old miser Demetrius, the Hungarian Miggs, Clementina, the frivolous Countess Kengyelesy), are not without a mild Dickensian flavour, while in that rugged but good-natured and chivalrous Nimrod, Mr. Gerzson, the Hungarian novelist has drawn to the life one of the finest types we possess of the better sort of sporting Magyar squires.

Finally, this fascinating story possesses in an eminent degree the charm of freshness and novelty, a charm becoming rarer every year in these globe-trotting days, when the ubiquitous tourist boasts that he has been everywhere and seen everything. Yet it may well be doubted whether even he has penetrated to the heart of the wild, romantic, sylvan regions of the Wallachian and Transylvanian Alps, which is the theatre of the exploits of that prince of robber chieftains, the mighty and mysterious Fatia Negra, and the home of those picturesque Roumanian peasants whom Jókai loves to depict and depicts so well.

R. NISBET BAIN.

Contents

CHAPTER		PAGE
I.	Boredom	1
II.	A New Mode of Duelling	18
III.	An Amiable Man	29
IV.	Childish Nonsense	34
V.	She is Not for You	64
VI.	Bringing Home the Bride	79
VII.	The Cavern of Lucsia	115
VIII.	Strong Juon	142
IX.	The Geina Maid-Market	157
X.	The Black Jewelry	166
XI.	Two Tales, of which only One is True	190
XII.	The Soirées at Arad	210
XIII.	Tit for Tat	225
XIV.	The Mikalai Csarda	250
XV.	Who It was that Recognized Fatia Negra	261
XVI.	Leander Baberossy	298
XVII.	Mr. Margari	312
XVIII.	The Undiscoverable Lady	329
XIX.	The Shaking Hand	353
XX.	The Fight for the Gold	360
XXI.	The Hunted Beast	375
XXII.	The Sight of Terror	402
XXIII.	The Accommodation	416
XXIV.	Conclusion	421

POOR PLUTOCRATS

CHAPTER I

BOREDOM

"Was it you who yawned so, Clementina?"

Nobody answered.

The questioner was an old gentleman in his eightieth year or so, dressed in a splendid flowered silk Kaftan, with a woollen night-cap on his head, warm cotton stockings on his feet, and diamond, turquoise, and ruby rings on his fingers. He was reclining on an atlas ottoman, his face was as wooden as a mummy's, a mere patch-work of wrinkles, he had a dry, thin, pointed nose, shaggy, autumnal-yellow eyebrows, and his large prominent black eyes protected by irritably sensitive eyelids, lent little charm to his peculiar cast of countenance.

"Well! Will nobody answer? Who yawned so loudly behind my back just now?" he asked again, with an angry snort. "Will nobody answer?"

Nobody answered, and yet there was a sufficient number of people in the room to have found an answer between them. In front of the hearth was sitting a young woman about thirty or thirty-five, with just such a strongly-pronounced pointed nose, with just such high raised eyebrows as the old gentleman's, only her face was still red (though the favour of Nature had not much to do with that perhaps) and her eyebrows were still black; but her thin lips were just as hermetically sealed as the old man's, when she was not speaking. This young woman was playing at Patience.

In one of the windows sat a young girl of sixteen, a delicate creature of rapid growth, whose every limb and feature seemed preternaturally thin and fragile. She was occupied with some sort of sewing. At another little sewing-table, immediately opposite to her, was a red-cheeked damsel with a frightful mop of light hair and a figure which had all the possibilities of stoutness before it. She was a sort of governess, and was supposed to be English, though they had only her word for it. She was reading a book.

On the silk ottoman behind lay the already-mentioned Clementina, who ought to have confessed to the sin of yawning. She was a spinster already far advanced in the afternoon of life, and had cinder-coloured ringlets around her temples and a little bit of beard on her chin. She was no blood relation of the family but, as an ancient companion to a former mistress of the house, had long eaten the bread of charity under that roof. She was now engaged upon some eye-tormenting, fine fancy work which could not have afforded the poor creature very much amusement.

The old gentleman on the sofa used to divert himself the whole day by assembling as many human beings around him as possible and driving them to desperation by his unendurable nagging and chiding; they, on the other hand, had by this time discovered that the best defence against this domestic visitation was never to answer so much as a word.

"Of course! Of course!" continued the old gentleman with stinging sarcasm. "I know what a bore it is to be near me and about me. I see through it all. Yes, I *know* that I am an unendurable old fellow on whom not a single word should be wasted. I know well enough that you are not sitting here beside me because you like to be here. Who compels you to? I certainly shall not prevent anybody's petticoat from going away by laying hold of it. The gate is not closed. Nothing easier than to be off. Yet nobody likes the idea, eh? Ah-ha! It is possible that when the eye of old Lapussa no longer sees, the heart of old Lapussa may no longer remember. Besides, nobody can tell exactly when the old man may die. Indeed they are waiting for his death every hour—he is beyond eighty already. A most awful bore certainly. Ah ha! The old fool is unable to get up any more, he is not even able to strike anybody. If he cries out, nobody is afraid of him; but, at any rate, he has strength enough to pull the bell-rope, send for his steward, tell him to go to the office of the *alispán** there ferret out and bring back his last will and testament—and then he can dictate another will to his lawyer quite cosily at his ease."

And in order to emphasize his words more terribly, he there and then gave a tug at the bell-rope.

Yet for all that nobody turned towards him; the lady kept dealing out the cards, the young girl continued working beads into her sampler, the governess went on reading, and the old spinster was still intent upon some delicate operation with her needle—just as if nobody had spoken a word.

In answer to the bell an ancient serving-man appeared in the doorway, and the old gentleman, after waiting a little to see from the countenances of those present (he could observe them in the mirror opposite) whether his allusion to his will had produced any effect, and finding no notice taken of it whatever, said in a sharp, petulant voice: "Louis!"

The servant approached the sofa and then stood still again.

"My dinner!"

This was the end of the awe-inspiring threat.

The old gentleman observed, or rather, suspected, some slight amusement in the company present.

"Miss Kleary!" he observed irritably, "don't you observe that Henrietta is looking out of the

---

* Vice-lieutenant of the county.

window again? I am bound, Miss, to direct your attention to the fact that I consider such a thing decidedly unbecoming in a young lady."

"Dear Grandpapa.....!" began the accused.

"Silence! I did not speak to Henrietta, I spoke to Miss Kleary. Miss Henrietta is still a child who understands nothing. I neither address her nor attempt to explain anything to her. But I keep Miss Kleary in this house, I pay Miss Kleary a princely salary, in order that I may have some one at hand to whom I can explain my educational ideas. Now my educational ideas are good; nay, Miss, I think I may even say that they are very good. I will therefore beg you to do me the favour to stick to them. I know what ought and what ought not to be allowed young girls; I know that....."

The young girl's face blushed beneath the reproachful look of the old tyrant, whilst the governess rose defiantly from her place, and in order that she might wreak her anger upon some one, industriously proceeded to pick holes in Henrietta's sewing and effectually spoil her whole day's work.

Thus, it will be perceived, only one person had the right to speak; the only right the other people had was not to listen to him.

But there was someone else in the background who had better rights than anybody, and this someone now began to hammer with his fists on the door, that very door at which the oldest and most trusty domestics hardly dared to tap—began, I say, to hammer with his fists and kick with his heels till everyone was downright scared.

This was the little grandson, the old gentleman's spoiled darling little Maksi.

"Why don't you let in little Maksi?" cried the old gentleman, when he heard him. "Open the door for little Maksi; don't you know that he is not tall enough to reach the door-handle? Why don't you let him come to me when he wants to come?"

At that moment the footman opened the door and the little family prince bounded in. It was a pale little mouldy sort of flower, with red eyes and a cornerless mouth like a carp, but with the authentic family nose and the appurtenances thereof, which took up so much room as to seriously imperil the prospects of the rest of the head growing in proportion. The little favourite was wearing a complete Uhlan costume, even the four-cornered chako was stuck on the side of his head; he was flourishing a zinc sword and grumbling bitterly.

"What's the matter with little Maksi? Has anybody been annoying him?"

Grandpapa succeeded at last in making out that on running out Maksi had tripped over his sword, that his tutor had wanted to take it away, that Maksi had thereupon drawn his weapon and made the aggressor's hand smart with it, and that finally he had fled for refuge to grandpapa's room as the only place where he was free from the persecutions of his instructors.

Grandpapa, in a terrible to do, began to question him: "Come here! Where did you hit yourself? On the head, eh! Let us see! Why, it is swollen up—quite red in fact! Put some opodeldoc on it! Clementina, do you hear?—some opodeldoc for Maksi!" So the family medicament had to be fetched at once; but Maksi, snatching it from the worthy spinster's hand, threw it violently to the ground, so that the whole carpet was bespattered with it.

Nobody was allowed to scold him for this, however, as grandpapa was instantly ready with an excuse: "Maksi must not be vexed," said he. "Does not Maksi wear a sword by his side already? Maksi will be a great soldier one of these days!"

"Yes," replied the lad defiantly, "I'll be a general!"

"Yes, Maksi shall be a general; nothing less than a general, of course. But come, my boy, take your finger out of your mouth."

The English governess here thought she saw an opportunity of insinuating a professional remark.

"He who would be a general, must, first of all, learn a great deal."

"I don't want to learn. I mean to know everything without learning it. I say, grandpapa, if you've lots of money, you will know everything at once without learning it, won't you?"

The old man looked around him triumphantly.

"Now that I call genius, wit!" cried he.

And with that he tenderly pressed the little urchin's head to his breast and murmured: "Ah! he is my very grandson, my own flesh and blood."

He was well aware how aggravated all the others would be at these words.

Meanwhile the footman was laying a table. This table was of palisander wood and supported by the semblance of a swan. It could be placed close beside the ottoman and was filled with twelve different kinds of dishes. All these meats were cold, for the doctor forbade his patient hot food. The old gentleman tasted each one of the dishes with the aid of his finger-tips, and not one of them pleased him. This was too salt, that was too sweet, a third was burnt, a fourth was tainted. He threatened to discharge the cook, and bitterly complained that as he did not die quickly enough for them, they were conspiring to starve him. They might have replied that he had ordered all these things himself yesterday; but nobody took the trouble to contradict him any longer, so gradually the storm died away of its own accord and the old man, turning towards Maksi, tenderly invited him to partake of the disparaged dishes.

"Come and eat with me, Maksi, my darling."

"That I will," cried the little horror, grabbing at everything simultaneously with both hands.

"Oh, fie, fie!" said grandpapa gently. "Take Maksi out for a ride and let the lacquey go with him instead of his tutor!" The old gentleman then pushed the little round table aside and signified to the footman that he was to put all the dishes carefully away, as he should want to see them again on the morrow. The footman conscientiously obeyed this command—which was given regularly every day—and locked up all the dishes well aware that he would get a sound jacketting if he failed to produce a single one of them when required to do so.

The old man knew well enough that there was not a servant in the house who, for any reward on earth, would think of touching any food that had ever lain on his table; indeed, they held it in such horror that they used regularly to distribute it among the poor. In order therefore that the very beggars might have nothing to thank him for, he had the food kept till it was almost rotten before he let them have it. As for his own family, he had not dined at the same table with them for ten years.

It was certainly not a sociable family. For example, the old gentleman's widowed daughter, red-cheeked Madame Langai, did not exchange a single word with her father for weeks at a time. At first he had expected her to remain in the same room with him till nine o'clock every evening, dealing out cards for him or boring herself to death in some other way for his amusement. She endured it for a whole month without a word; but at last, one evening, at seven o'clock, she appeared before him in evening dress and said that she was going to the theatre.

Old Lapussa glared at her with all his eyes.

"To the theatre?" cried he.

"Yes, I have ordered a box."

"Really? Well, I hope you will enjoy yourself!"

The lady quitted him with a shrug. She knew that from that moment she would inherit a million less than her elder brother; but nevertheless she went to the theatre regularly every day, and never stirred from her box so long as there was any one on the stage who had a word to say.

The Lapussa family was of too recent an origin for the great world to take much notice of it, and the fame of its fabulous wealth went hand in hand with the rumour of a sordid avarice which was not a recommendable quality in the eyes of the true gentry. The Lapussas were, in fact, not of gentle blood at all, but simply rich. Madame Langai's elder brother, John, was notoriously the greatest bore in the town, whom nobody, from the members of his own family down to his coffee-house acquaintances, could endure for a moment. Only his father made much of him. For all his great wealth, he was very stingy and greedy; he even lent money at usury to his best friends. Our amusing little friend Maksi was this man's son. The slender, fanciful damsel, Henrietta, who appeared in that family like an errant angel specially sent there to be tormented for the sins of her whole race, was the orphan daughter of another son of old Lapussa, who had lost father and mother at the same time in the most tragical manner; they had both been drowned by the capsizing of a small boat on the Danube. Henrietta herself had only been saved with the utmost difficulty. She was only twelve years old at the time, and the catastrophe had had such an effect upon her nerves that ever afterwards she collapsed at the least sign of anger, and often fell a weeping for no appreciable cause. Since the death of her parents, who had loved her dearly, Henrietta had been obliged to live at her grandfather's house, where nobody loved anybody.

But no, I am mistaken. She had a brother, Koloman by name, who was a somewhat simple but thoroughly good-natured youth. He used to appear very rarely among his relations because they always fell foul of him. The poor fellow's sole fault was that he was in the habit of regularly selling his new clothes. Still, I am doubtful, after all, whether this can fairly be imputed to him as a fault at all, for although it was always being dinned into his ears that his family was immensely rich, he was never blessed with a penny to spend in amusing himself with his comrades, and therefore had to do the best he could to raise the wind. Another failing of Koloman's was that he would not learn Latin, and in consequence thereof he had to suffer many things. Old Lapussa and his son John indeed had no notion whatever of the

Latin tongue. The former in his youthful days had never gone to school at all, because he was occupied in building up a business. The latter had not gone to school in *his* youth because by that time his people were already rich and he considered it beneath him. The consequence was that neither father nor son had a proper idea on the simplest subjects, except what they picked up on their travels. Still that was no reason why Koloman should not learn, but as the tutor had his hands full already with little Maksi, Koloman was obliged to go to the national school in order to become a wiser man than his forbears.

Poor Henrietta often slaved away for hours at a time with her younger brother sitting at the table by her side, helping him to struggle through the genders, declensions, conjugations, or whatever else the infernal things were called; and the end of it all was that, at last, she learnt to know Latin better than Koloman, and secretly translated all his exercises from Cornelius Nepos and the Bucolics of Virgil for him.

But we must not linger any longer over these Latin lessons, for a much more important event claims our attention—Mr. John is coming home, and we must hasten forward to admire him.

Mr. John Lapussa was a perfect prototype of the whole family. His extraordinarily lanky pinched figure seemed even lankier than it was by nature because he always carried his head so high: he peered down from that elevation upon humanity at large as if there was something the matter with his eyes which prevented him from properly raising the lids. In him the dimensions of the family nose were made still more remarkable by an inordinately tiny chin and thin compressed lips. His moustache was shaved down to the very corners of his mouth, only a little mouse-tail sort of arrangement being left on each side, which was twisted upwards and dyed black with infinite skill. His costume was elegant and ultra-refined, and only differed from the fashion in being extra stiff and tight-fitting. Moreover, all the buttons of his shirt and his waistcoat were precious stones, and he had a plenitude of rings on his fingers which he delighted to show off by ostentatiously adjusting his cravat in the course of conversation, or softly stroking the surface of his superfine coat.

Mr. John entered the room without looking at a soul, and paced up and down it with his hands behind his back. Then he suddenly caught sight of his father, kissed his hand and resumed his dignified saunter. It was evident that he was bursting for some one to speak and ask him what was the matter.

Clementina was the first to speak.

"Your honour!" said she.

"What is it?" he asked, lifting his head still higher.

"I have finished the embroidery for your shirt front which your honour was pleased to command."

His honour with a haughty curl of the lip condescended to glance down upon the proffered embroidery. I am afraid Clementina was a poor physiognomist, she might have noticed from his face how utterly indifferent he was to her and her embroidery, which he regarded with puckered eyes and screwed-up mouth.

"No good. Those flowers are too big; it is the sort of thing the Wallachian peasants stitch on to their shirts." And with that he took up Clementina's scissors from the work-table and deliberately snipped into little bits the whole of the difficult piece of work which the worthy woman had been slaving away at for a week and more, finally pitching it away contemptuously while she sat there and stared at him dumfounded.

"John, John!" said the old man in mild remonstrance.

"To show me such rubbish when I am mad! When I am wroth! When I am beside myself with fury!"

"Why are you angry, and with whom?"

John went on as if he did not mean to tell the cause of his anger. He flung himself into an armchair, crossed his legs, plunged his hands into the depths of his pockets and then, starting up, began to pace the room again.

"I am furious."

"Then what's the matter?" enquired the old man anxiously.

John again flung himself into an armchair and cocked one leg over the arm of the chair: "It is all that good-for-nothing Hátszegi!" he cried. "The fellow is a villain, a scoundrel, a robber!"

"What has he done?"

"What has he done?" cried John, leaping to his feet again, "I'll tell you. Yesterday he sent word to me by his broker that he would like to buy those houses of ours in the Szechenyi Square which I have offered for sale. Wishing to save broker's expenses I went to see him myself at twelve o'clock. Surely that is the most convenient time for paying business calls. At least I have always supposed so. I entered his ante-chamber and there stood a flunkey. He told me I must wait! Told *me* forsooth—*me,* John Lapussa—that I must cool my heels in an ante-chamber, at an inn, to please that wretched Hátszegi. Very well. I waited. I sent him a message that I *would* wait. Meanwhile I found I could not sit down anywhere, for the rascal had piled dirty boots and brushes on all the chairs. Presently the rascal of a servant came back and told me that his master could not see me then, would I come back again in the afternoon— I, John Lapussa, forsooth! Absolutely would not speak to me, but told me to come again another time! Thou dog, thou wretched rascal! But wait, I say, that's all!"

At this the old man also grew excited.

"Why did you not box his ears?" cried he.

"I'll do it, and do it well. I'll not stand it.

What! send a Lapussa packing! It cannot be overlooked. I shall immediately go and find two seconds and challenge him to a duel."

"Nay, John, don't do that! Don't even box his ears in the street, but give a street-porter ten shillings to cudgel him well as he comes out of the theatre; that will be best!"

"No, I will kill him. I will shed his blood. He who insults me in a gentlemanly manner must be shown that I can revenge myself like a gentleman. I will wipe off the score with pistols—with pistols I say."

The old man and the female members of the family were duly impressed by this bragging, or rather all except Madame Langai, who was getting ready for the theatre and took no notice of the general conversation.

Mr. John was much put out by her indifference. "Matilda," he asked, "what do *you* say? Ought I not to fight, after such an insult?"

Madame Langai answered the unavoidable question with a cold smile: "I would only say that if anyone angers you another time you had better expend your wrath upon him before dinner, for if you nurse your wrath till after dinner you spoil the whole thing."

Mr. John listened to her in silence and then resumed his promenade with his hands behind his back snorting furiously. Suddenly he snatched up his cap and rushed out.

"John, John, what are you going to do?" the

old man called after him in a supplicating voice.

"You'll very soon see, I'll warrant you," and he banged the door behind him.

The old man turned reproachfully towards Madame Langai. "Why did you irritate him when he was mad enough already?" he cried. "What will you gain by his death? He has a son who will inherit everything, you know. Yes, everything will belong to little Maksi."

Madame Langai calmly went on tying her bonnet strings.

"I know what fiery blood he has," mumbled the old man. "When he is angry he will listen to nobody, and is capable of facing a whole army. We must prevent this duel somehow. And you are actually preparing to go to the theatre when things have come to such a pass? You are actually going to see a comedy!"

"The actor Ladislaus plays just the same parts on the stage as John does off the stage," replied Madame Langai bitterly. "And I am as little afraid of John's rhodomontade as I am of the result of stage duels. Don't be afraid! He'll come to no harm."

A lacquey now entered to announce that the coach was ready, and Madame Langai, adjusting her mantilla, went to the playhouse where the actors were, at least, amusing.

CHAPTER II

A NEW MODE OF DUELLING

OLD LAPUSSA always liked to have under his eye, night and day, some one or other whom he could plague and worry. Till eight o'clock every evening he was fully occupied in tormenting the whole family. Then Madame Langai went to the theatre and Henrietta and the governess had to sit down at the piano in the large drawing-room till it was time to put the child to bed. But when Clementina and the domestics had had supper and there was no longer anybody else with him, the turn of the night nurse began.

The duties of a night nurse are never very enviable or diverting at the best of times, yet penal servitude for life was a fate almost preferable to being the nocturnal guardian of old Demetrius Lapussa. The unhappy wretch who was burdened with this heavy charge had to sit at Mr. Lapussa's bed from nine o'clock at night till early the following morning and read aloud to him all sorts of things the whole time. Old Demetrius was a very bad sleeper. The whole night long he scarcely slept more than an hour at a time. His eyes would only close when the droning voice of some one reading aloud made his head dizzy, and then he would doze off for a short time. But at the slightest pause he would instantly awake and angrily ask the reader why he left off, and urge him on again.

The reader in question was a student more than fifty years old, who, time out of mind, had been making a living by fair-copying all sorts of difficult manuscripts. He was an honest, simple creature who, in his time, had tried hard to push his way into every conceivable business and profession without ever succeeding till, at last, when he was well over fifty, he was fortunate enough to fall in with an editor who happened to know that Demetrius Lapussa wanted a reader, and recommended the poor devil for the post. He knew Hungarian, Latin, and Slovack well enough to mix them all up together; German he could read, though he did not understand it, but this was not necessary, for he was not expected to read for his own edification.

This worthy man, then, grew prematurely old in reading, year out year in, aloud to Mr. Demetrius, one after another, all the German translations of French novels procurable at Robert Lempel's circulating library without understanding a single word of them. Mr. Demetrius had, naturally, no library of his own, for reading to him, in his condition, was pretty much the same as medicine, and who would ever think of keeping a dispensary on his own premises? I may add that the reader received free board and lodging and ten florins a month pocket-money for his services.

On that particular night when Mr. John flung out of the house in such a violent rage, Mr. Demetrius was particularly sleepless. I know not whether Monte Cristo, the first volume of which honest Margari happened to be reading just then, was the cause of this, or whether it was due to the old man's nervousness about the terrible things John was likely to do, but the fact remains that poor Margari on this occasion got no respite from his labours. At other times Margari did manage to get a little relief. Whenever he observed that Mr. Demetrius was beginning to draw longer breaths than usual he would let his head sink down on his book and fall asleep immediately till the awakened tyrant roused him out of his slumbers and made him go on again. But now he was not suffered to have a moment's peace.

Monte Cristo had already been sitting in his dungeon for some time when Madame Langai's carriage returned from the theatre. Then Mr. Demetrius rang up the porters to inquire whether Mr. John had also returned home. No, was the answer. At eleven o'clock Mr. John had still not returned. Meanwhile Monte Cristo's neighbour had traced the figure on the floor of the dungeon. Mr. Demetrius here demanded a fuller explanation of the circumstances. "How was that, Margari?" he enquired.

"I humbly beg your honour's pardon, but I don't understand."

"Very well, proceed!"

A NEW MODE OF DUELLING

Every time a door below was opened or shut, Mr. Demetrius rang up the porter to enquire whether Mr. John had come in, to the intense aggravation of the porter, who appeared in the door of the saloon with a surlier expression and his hair more and more ruffled on each occasion, inwardly cursing the fool of a student who had not even wit enough to send an old man asleep, and envying the other servants who at least were able to sleep at night without interruption.

And still Margari went on reading.

By this time Monte Cristo had had himself sewn up in a sack and flung into the sea as a corpse.

Would you have dared to have that done to you, Margari?" interrupted Mr. Demetrius.

"If I had a lot of money I might, begging your honour's pardon, but a poor devil like me is only too glad to live at any price," replied Margari, whose answer naturally had no relation whatever to the text, not a word of which he understood.

"You are a simple fellow, Margari; but go on, go on!"

Margari gaped violently, he would have liked to have stretched himself too, but he bethought him in time that his coat had already burst beneath his armpits, and he had no wish to make the rent still larger, so he let it alone and proceeded with his bitter labour.

By the time Monte Cristo had swum back to dry land, Margari's eyelids were almost glued to his eyes and still the old gentleman showed no sign of drowsiness. Mr. John's threat had kept Mr. Demetrius awake all night, and consequently had kept poor Margari awake too. Once or twice an unusually interesting episode excited the old man's attention, and for the time he forgot all about John's duel—for example, when Monte Cristo discovered the enormous treasure on the island—and he would then rouse up Margari and make him go and find a map and point out the exact position of Monte Cristo's island. Margari searched every corner of the sea for it, and at last looked for it on the dry land also without finding it. Tiring at length with the fruitless search he proposed, as the best way out of the difficulty, that he should write on the afternoon of the following day to Monsieur Alexander Dumas himself to explain to his honour where the island used to be and whether it still existed.

"What a blockhead you are," said the old man, "but go on, go on!"

Margari gave a great sigh and looked at the clock on the wall, but, alas! it was still a long way from six o'clock. At last, however, while he was still reading, the clock *did* strike six. Margari instantly stood up in the middle of a sentence, marked the passage with his thumb-nail so as to know at what word to begin again on the following evening, turned down the leaf and closed the book.

"Well! is that the end of it?" enquired Mr. Demetrius in angry amazement.

"I humbly beg your honour's pardon," said Margari with meek intrepidity, "there's nothing about reading *after six* in our agreement"— and off he went. Mr. Demetrius thereupon flew into a violent rage, cursed and swore, vowed that he would dismiss his reader on the spot, and as the morning grew lighter fell into a deep, death-like, narcotic sleep from which he would not have awakened if the house had come tumbling about his ears. When he did awake, about ten o'clock, his first care was to make enquiries about Mr. John. Then he sent the porter to the police station to inform the authorities that his son and Mr. Hátszegi, who were both staying at the Queen of England inn, were going to fight a duel, which should be prevented at all hazards. A police constable, at this announcement, flung himself into a hackney-coach and set off at full speed to make enquiries. Half an hour later a heyduke was sent back to the porter to tell him that either the whole affair must be a hoax, as nothing was known of a duel, or else that the two combatants must already be dead and buried, as not a word could be heard of either of them. Luckily, towards the afternoon, Mr. John himself arrived in a somewhat dazed condition, like one who has been up drinking all night. The members of the family were all sitting together as usual in Mr. Demetrius's room, listening in silence to his heckling, when the tidings of

Mr. John's arrival reached him. Demetrius immediately summoned him. He sent back word at first that he was lying down to try to sleep, which was an absurd excuse for even the richest man to give in the forenoon; on being summoned a second time he threatened to box the porter's ears; only the third time, when Clementina was sent with the message that if he did not come at once, his sick father would come and fetch him, did he respond to the call and appear before them in a pet.

"Well, thou bloodthirsty man, what has happened? What was the end of it?"

"What has happened?" repeated John with monstrously dilated eyes. "What marvel do you expect me to relate?"

"Clementina, Miss Kleary, Henrietta, retire," cried the old man; "retire, go into the next room. These are not the sort of things that children should hear."

When they had all withdrawn except Madame Langai, Demetrius again questioned his son: "Now then, what about this affair, this *rencontre* with Hátszegi; did you challenge him, did you meet him?"

"Eh? Oh—yes! Naturally. Of course I sought him out, I have only just come from him. We have been making a night of it together at the Queen of England. I can honestly say that he is a splendid fellow, a gallant. charming gentleman. He has really noble qualities. I am going to bring him here this afternoon. You shall all see him.

Even you will like him, Matilda. But now, adieu, I must really have a little sleep, we were drinking champagne together all night. Oh, he is a magnificent, a truly magnificent character."

Mr. Demetrius said not a word in reply, but he compressed his thin lips and wagged his head a good deal. Nobody made any observation. Mr. John was allowed to go to bed according to his desire. A little time after he had withdrawn, however, the old man said to Madame Langai: "What are you doing Matilda?"

"I am trying to guess a rebus which has just appeared in 'The Iris.'"

"Don't you think that what John has just said is rather odd?"

"I have not troubled my head about it one way or the other."

"I can see through it though. John wants to pay off Hátszegi in his own coin. He has invited him here this afternoon in order to keep him waiting in the ante-chamber, and then send him word that he can't see him till to-morrow. Oh! Jack is a sly lad, a very sly lad, but I can see through him. I can see through him."

* * * * * * *

Mr. John passed the whole afternoon in his father's room: he did not even go to his club. No doubt he was awaiting his opportunity for revenge. He amused himself by sitting down beside his niece, stroking her hand, admiring the whiteness of her skin, and, drawing the governess into the conversation, enquired how Henrietta was getting on with her studies, whether she had still much to learn in English and French, and whether she was not, by this time, quite a virtuoso at the piano. He insinuated at the same time that it would be just as well, perhaps, if she made haste to learn all that was necessary as soon as possible, because she was no longer a child, and when once a woman is married she has not very much time for study.

"By the way, Henrietta," he added suddenly, "have you chosen a lover yet?"

Henrietta was too much afraid of him even to blush at this question, she only glanced at him with timid, suspicious eyes and said nothing.

"Don't be afraid, sisterkin," continued Mr. John encouragingly. "I'll bring you such a nice bridegroom that even your grandpapa, when he sees him, will snatch up his crutches in order to go and meet him half-way." Here the old man growled something which John smothered with a laugh. "Yes, and if he won't give you up we'll carry you off by force."

Henrietta shuddered once or twice at her uncle's blandishments, like one who has to swallow a loathsome medicine and has caught a whiff of it beforehand.

The porter interrupted this cheerful family chat by announcing that his lordship Baron Hátszegi wished to pay his respects to Mr. Lapussa.

A NEW MODE OF DUELLING 27

Mr. Demetrius immediately raised himself on his elbows to read from Mr. John's features what he was going to do. Would he tell the lacqueys to turn Hátszegi out of the house? or would he send him word to wait in the ante-chamber, as he himself had waited at Hátszegi's, and then put him off till the morrow? Oh! John would be sure to do something of the sort, for a very proud fellow was John.

But, so far from doing any of these things, Mr. John rushed to the door to meet the arriving guest and greeted him aloud from afar in the most obliging, not to say obsequious, terms, bidding him come in without ceremony and not make a stranger of himself. And with that he passed his arm through the arm of his distinguished guest and, radiant with joy, drew him into the midst of the domestic sanctum sanctorum and presenting him in a voice that trembled with emotion: "His lordship, Baron Leonard Hátszegi, my very dear friend!"

And then he was guilty of the impropriety of introducing his guest first of all to his father and his niece, simply because they happened to be the nearest, only afterward he bethought him of turning towards Matilda to introduce her, whereupon Matilda's face assumed a stony expression like that of the marble maiden in Zampa, to the great confusion of John, who felt bound to enquire in a half-whisper: "Why, what's the matter?"

"You dolt," she whispered back, "have you not

learnt yet that the lady of the house should be introduced to her guests not last, but first?"

John's first impulse was to be shocked, his second was to be furious, but finally he thought it best to turn with a smile to Baron Hátszegi, who courteously helped him out of his embarrassment by observing: "It is my privilege to be able to greet your ladyship as an old acquaintance already. Many a time have I had the opportunity of secretly admiring you in your box at the theatre."

"Pray be seated, sir. . . !"

CHAPTER III

AN AMIABLE MAN

BARON HATSZEGI was certainly a very amiable man. He had a handsome face full of manly pride, sparkling eyes, and a powerful yet elegant figure. He moved and spoke with graceful ease, bore himself nobly, picked his words—in short, was a perfect gentleman. Mr. Demetrius was quite taken with him, although Hátszegi hardly exchanged a word with him, naturally devoting himself principally to the widowed lady who played the part of hostess. What the conversation was really about nobody distinctly recollected—the usual commonplaces no doubt, balls, soirees, horse-racing. Henrietta took no part in the talk; Mr. John, on the other hand, had a word to say on every subject, and, although nobody paid any attention to him, he enjoyed himself vastly.

When Hátszegi had departed, John, with a beaming face, asked Madame Langai what she thought of the young man.

Instead of replying, Madame Langai asked what had induced him to bring him there.

"Well, but he's a splendid fellow, isn't he?"

"You said yesterday that he was a vagabond."

"I said so, I know, but it is not true."

"You said, too, that he was a robber."

"What! I said that? Impossible. I didn't say that."

Old Demetrius here intervened as a peacemaker.

"You said it, John, you did indeed; but you were angry, and at such times a man says more than he means."

"So far from being a robber or a vagabond," replied John, "he is one of the principal landowners in the Hátszegi district. How *could* I have said such things! He has a castle that is like a fortress. He is like a prince, a veritable prince in his own domains. He is just like a petty sovereign. I must have been downright mad to call him a vagabond. . . ."

"Yet, yesterday, you would have called him out," continued Madame Langai teasingly.

"Yes, I was angry with him then, but there are circumstances which may reconcile a couple of would-be duellists, are there not?"

"Oh, certainly, if a man is a man of business before all things, or has perhaps a valuable house or two on his hands."

"This has nothing to do with business or selling houses. If you must know," he continued, lowering his voice, "it is about something entirely different, but of the very greatest importance."

"Indeed?" returned Madame Langai, "a new Alexander the Great, I suppose, who has gone forth to conquer, and who has come to look not for a house, but for a house and home perhaps?"

She thought to herself that it was some adventurer whom her brother John would palm off upon her as a husband so as to get her away from the old man.

"Something of the sort," replied John. "Yes, you have guessed half—but the wrong half."

"I am glad to hear it."

"Ah!" put in the old man sarcastically, Matilda will never marry again, I'm sure; she loves her old dad too much and feels far too happy at home to do that."

"Ho, ho, ho!" laughed John scornfully, "I did not mean Matilda, I was not thinking of her. Ho, ho, ho! Madame Langai imagines that *she* is the only person in the house whose hand can be wooed and won."

Dame Langai, with a shrug, looked incredulously round the room to see if there was anybody else who could possibly become the object of the baron's sighs. All at once her eyes accidentally encountered those of Henrietta, and immediately she knew even more than her brother John did. For she now clearly understood three things: the first was that Henrietta had taken in John's meaning more quickly than she had done, the second was that John had brought the suitor to the house on Henrietta's account. and the third was that Henrietta loathed the man.

She at once bade Miss Kleary give Henrietta an extra lesson on the piano in the adjoining room, and when they had taken her at her word and disappeared, she said to John in her usual quiet, mincing tone:

"You surely do not mean to give Henrietta to that man?"

"Why not, pray?"

"Because she is still a mere child, a mere school-girl; five years hence it will be quite time enough to provide her with a husband."

"But the girl is sixteen if she is a day."

"Yes, and delicate, sickly, and nervous."

"She will soon be well enough when she is married."

"And who, may I ask, *is* this suitor of yours. Is it not your duty, Demetrius Lapussa, as the girl's grandfather, to make the fullest enquiries about any man who may sue for your grand-daughter's hand? Is it not your duty, I say, to find out who and what he is and everything relating to him? For brother John may be very much mistaken in fancying his dear friend to be a wealthy and amiable nobleman. Whether he be amiable or not does not concern you personally, I know; but you ought certainly to know how he stands, for he may have castles and mansions and yet be up to the very ears in debt. In such a case if he is a nobleman so much the worse for you: for he will then have all the greater claim upon you. It may cost you dearly to admit a ruined baron into the bosom of your family."

John grew yellow with rage: "How dare you

talk like that of anyone you do not know?" he cried.

"Then, do you know him any better?"

But here the old man intervened:

"You're a fool, John," said he. "Matilda is right. I will send for my lawyer, Mr. Sipos. He understands all about such things and will advise us in the matter. We *must* find out how the baron stands."

CHAPTER IV

CHILDISH NONSENSE

Meanwhile Hátszegi continued to call every day, dividing his attention equally between the widow and Henrietta; and at the end of a fortnight everyone was charmed with his personal qualities. It could not be denied that he was a delightful companion, always merry, lively, frank, and entertaining. He even made the old gentleman laugh aloud more than once; in fact Demetrius Lapussa grew quite impatient if Hátszegi was five minutes late. Mr. John was more delighted with him than ever. They took walks together, invariably drove in the same carriage to the park, and John was to be seen every night in the baron's box at the theatre, talking at the top of his voice so that everybody might become aware of the fact. Nay, he succeeded, through the courtesy of his new friend, in making the acquaintance of one or two magnates who subsequently lifted their hats to John in the street and thus gratified the dearest desire of his heart.

The enquiries made about Hátszegi also proved extremely satisfactory. He was certainly sound and solid financially, had never had a bill dishonoured, had no dealings with usurers, always paid cash and was never even in temporary embarrassment, as is so often the case with most landed proprietors when the crops fail. In fact, he seemed to have unlimited funds constantly at his disposal and to be scarcely less wealthy than old Lapussa himself.

So far then, everything was as it should be, and everyone was enchanted with him personally.

But what of Henrietta, the intended bride?

Oh! she was not even consulted in the matter; it is not usual, and besides she had neither mind nor will enough to have a voice in so important a matter as the disposal of her hand. Nay, she was not even told that she was going to be married. She only got an inkling of it from various phenomena that struck her from time to time, such as the polite attentions of the baron, the whispering of the domestics, the altered attitude towards her of the various members of the family—who now addressed her in the tone you employ when speaking to a baroness that is to be. And then there was Clementina's chatter! Clementina was now for ever talking of all the sewing and stitching that had to be done for the young lady, and of the frightful quantities of linen and lace and silk that were being made up into dresses and other garments. Six seamstresses were hard at work, she said, and she was helping them and yet they had to make night into day in order to get the necessary things ready in time.

So gradually they accustomed her to the idea of

it, till at last one day Madame Langai took her aside and lectured her solemnly as to the duties of women in general and of women of rank in particular, pointing out at the same time how much such women owed to their own families for looking after and providing for them and expressing the hope that Henrietta would be duly grateful to the end of her days to *her* family—from all which she was able to gather that any opposition on her part would not be tolerated for a moment.

The day was already fixed for the exchange of the bridal rings, but the night before that day, Henrietta suddenly fell ill, and, what is more, dangerously ill, so that they had to run off for the family physician incontinently. The doctor was much struck by the symptoms of the illness and the first thing he did was to make the patient swallow a lot of milk and oil. Then he drove the servants headlong to the chemist's, and descending into the kitchen closely examined every copper vessel there by candle light, scolded the cook and the scullery maids till they were in tears, and terrified Clementina by telling her she was the cause of it all to the speechless confusion of the innocent creature. Not content with this, he made his way at once to Mr. Demetrius's room and there cross-examined everyone with the acerbity of an Old Bailey judge. What had the young lady been in the habit of eating and drinking? They must fetch what had been left over from her meals, he must see and examine everything. What had she eaten yesterday evening? Preserves? Then what sort of sugar was used, and where was the spoon? He insisted on seeing everything.

"But doctor," whined old Lapussa, "you surely don't mean to say that the child has been poisoned?"

"I do indeed, and with copper oxide too."

"How is that possible?"

"Why, simply because some of her food, preserve, for instance, has been allowed to stand too long in a copper or silver vessel and copperas has been developed."

The old man did not know enough of chemistry to understand how copperas could be developed from silver, but he was seriously alarmed.

"I hope there's no danger?" said he.

"It is a good job you sent for me when you did," replied the doctor, "for otherwise she would have been dead before morning. Copperas is a very dangerous poison, and if it gets into one's food in large quantities there is practically no antidote. A vigorous constitution, indeed, has a good chance of throwing it off; but, taking into consideration the state of the young lady's nerves and her general debility, I should say that her case was downright dangerous; anyhow she will be ailing for some time."

"Oh, doctor, doctor! and we all love Hetty so much, she is the very light of our eyes! I cannot tell you how anxious I am, on her account I should be so glad, doctor, if you could stay with her night and day and never leave the house. I would richly recompense you."

"I will do all I can, though I can't do that, and unless any unforeseen accident arise, I think I can answer for the result. But one thing I must insist upon, all these copper and silver vessels of yours must go to the devil. I'll come to-morrow and examine thoroughly the whole lot of them by daylight. The health of the family must not be endangered by such recklessness. And let me tell your honour something else. Are you aware that your honour's business-man, Mr. Sipos, who is only a lawyer and, therefore, can ill afford to do so in comparison with your honour, are you aware, I say, that he has on this very occasion sent all his copper vessels to the lumber-room?"

"On this occasion! what do you mean?" enquired the old man eagerly.

"I mean that I have just come from him and a similar case has happened in his house. His assistant—a fine young fellow, you know him, perhaps?—has also been poisoned by copperas. I have only this instant quitted him."

"What an odd coincidence."

"Very odd, indeed. Two exactly similar cases of poisoning at the same time and all because copper vessels were used and not properly cleaned."

"And how is the young man progressing? Is he out of danger?"

"Fortunately; although at the outset his was an even worse case than the young lady's. But then he is so much stronger. Well, good-bye! I will look in again to-morrow."

"But I should be so much easier, doctor, if you never left my grandchild's side."

"I would willingly do even that if I had not other patients in the town to attend to."

"Could you not entrust them to someone else?"

"Impossible. My reputation would be at stake. Besides I do not often have the chance of studying two such interesting parallel cases of poisoning at the same time."

"Very well, doctor. All I ask of you is to cure our little one."

"I hope to save the pair of them. And now I'll go up and have a look at her, and then I must return to Mr. Sipos's house. But I shall be here again in an hour or so."

And with that the old man had to be content.

During the whole course of Henrietta's illness he sent to enquire after his grandchild every hour. Clementina and an old maid-servant took it in turns to watch by her bedside. It was strictly forbidden to leave Henrietta alone for an instant, and Mr. Demetrius gave special orders that her brother Koloman was not to be allowed to approach within six paces of her bed because he was sure to bring cold air into the room, or convey to her surreptitiously something which she ought not to have and behave like a blockhead generally. So he was obliged to keep his distance.

At last when weeks and weeks had flown by,

God and blessed nature helped the doctor to triumph over the effects of the poison. Henrietta slowly began to mend. She was still very weak, but the doctor assured them that she was quite out of danger and that the little capricious fancies of convalescence might now be safely humoured.

Madame Langai, in the doctor's presence, asked the sick girl whether there was anything in particular she would like, any food she fancied, any pastime she preferred.

The pale, delicate-looking child languidly cast down her eyes as if she would say: "I should like to lie in the grave—deep, deep, down." But what she really did say was: "I should like to read something. I feel so dull."

"That I cannot allow," said the doctor, "it would make your head ache, but I have no objection to someone reading to you some nice, amusing novel, Dickens's "Pickwick Papers," for instance, or a story of Marryat's, something light and amusing, I mean, which will not excite you too much."

"I should like that," said Henrietta and the choice fell on the "Pickwick Papers." But as the English governess complained that she could never read aloud for ten minutes at a time without growing hoarse and Clementina's eyes were too weak for any such office, it was suggested that Margari should be asked to submit to this extra sacrifice, and Clementina succeeded in persuading him to do so by promising him a liberal reward.

So she brought him back with her and seated him behind a curtain so that he could not see the invalid (that would have been scarcely proper), and put the book into his hand.

But scarcely had Margari struggled through a few lines when Henrietta again became fidgety and said she longed for something to eat. The good-natured Clementina jumped with joy at this sign of returning appetite, and asked her what she would like and how she would like it. Henrietta thereupon directed her to have prepared a soup of such a complicated character (only the morbid imagination of an invalid could have conceived such a monstrosity), that Clementina felt obliged to descend to the kitchen herself to superintend its concoction herself, for it was certain that any servant would have forgotten half the ingredients before she could get down stairs.

Scarcely had Clementina shut the door behind her when Henrietta interrupted Margari's elocution.

"For Heaven's sake, come nearer to me," she said, "I want to speak to you."

The worthy man was so frightened by this unexpected summons that he had half a mind to rush out and call for assistance. He fancied that the young lady had become delirious—it was such an odd thing to ask him to draw nearer. But the sick girl, pressing together her trembling hands, looked at him so piteously that he could hesitate no longer but approached her bedside.

Henrietta did not scruple to sieze the hand of the embarrassed gentleman.

"For God's sake, help me, my good Margari," she whispered. "I am plagued by an anxiety which prevents me from closing my eyes. Even here when I sleep it follows me into my dreams. You can free me from it. In you alone have I confidence. You suffer in this house as much as I do. You have no cause to torment or persecute me. Will you do what I ask you, my dear, good Margari?"

It occurred to Margari that the young lady was wandering in her mind, so to humour her, he promised to do whatever she asked him without hesitation.

"I will be very good to you, I will never forget all my life long the kindness you are about to do me."

"Your humble servant, Miss! but you have always been good to me. As far as I can remember, while the others took a delight in vexing me, you were the only one who always took my part. I don't forget that either. Command me! I will go through fire and water for you."

"Look, then!" said the girl, drawing from her bosom a little key attached to a black cord, "this is the key of my toilet casket. Open it and you will find a bundle of documents tied together with a blue ribbon, take them. All through my illness I trembled at the thought that they might ransack my things and find them, and when I came to myself I was worrying myself with the idea that I might perhaps have spoken about these papers in my delirium. Oh! it would have been frightful if my relations had seized them. Take them, quickly, before Clementina returns. I must conceal everything, even from her."

Margari accomplished the task with tolerable dexterity. He only broke the looking-glass while he was opening the casket, and that was little enough for him. There the documents were right enough, nicely tied together.

And then Henrietta seized his hand and pressed it so warmly and looked at him with her lovely, piteous, imploring eyes—a very lunatic might have been healed by such a look.

"I know you for an honourable man," continued she, "promise me not to look at these papers, but give them to my brother Koloman, he will know what to do with them. You will do this for my sake, dear Margari, will you not? It is just as though one of the dead were to come back to you from the world beyond the grave and implore you, with desperate supplications, to free its soul from a thought which rested upon it like a curse and would not let it rest in the grave."

Margari shuddered at these words. A corpse that returns from the world beyond the grave! This young gentlewoman certainly had a terrifying imagination. Nevertheless he swore by his hope of salvation that he would not bestow a glance upon the papers, but would give them to young Koloman.

"Hide them, pray!"

And indeed it was high time that he should bestow them in the well-like pocket of his long coat, for Clementina's steps were already audible in the adjoining chamber. When she appeared, however, he was sitting behind the curtain again, reading away as if nothing had happened.

When the clock struck four, at which time Koloman usually returned from school, Henrietta said to Margari that she had had enough of romance-reading for that day, but thanked him for his kindness and asked him to come again on the morrow if he would be so good. Margari protested that he should consider it the highest honour, the greatest joy. He would willingly read even English to her, if she liked, and without any special honorarium either, and then off he went to seek young Koloman.

Now it so happened that young Koloman did not come home at the usual time that day, and Margari after looking for him in vain became very curious as to the contents of the packet entrusted to him. What sort of mysterious letters could they be which Miss Henrietta was afraid of falling into the hands of her family. Hum! how nice it would be to find out!

The packet was tied up—naturally! But it was possible to undo and then retie the knots in just the same way as before, so that nobody would be any the wiser. To an honourable man, indeed, the mere knowledge that another's secret was concealed therein which he was bidden to guard would have been as invincible an impediment as unbreakable bolts and bars; but the worthy fellow reassured himself with the reflection that, after all, he was not going to tell anybody the contents of these documents, and he so very much longed to know what it could be that Miss Henrietta was so anxious to hide away, and old Lapussa would so much like to find out. As if he would ever betray the secret of such a nice, kindly creature to such an old dragon! Why, he would rather have his tongue torn out than betray it!—but know it he must and would!

So he locked himself up in his little room on the third storey, and very cautiously opened the bundle which was enwrapped in I know not how many folds of paper and greedily devoured the contents of the various documents.

But how great was his fury when, instead of the expected secrets, he found nothing but dull Latin exercises, wearisome rhetorical commonplaces on such subjects as the charms of spring and summer, the excellence of agriculture, the advantages of knowledge, the danger of the passions, and similar interesting themes. He was just about to tie the bundle up again, when it occurred to him to read one of these tiresome dissertations to the end, just to see what sort of style the young scholar affected. And now a great surprise awaited him, for he found that after the first five or six lines the theme suddenly broke off and there followed something altogether different, which though also written in the Latin tongue had nothing whatever to do, either with the beauties of spring or the excellencies of agriculture, but was, nevertheless, of the most interesting and engrossing character.

Now, indeed, he read every one of the exercises from beginning to end, and, when he had done so, he clearly perceived that if old Demetrius Lapussa had very particular reasons for ferreting out these things, Miss Henrietta had still greater reason for concealing them.

After having neatly tied up the packet again, he bethought him what he had better do next. Miss Henrietta had confided the secret to his safe-keeping, but Mr. Demetrius had commanded him to keep an eye upon Koloman and his Latin exercises —which of them had the best right to command in that house? But was it right to divulge a secret? Ah! that was another question. It is true that, as a general rule, it is wrong to betray secrets; yet, it is nevertheless true, that to betray a secret that ought to be known is at least justifiable. Moreover, was it not a Christian duty to let the grandfather know as soon as possible what extraordinary things his granddaughter was turning over in her noddle? And finally—there was money in it!—good solid cash! If old Lapussa did not choose to pay a price for it, and a liberal price too, he should be told nothing at all and Margari would show the old miser that he had a man of character to deal with. For after all poor Margari had to live, and this was worth as much as a thousand florins to him or its equivalent anyhow. Surely Miss Henrietta could not be so unreasonable as to expect poor Margari to chuck such a piece of good fortune out of the window, especially as she had given him nothing herself.

At that moment someone knocked at the door and enquired whether Mr. Margari was there.

Margari was so frightened that he bawled out: "No, I am not!"—so of course he was obliged to open the door, but he concealed the packet of letters in his pocket first.

It was the lacquey who came to ask whether Mr. Margari was aware that it was past seven o'clock; he must come and read to the old gentleman.

Margari could not endure to hear the domestics speaking to him familiarly.

"Seven o'clock! What do you mean?" said he. "Am I bound to know when it is seven o'clock? Am I a clockmaker or a bell-ringer? If your master wants me to know what a clock it is, let him send me, not a lacquey, but a gold repeater watch!"

And salving his wounded dignity with these and similar effusions, Margari trotted alongside the lacquey to the room of Mr. Demetrius, to whom he immediately notified the change in the situation by sinking down into a soft and cosey arm-chair instead of sitting down on the edge of the hard leather-chair, expressly provided for him.

Demetrius measured him from head to foot with his terrible eagle eyes and observed in an even more stridently moral voice than usual: "Well, Margari, when are we going to have our novel reading?"

"We will have our reading presently, but it won't be a novel to-day."

"What do you mean, sir?"

"I humbly beg to remind your honour that you were pleased to commission me to lay hands upon certain Latin exercises of your grandson Koloman. I humbly beg to inform you that they are now in my possession."

"Oh!" said old Lapussa, with a forced assumption of *sang froid,* "you may give them to me to-morrow, I will look them through."

"Crying your honour's pardon, they are in Latin."

"Well, I can get someone to look them through for me."

"I beg humbly to represent that it would not be well to put them into anybody's hands, for strange things are contained therein."

"What!" cried the old man angrily, "you don't mean to say *you* have looked into them?"

"Yes, I have read them all through."

"I did not tell you to do that."

"No, but you were graciously pleased *not* to forbid me to do so. Now, I know everything. I know the cause of the young lady's illness. I know why she does not wish to become the wife of Count Hátszegi. Nay, I even know what will happen in case she does. I know all that I say—and here it is in my pocket."

"And what presumption on your part to read other people's letters!"

"I beg your honour's pardon, but it is not presumption; I only wanted to know the value of the wares I have obtained for your honour. I wanted to know whether they were worth one florin, two florins, a hundred florins, a thousand florins, lest you should do me the favour to say to me: 'look, ye, Margari, my son, here are some coppers, go and drink my health!'—and so get the better of me."

"You are becoming impertinent! Do you want me to ring for the footman?"

"Pray do not give yourself the trouble! If you are determined to take the documents away from me by force I will fling them into the fire that is burning there on the hearth before the footman can come in and there will be an end to them."

"Then it is money you want, eh? How much?"

This question made Margari still more bumptious.

"How much do I want? A good deal, a very good deal, I can tell you. In fact I cannot tell at present how much."

But then he suddenly reassumed his obsequious

cringing mien and added: "I tell you what, your honour, procure me some petty office at Count Hátszegi's. I don't care what it is, so long as I get a life-long sinecure—suppose we say his bailiff, or his librarian, or his secretary? A single word from your honour would do it."

An idea suddenly occurred to Mr. Demetrius.

"Very good, Margari, very good. So it shall be. I give you my word upon it—you shall be Hátszegi's secretary."

"But it must be life-long. I humbly beg of you, it must be till the term not of his but of my natural life."

"Yes, yes, till the term of your natural life."

"But if he won't have it?"

"I'll pay you myself. You shall receive your regular salary from me without including whatever you may get over and above from him. Will you be satisfied with a yearly salary of three hundred florins with your board and keep?"

At these words Margari's breath failed him. It was not without difficulty that he put the rapacious question: "Will your honour do me the favour to give me this promise in writing?"

"Certainly! Bring writing materials and I will dictate it to you on the spot."

And so an agreement was duly drawn up whereby Mr. Margari, in consideration of a yearly salary of 300 florins to be punctually sent to him at the beginning of every quarter, undertook in his capacity of secretary to Baron Hátszegi, to keep his Honour Demetrius Lapussa informed of all that he saw and heard at the residence of that gentleman, Henrietta's future husband, and this obligation of maintaining Margari was to be transferred on the death of Mr. Demetrius to his son John. And no doubt Mr. Demetrius knew very well what he was about.

This document signed and sealed, Mr. Margari, with the greatest alacrity, produced the Latin exercises in question, first of all, however, respectfully kissing the hand of his patron.

It took till midnight to read and translate all these documents one by one. Mr. Demetrius was very well satisfied with the result, that is to say so far as concerned the fidelity of the translation, —with the tenor of the original text he had not the slightest reason to be pleased.

When, shortly after midnight, these revelations were concluded, Mr. Demetrius commanded Margari to go up into his room and have a complete translation of all this Latin rigmarole written down in honest Hungarian by the morning and to encourage him in his task he gave him two guldens and an order on the butler for as much punch as he could drink. By the morning all the punch was drunk, but the translation also was finished, to the tune of bacchanalian songs which Margari kept up with great spirit all night long.

* * * * * * *

Next day, punctually at the appointed hour, the lawyer, Mr. Sipos, appeared at the house of the

Lapussas, with the necessary documents neatly tied up with tape, under his arm as usual; he was not like our modern lawyers who carry their masterpieces in portfolios as if they are ashamed of them. The only persons in the reception room besides the old man, were Madame Langai and Mr. John. Henrietta, still an invalid, had been allowed to take a stroll to the woods near the town in order to visit her favourite flowers once more and possibly take leave of them for ever. She had received no invitation-card for this lecture. Why, indeed, should a bride know anything of her bridegroom's biography before marriage! The lawyer took his place at the table, untied his pile of documents and began to read.

It appeared from these documents that the founder of the Hátszegi family, the great grandfather of the present baron, was one Mustafa, who had been a Defterdar* at Stamboul, and had used his unrivalled opportunities for making money so well that he found it expedient to fly from Jassy to Transylvania, where he made haste to get baptized and naturalized. His son, now an Hungarian nobleman, cut a fine figure at court and gallantly distinguished himself in the Turkish wars against his former compatriots, his exploits winning for him the estate of Hidvár and the title of baron. His son again was a miser of the first water who could be enticed neither to court nor into the houses of his neighbours. He was con-

---

*The chief of the financial department in the Turkish vilagets.

CHILDISH NONSENSE

tinually scraping money together and was not over particular in the choice of his scraper. By adroit chicanery he acquired possession of the gold mines of Verespatak, which he exploited with immense advantage, and by means of money lending and mortgages got into his hands the vast estate of Hátszegi in the counties of Hunyad and Feher, so that when he died it took thirty heavy wagons to convey his ready money in gold and silver alone from the Vadormi caverns, where he had concealed it to the castle of Hidvár, which his only son, Leonard, chose as his residence after his father's death. All these details were certified by unimpeachable documents in schedules B. C. and D.

Moreover, the blood of many nationalities circulated in the veins of Baron Leonard. The Defterdar himself was a Turk of Roumelian origin, whose only son was the child of his Hindu concubine. He again married the daughter of a Polish countess at the court of Vienna. The wife of Baron Leonard's father was a wallachized Hungarian lady, whom he married for her wealth. It was not wonderful, therefore, if the noble baron possessed the qualities of five distinct races. Thus he had something of the voluptuousness of the Turk, the ostentation of the Hindu, the flightiness of the Pole, the foolhardiness of the Hungarian, and the obstinacy of the Wallach.

"For, I speak of his faults first," the lawyer proceeded, "because I consider that they outweigh his good qualities. That the baron is a rich man is evident from the accounts and inventories classed under schedule E; that the baron is a handsome man is evident from the photograph under schedule H; that the baron is physically sound is clear from the certificates annexed to schedules I and K, one of which is supplied by his physician and the other by his hunting comrades. Those who require nothing from a man save health, wealth, strength, and beauty, will of course consider him fit and proper to make a woman happy. Yet having regard to the following facts (1) that the aforesaid baron is not merely unstable in love affairs but capricious to the verge of eccentricity, and a winebibber and gourmand to boot; (2) that he is as vain as an Indian prince who takes unto him a wife for the mere pomp and show of the thing; (3) that he is violent and brutal, sparing nobody in his sudden fits of passion and, as the documents testify, has frequently inflicted mortal injuries on those who have come in his way while he was in an ill-humour; (4) that he has an odd liking for rowdy adventures, which do not reflect much credit upon him; and (5) that, according to the whispers of those nearest to him there is a strange mystery pervading his whole life, inasmuch as mysterious disappearances, which nobody can make head or tail of, occupy an incalculable number of his days and weeks which remain unaccounted for, and make a pretty considerable hiatus in every year of his life—taking all these things into consideration, I am constrained to give it as my opinion that I do not consider such a man a fit and proper husband for such a tender, sympathetic young lady as the Miss Henrietta in question, and let the world if it likes consider such a match as the greatest piece of good fortune imaginable, I, for my part, would nevertheless call it a calamity to be avoided at any price. And now would you do me the honour to examine the original documents I have brought with me as exhibits in corroboration of my statements—though I would mention," he quickly added, perceiving that Madame Langai had greedily clutched hold of them, "that among those documents there are sundry by no means suited for a lady's perusal."

"When I come across any such I will pass them over," said she. Of course these were the very passages she proceeded to search for straight away.

Meanwhile Mr. Demetrius also had drawn a packet of papers from underneath the cushions of his sofa and handed them to Mr. Sipos.

"Then you do not advise me to give Henrietta to Baron Hátszegi to wife? Good! And now, perhaps, while we run through the exhibits and schedules, perhaps you'll be so good as to cast your eye over these papers. I don't think they will bore you."

These documents, by the way, were the Latin documents discovered by Mr. Margari—*in natura*.

Mr. John was marching pettishly up and down

the room, and Madame Langai was reading her documents with the greatest attention so that nobody observed the surprise, the confusion reflected in the countenance of the lawyer as he looked through the fatal Latin manuscripts. He kept shaking his head and twisting his moustache right and left, fidgeted in his armchair, and the beads of perspiration which stood out on his forehead gave him enough to do to wipe them away with his pocket-handkerchief; at last he had read the papers, and then he laid the whole bundle on the table and stared silently before him like one whose reason for the moment had no counsel to give him.

Just about the same time Madame Langai had completed the perusal of *her* documents, and now she too seemed to be in an extreme state of agitation. During the course of her reading, she had been unable to restrain herself from exclaiming at intervals: "the monster! the scoundrel!"

Mr. Demetrius had been amusing himself all this time by carefully observing the various mutations of expression in the faces of the readers, which certainly afforded considerable entertainment to an onlooker with any sense of humour.

When every document had produced its expression, he remarked in a soft gentle voice: "Well, my daughter, what do *you* think of the affair?"

Madame Langai clapped to her eyeglass and, with the air of one who had made up his mind once for all, replied instantly: "I would not allow

CHILDISH NONSENSE

a decent chambermaid to become Baron Hátszegi's wife, let alone a Henrietta Lapussa."

"And what is your opinion, Mr. Lawyer?" enquired the old man turning to Mr. Sipos.

"I?" replied the honest man, visibly perturbed, with a voice full of emotion: "I would advise that the young lady should be married to the baron as quickly as possible."

Madame Langai regarded him with wide-open eyes.

"What! After all that is in these papers?"

"No, after all that is in those other documents."

"What are they?" cried Madame Langai pouncing upon them incontinently and extremely vexed, the next moment, to find them all written in Latin. She perceived that they were Koloman's exercises, and that was all. She did not understand their connection with the case in point.

"I'll take those documents back please," said old Demetrius, stretching out a skinny hand towards them. "They will be of use to us though I have a translation of them besides. Then, you think, Mr. Lawyer, it will be as well to marry Henrietta to the baron, eh? Very well! Let me add that on the day when Henrietta goes to the altar with Baron Leonard, I will make you a present of all this scribble. Till then I shall require them. Do you understand?"

Mr. Sipos was completely beaten; you might have knocked him down with a feather. He had never been so badly worsted in his professional capacity. Madame Langai would have besieged him with questions, but he avoided her, put on his hat and departed.

Madame Langai thereupon turned to her father: "What is the cause of this wondrous change?" she cried. "What secrets do those miraculous papers contain?"

Mr. Demetrius tucked the documents in question well beneath him and replied: "They contain secrets the discovery whereof will be a great misfortune and yet a great benefit to the parties concerned."

"Have they any connection with Henrietta's wedding?"

"They have a direct bearing thereupon, and, indeed, necessitate it!"

"Poor girl!" sighed Madame Langai.

*   *   *   *   *   *   *

Mr. Sipos passed by his own dwelling three times before he knew that he had reached home, so confused was he by what he had just learnt. When he *did* get inside the house he walked for a long time up and down his consulting room as if he were trying to find a beginning for a business he would very much have liked to be at the end of. At last he gave the bellrope a very violent pull and told the clerk who answered the bell to send him his assistant, Mr. Szilard, at once.

Szilard appeared on the very heels of the messenger. His was one of those faces which women never forget. There was ardent passion in every feature and the large flaming black eyes, which spoke of courage and high enthusiasm, harmonized so well with the wan hue of the pallid face.

"Well, my dear fellow, do you feel quite well again now?" asked Mr. Sipos in a tone of friendly familiarity; "did the doctor call to see you to-day?"

"I have no need of him, there's nothing the matter with me."

"Nay, nay! Not so reckless! You have been working again, I see. You know the doctor has forbidden it."

"I only work to distract my thoughts."

"You should seek amusement rather. Why don't you mix in society like other young men? Why don't you frequent the coffee-houses and go to a dance occasionally? Why, you slave away like a street-porter! Young blood needs relaxation."

"Oh, I am all right. My dear uncle, you are very kind, but you worry about me more than I deserve."

"That is my duty, my dear nephew. Don't you know that your poor father confided you to my care on his death-bed, bade me be a father to you. Don't you remember?"

"I do," replied the young man, and catching hold of his guardian's hand he pressed it, murmuring in a scarcely audible voice: "You have indeed been a second father to me!"

But Mr. Sipos tore his hand passionately from the young man's grasp and said in a somewhat rougher tone: "But suppose your dead father were to say: 'That is not true! You have *not* watched over my son as a father should! You have lightly left him to himself. He was in danger and you were unaware of it. He hovered on the edge of the abyss and you were blind and saw nothing. And if God and my dead hand had not defended him, he would have become a suicide and you knew it not—wherefore?' "—

The young man trembled at these words, he grew even paler than before and gazed with a look of stupefaction at his chief. Then the old man approached him, and took him by the hand as if he would say: "I am going to scold you, but fear nothing. I am on your side."

"My dear Szilard," said he, "don't you recollect that when you were a little child and did anything you should not have done, and your father questioned you about it, did he not always say to you: 'when you have done wrong and are ashamed to confess it, keep silence! press your teeth together! but don't lie, don't deny it, never think of taking refuge behind any false excuse, for your name is Szilard,* and cowardice does not become the bearer of such a name!' You understood him. You acted as he would have had you act. And now I also would remind you once more that you were christened Szilard and I ask you therefore

---

*Strong, firm.

CHILDISH NONSENSE 61

to listen calmly to what I am about to say to you. Don't interrupt, don't attempt to deceive me. If you don't want to answer my questions, simply shake your head! And now sit down, my son! You are still barely convalescent. Your head is weak and what I have to say to you might very well make it reel again."

Then the old lawyer tenderly pressed the youth into a chair and sighing deeply, thus continued: "You fell in love with the daughter of a great family and she with you. You got acquainted at a dance and the intimacy did not stop there. Every conceivable obstacle intervened between you, but love is artful and inventive and you found a way. The rich girl had a neglected brother whom his relations sent to the grammar school and the rascal frequently took refuge with me, the family attorney, when he was ill-treated at home, and here you came across him. You cared for him and explained to him the difficulties in his lessons which he was unable to do for himself. The boy grew very fond of you. He spoke to you of your beloved, and he spoke to her of you, and he was always praising each of you to the other. The grandfather, the uncle, the aunt, the governess, the domestics who never took their eyes off the girl for an instant, had no idea that she was already involved in a love affair. But amazing is the ingenuity of love and lovers! You knew that none of the older members of the family understood the classical language of the orators, and the girl loved so dearly that she did not consider it too great a labour to learn a dead tongue which could be of no further use to her in order to be able to say to her beloved: *Ego te in aeternum amabo!* One must admit that that was a great and noble sacrifice. Every day you corresponded with each other. Before school time the girl dictated his lessons to her young brother, beginning with the usual scholastic flowers of rhetoric but ending in the passionate voice of love, and after school was over, you, in your turn dictated a similar lesson for the lad to carry back with him. Naturally, *this* lesson book he *never* took to school with him; you kept the other here, the genuine one which he had to show to his masters. And this ingenious smuggling was carried on beneath the very eyes of the family without their perceiving it. Yet at last it *was* discovered. This very day, only an hour ago, the old head of the family placed these papers in my hands that I might read them, informing me at the same time that he had already read a translation of them. Terrible were the things I discovered in these papers. The appearance of a rich and noble suitor who, according to the notions of the world, was just made for the girl, frustrated all your plans of waiting patiently for better times. The family forced this union upon the girl. You, in your despair, racked your brain as to what you should do. At first you resolved upon an elopement, but the redoubled vigilance with which every step of the young girl was watched made this impossible. Then a black and terrible thought occurred to you both. You resolved to kill yourselves—it was your one remaining means of deliverance. Yes, you resolved to kill yourselves at once, on the self-same day, in the self-same manner. For many days you deliberated together as to the best way of accomplishing your design. Great caution was necessary. You had to pick your words lest the little brother who wrote them down from dictation should have guessed your intentions. The girl asked you, at last, to send her a book on natural science. You sent it to her. She, with the help of it tried to find out what sorts of poisons could be most easily procured. For two whole days you deliberated together as to the best way of obtaining matches, the phosphorus of which is the most efficacious of poisons. But in vain. In great houses only the domestics have charge of the matches, it was impossible to get any. At last the girl hit on an expedient. She discovered that if you put a copper coin in a glass dish and pour strong vinegar over it, verdegris will be formed and verdegris is poison. Your minds were at once made up. The girl prepared poison for herself and taught you to do the same. . . Merciful Heaven! what notions children do get into their heads to be sure."

CHAPTER V

SHE IS NOT FOR YOU

Up to this moment the youth had listened to the lecture in silence, but now he arose and said in a calm clear voice: "'Tis all true; it is so!"

"I should say it was all very bad, very bad indeed!" said the lawyer vehemently, as if completing a broken sentence. "What! Children to meditate suicide because things in this world don't go exactly according to their liking! Have you never regarded the affair from its practical side? Did you imagine that the girl's relations would support you? And would you yourself endure to be their pensioner, their butt, the scorn of the very domestics, for a poor son-in-law is the standing jest of the very flunkeys—you ought to know that!"

Szilard's face burned like fire at these words, but the old man hastened to soothe him.

"No, you could never reconcile yourself to that, I am sure. But you thought, perhaps, that the girl might descend to your level and share your poverty. There are in the world many a poor lad and lass who endow one another with nothing but their ardent love and yet make happy couples enough. So, no doubt, you argued, and herein lies the fallacy that has deceived you. If you had been enamoured of a poor girl, I should have said: it is rather early to think of marriage, but if it be God's will, take her! Work and fight your way through the world where there is room enough for every one. The lass, too, is used to deprivation, and you are also. She will be content with little. She can sew, she will do your cooking for you, and, if need be, your washing likewise! She can make one penny go as far as two. When there is a lot to do she will sing to make the work lighter, and when your supper is slender, her good humour and her loving embraces will make it more. But my dear boy! how are you going to make a poor housewife out of a girl who has been rich? How can she ever feel at home in a wretched, out-of-the-way shanty, where she will not even have you always by her side, for you will have to be looking after your daily bread? She will say nothing, she will make no complaint, but you will perceive that she misses something. She will not ask you for a new dress, but you will see that the one she wears is shabby and it would break your heart to reflect that you have fettered the girl you love to your step-motherly destiny, and your manly pride would one day blush for the recklessness which led you to drag her down with you."

"My dear guardian," said Szilard, "to prove to you that I did think of all these things let me tell you that I have put by from my salary and commissions enough to enable us to live comfortably for at least a twelvemonth. For a whole year I have lived on two pence a day in order to save, and during all that time I am sure you have not heard from me one word of complaint."

Mr. Sipos was horrified. It was an even worse case than he had imagined. What! to live for a whole year on two pence a day in order to scrape together a small capital for one's beloved! It would be very difficult to cure a madness which took such a practical turn as this!

"But my dear boy!" he resumed, "what is the good of it all? What can you do now that your secrets are discovered? It would have served you right if the girl's parents had proceeded against you on a charge of murder, for you were an accomplice in this poisoning business; but I am pretty sure they will only threaten to do so in case she refuses the baron. And what, pray, can you do in case they thus compel her to become his wife?"

"Whoever the baron may be," rejoined Szilard, "I suppose he is at least a gentleman; and if a woman looks him straight in the face on the wedding day and says to him: 'I cannot love you because I love another and always will love another,' —I cannot think he will be so devoid of feeling as to make her his wife notwithstanding."

"And if she does not say this, but voluntarily gives him her hand in order to save you from the persecutions of her family, what then?"

"Hearken, my dear guardian! She may be compelled to write to me that she loves me no more and I must forget her, but I shall not believe it till she pronounces or writes down a word the meaning of which only we two understand and nobody else in the world can discover. So long as this one word does not get into the possession of a third person, I shall know that she has not broken with me and no power in this world shall tear her from my heart. She may be silent, because she is not free to speak; she may speak because she is commanded to speak; yet, for all that, this religiously guarded word tells me what she really feels—and what no other human intelligence can understand. If you like, my dear guardian, you may betray this confession of mine to Henrietta's relatives and they will torment the girl till they get her to pronounce the mysterious word which once pronounced will burst the bonds that unite us. She will be driven to say something. But oh! women who love are very crafty. The word they will report to me will not be the right one. It is possible, too, that they may take her far away from me. Let them guard her well I say, let those who watch over her never close an eye. And if they give her a husband, they had best pray for his life for they know not what a fated thing it is to give away in marriage a girl who bears about in her heart the secret of a third person."

"My dear young friend, I see that we shall not come to an understanding with each other. You are bent upon plunging into ruin a poor defenceless girl in the name of what you call love, and will not renounce, though you have not the slightest hope of winning her—that I do not understand. I, on the other hand, am the legal adviser of the young lady's family, and, in that capacity, I considered it my duty to protest very energetically against the match in question. But when they placed those precious papers in my hands, I said at once that they must marry her to this man in any case. Otherwise they would have fancied I was advocating your crazy hopes, that I was an interested party and simply opposed the family candidate in order to smuggle in a kinsman of my own in his stead. That idea I was determined to knock out of their heads, happen what would. But that of course you do not understand. And now you had better return to your room. Destiny will one day explain to all of us what we do not understand now."

* * * * * * *

At about the same hour the second act of this drama was proceeding in the torture-chamber of the Lapussa family.

Henrietta had returned home from her little tour laden with flowers, when old Demetrius sent word to her that he would like to see her in his room. He had taken the precaution of sending Madame Langai away shortly before and Mr. John was absent at the Corn Exchange.

"My little maid, Hetty, come nearer to me," said the old gentleman, turning sideways on his

SHE IS NOT FOR YOU 69

couch and ferreting out from beneath his pillows a concave snuff-box, "pray do not be angry with me for putting you to inconvenience. Bear with me for the little time I have still to live. But if you find living under the same roof with me unendurable, all the greater reason for you to seize the opportunity of releasing yourself as quickly as possible."

Henrietta was too much used to these choleric outbursts to think of replying to them.

"Pray, put your hand beneath my pillow. You will find a packet of papers there. Take them out and look at them."

Henrietta did with stolid indifference what the old man bade her and drew forth from this peculiar repository—which served as a sort of lair for snuff-boxes, pill-boxes and odd bits of pastry—a large bundle of manuscripts which she recognized at the first glance. The apprehended papers, which during her illness had prevented her from sleeping, which had made it impossible for her to get well, were now in the possession of him from whom she had been most anxious to conceal them. The criminal stood face to face with the witness whose damning evidence was to condemn her. There was no escape, no defence.

"My little maid," said the old man, exultantly stuffing his eagle nose full of that infernal heating material which goes by the name of snuff, "don't be angry with me for directing your attention to this scribble. I don't want to make any use of it.

I know quite enough of it already, but be so good as to listen to me!"

Henrietta absolutely could not look away from her grandfather's blood-shot eyes; it seemed to her as if those eyes must gradually bore through to her very heart.

"You won't marry an eminent and wealthy man who bestows an honour upon your family by asking for your hand, and yet you would run away with a worthless fellow who does not even know why he was put into the world, and when your family steps in to prevent it, you would violently put yourself to death in order to die with him, to our eternal shame and dishonour. That was not nice of you. But sit down. I see you are all of a tremble. I would fetch you a chair myself if it was not for this infernal gout of mine."

Henrietta accepted the invitation and sat down, otherwise she must have collapsed.

"Now look ye, my dear little girl! if you had to deal with an unmerciful, austere old fellow, a veritable old tiger, in fact, as I have no doubt you fancy I am, he would make no bones about it but pack you straight off to a nunnery and so cut you off from the world for ever."

Henrietta sighed. Such a threat as that sounded to her like a consolation.

"In the second place, an old tyrant, such as I am imagining, would have sent that rip of a brother of yours, who is not ashamed to lend a hand in the seduction of his own sister, would have sent him, I say, to a reformatory. I may tell you there are several such institutions, celebrated for their rigour, whither it is usual to send precocious and incorrigible young scapegraces. And richly he would have deserved it, too."

"Poor Koloman!" thought the little sister. They were tenderly devoted to each other.

"In the third place, our old tiger would have prosecuted at law that reckless youth who had a share in this fine suicide project of yours. For death, my dear, is no plaything and jests with poison are strictly forbidden. He would certainly be condemned to hard labour for five or six years, which would be a very wholesome lesson for him."

"Grandfather!" screamed the tortured child. This last allusion dissolved her voice in tears. She fell down on her knees before him and shed innocent tears enough on his hand to wash out all the old specks and stains on it.

"I am glad to see those tears, my dear little girl, they show that you have confidence in me. I am not a tiger who eats little children, what I have said *might* happen but I don't say it necessarily *must*. I don't want to be cruel and vindictive. I don't want to recollect anything of the insults showered upon me in that scribble of yours, all I ask of you is that you will not stand in your own way. Get up and don't cry any more or you will be ill again. Go up into your own room and ponder deeply what you ought to do! In two hours' time I shall send for you again, and in the meantime make up your mind about it. You have the choice between accepting as your husband an honourable gentleman of becoming rank and at the same time renouncing and forgetting a fellow who will never be able to raise himself to your level, or of taking the veil and bidding good-bye to this world. In the latter case, however, your brother will be sent to a reformatory and an action will be commenced against your accomplice. It is for you to choose. You have two whole hours to turn the matter over in your mind. In the meantime I shall send for my lawyer and, according to your decision, I shall get him to draw up a marriage contract or a summons to the criminal court. It all depends upon you. And now put back those documents beneath my head. Remember that you will only receive them back from me as a bridal gift. Go now to your own room and reflect. For two hours nobody shall disturb you."

The girl mechanically complied with his commands. She put back the ominous documents in their receptacle and withdrew to her room. There she stood in front of a vase of flowers and regarded their green leaves for an hour without moving. In the vase was a fine specimen of one of those wondrous tropical plants whose leaves never fall off, one of those plants which the seasons leave unchanged and which, therefore, is such a beautiful emblem of constancy. This beautiful plant has a peculiar property. If one of its compact shining leaves be planted in the earth it takes root and grows into a shrub whose fragrant wax-like flowers diffuse an enchanting perfume. Three years before at a jurists' ball, when Henrietta and Szilard met for the first time, he had given her a bouquet, among the flowers of which was one of these green-gold leaves, and when she got home she had planted it in a jar and it had taken root, spread its shoots abroad and grown larger and larger every year. And Henrietta had called it Szilard and watched over its growth and cared for it as if it had been a living human creature. For a long time she stood before this flowering plant as if she would have spoken to it and taken counsel of it. At last she turned away and with her hands behind her head, she walked slowly up and down the room, and as often as she paused before the vase, she behaved like one whose heart is breaking. But time was hastening on, an hour is so short when one would have it stay. Alas! nowhere was there any help, any refuge. She was abandoned. She had nothing in the world but this one flowering plant which she called Szilard. And the moments swiftly galloping after one another called for a decision. There must be an end to it. Once more she approached her darling plant and kissed all the leaves of its beautiful flowers one by one. And now there came a knock at the door. Mr. Demetrius's messenger had come and a cold shudder ran through the girl's tender frame. "I am coming!" she cried. The next moment not a tear was to be seen on her face, nay, not a trace of sorrow, or fear, but only snow-white tranquillity.

All the members of the family were assembled together again in grandpapa's room. Mr. Sipos was also present, he had been told all about the business.

"Well my dear little grandchild," said Mr. Demetrius, motioning Henrietta to take her place at the table with the others, "have you made up your mind?"

"I have."

"Veil or myrtle wreath?"

"I will be married."

"To the baron?"

"Yes," replied the girl in a strangely calm and courageous tone, "but I also have my conditions to impose."

"Let us hear them."

"In the first place I must be sure that my brother Koloman will not be persecuted. I suppose you will not let him come with me?"

"No, that one thing cannot be allowed."

"But I cannot let him remain here. Send him to some other town. You are always talking of your rank and riches, give him an education to correspond."

The child in those two hours had grown older by ten years, she now spoke to the other members of the family with the air of a matron.

"Agreed!" cried Mr. Demetrius. "Besides it will be much better if we do not see him."

"My second request is that I may take the furniture I have been used to and my flowers along with me to the place where I have to go."

"Granted, a harmless feminine caprice. Be it so!"

"In the third place I should like the papers grandfather knows of to be given back to him whom it most concerns."

"Certainly," said Mr. Demetrius, "I promised, did I not, that it should form part of your marriage portion. Mr. Sipos, would you be so good as to place these documents in the hands—of the proper person?"

Mr. Sipos bowed and promised to carry out the mournful commission.

"And now, my girl, the marriage-contract is before you, the baron has already signed it and awaits your decision in the adjoining room. Show us what a nice hand you can write."

And Henrietta did show it. She signed her name there in such pretty little delicately rounded letters that it looked as if some fairy had breathed a spell upon the page.

"And just one thing more, my dear young lady," put in Mr. Sipos politely, "while the pen is still in your hand, would you be so good as to write down on the cover of the returned documents a particular word, that particular word, I mean, which is known only to yourself and one other person in the world, as a proof that your renunciation is genuine and irrevocable."

The girl fixed her mysterious black eyes for a long time on those of the lawyer. It was in her power to deceive him if she would and he knew it well. At last she gently stooped over the bundle of papers and pressing down the pen with unusual firmness she wrote that barbarously sounding name of a beautiful bright star: "Mesarthim" and then quietly laid down the pen. There was not the slightest sign of agitation in her face. Could it be the right word?

"And now the bridegroom can come in and the necessary pre-nuptial legal formalities can be carried out."

* * * * * * *

When Mr. Sipos got home he went straight up to the room of his young protegé.

"My dear fellow," said he, "I have brought you some medicine. As you know, medicine is generally nasty and bitter, but perhaps none the worse on that account. As I said beforehand, the young lady reconsidered her position, chose the better way and consented to the marriage with the baron. The betrothal is an accomplished fact and they signed the marriage contract before my eyes."

"Doubtless," returned Szilard coldly.

"My friend, the girl did not make such a sour face over it as you are doing. She was strong-minded and decided. I was amazed at the composure with which she addressed her family, she was like the capitulating commandant of a fortress dictating the terms of surrender. Not a tear did she shed in their presence and yet I believe she suffered."

"Oh, she has lots of courage."

"I wish you had as much. Here is your absurd scribble, its surrender was one of the conditions imposed. I am glad these mischievous exercises are safely in our hands again. Don't bother your head about them any more! The girl is going away, you will remain here, in a year's time you will have forgotten each other."

Szilard smiled frostily.

"And that word which binds us together or tears us asunder?" said he.

"Yes, I thought of that, too. She looked me straight in the eyes for a long time when I asked for it and I told her I wanted the real, the genuine word. She has written it on the back of these papers, look!"

Szilard stretched forth a tremulous hand towards the papers, seized them, turned them round, and cast one look at the word written there and then fell at full length on the floor, striking his head against the corner of the table so that the blood flowed.

Mr. Sipos, cursing the whole stupid business and wishing the papers at the bottom of the sea, raised the young man tenderly and bathed his head with cold water. He did not call for assistance (why should the whole world be taken into his confidence?), but when the youth came to again, he soothed and consoled him with loving words. And Szilard, unable to contain himself any longer, hid his head in the good old man's bosom, pressed his lips to his hand and wept long and bitterly.

*   *   *   *   *   *   *

A fortnight later the marriage of Baron Hátszegi and Henrietta Lapussa was solemnized with great pomp and befitting splendour. The bride bore herself bravely throughout the ceremony, and they tell me that her lace and her diamonds were fully described in all the fashionable papers.

CHAPTER VI

BRINGING HOME THE BRIDE

In those days there were no railways in Hungary. It took a whole week to travel post from Pest to the depths of Transylvania, with relays of horses provided beforehand at every station. On the very day after the wedding the young bride set out on her journey. She had only stipulated that they should set off very early before anyone was up and stirring. They travelled in two carriages. In the first sat the bride and Clementina, who had begged and prayed so urgently to be allowed to accompany the young lady that to get rid of her they had at last consented. The poor thing fancied she would better her position thereby: it was not from pure love of Henrietta that she had been so importunate. In the second carriage sat the baron and Margari. Margari was just the sort of man the baron wanted. He was a scholar who could be converted into a domestic buffoon whenever one was required. Now-a-days it is difficult to catch such specimens, all our servants have become so stuck-up. Henrietta did not dare to ask how far they were going, or where they were to pass the night, she felt so strange amidst her new surroundings. Her husband was very obliging and polite towards her,—in fact he gave her no trouble at all.

Towards the evening they stopped at a village to water the horses and there Hátszegi got out of his carriage and, approaching his wife's, spoke to her through the window: "We shall rest in an hour," said he. "We shall put up for the night at the castle of an old friend of mine, Gerzson Satrakovich. He has been duly apprised of our coming and expects us."

But the promised hour turned out to be nearly two hours. The roads were very bad here and it was as much as the carriage wheels could do to force their way through the marshy sand. The monotonous *Buczkak** which extended desolately, like a billowy sandy ocean, to the very horizon, were overgrown with dwarf firs that looked more like shrubs than trees. Not a village, not a hut was anywhere to be seen. From the roadside sedges, flocks of noisy wild-geese, from time to time, flew across the sky which the setting sun coloured yellow. At last a great clattering and rattling gave those sitting in the carriage to understand that they were passing into a courtyard and the carriage door was opened. Henrietta got out. The young wife looked around with the same sort of curiosity which a robber condemned to a long term of imprisonment and conveyed to a distant jail might feel on first surveying his new environment.

---
* Sand hills.

In the midst of a spacious courtyard, surrounded by stone walls, stood an old-fashioned mansion with a verandah in front of it, resting on quadrangular columns which one ascended by a staircase whose brick parapet served as a lounge both for the gentlemen guests and their heydukes whenever they wanted to take their ease, —though, of course, the gentlemen occupied one end of it and the heydukes the other. A couple of favourite dogs were also accommodated with a place there. But when the carriages stopped in front of the verandah, every one instantly quitted this favourite sun-lit resting place and rushed down to meet them—host, guests, heydukes, and dogs.

The first to reach the carriage door was a peculiar looking man, a more repulsively mutilated creature it was impossible to imagine. He might have been fifty, but it was difficult to read his age from his face. His features were scarred with ancient scars and a piece of his mouth was missing—and perhaps a tooth or two as well, if one could have seen through his thick grizzled moustache. An eye was missing on the same side, and half his face was tattooed with little black points as if from an exploded musket. His nose was bent sideways and quite flattened at the top, doubtless owing to a heavy fall. He had only three whole fingers on the right hand, the other two were fearfully mutilated. As for the left arm it was horribly distorted from its natural position, the elbow being twisted right round and the joint immovable. Add to this that one of his legs was shorter than the other. Yet, in spite of everything, this fraction of a man was so agile that he anticipated all the others and was the first to courteously kiss the hand of the descending lady, who shrank back horror-stricken at the contact of those crippled fingers.

"My wife—my friend Gerzson," said Hátszegi hastening to introduce them to each other. The master of the house professed himself delighted at his good fortune; pressed his friend's hand with his third remaining finger and presented his arm, the stiff one, to the lady who touched it as gingerly as if she was afraid of hurting it.

The master of the house laughed aloud at her misgivings.

"Lean on it hard your ladyship!" cried he, "it won't break, it is as strong as iron. Down Fecske, down sir!" (this to a dog who had expressed his joy at the sight of Henrietta by jumping on her shoulder.) "I rejoice that I have the felicity to welcome your ladyship. I have arranged a great fox hunt in your ladyship's honour for to-morrow. We are all fox hunters here. I hope your ladyship will take part in it?"

"I don't know how to ride," replied the child-wife simply.

"Oh! that's nothing, we will teach you. I have got a good nag who is as gentle as a lamb. We won't let your ladyship go till we have taught you."

When they reached the saloon a number of jackbooted, brass-buttoned, gentlemen of various ages were presented in turn to Henrietta who forgot all their names the moment after they were introduced and was quite delighted when she was conducted to her room and left alone with Clementina.

She had scarce time to change her travelling dress when supper was announced. The meal was laid on a large round table in the midst of a vast hall; there were more wine bottles than dishes; the handles of the knives and forks were made from the horns of elks and the antlers of stags,— the principal meats were cold venison, highly spiced and peppered stews and pickled *galuska.**

"I am afraid this is only a hunter's repast, my lady!" opined Mr. Gerzson conducting Henrietta to the table, at which she and Clementina were the only ladies present. "Unfortunately this house has no mistress and an old bachelor like me must serve others as he himself is served."

"Then why don't you marry?" bantered Hátszegi.

"I wanted to once, but it all come to nothing. The bride was already chosen and the day for the bridal banquet was fixed. My lady bride was a fine handsome lassie. On the eve of my wedding day, in order that the business might not escape

---

* A sort of large dumpling.

my memory, I told my heyduke to place by my bed in the morning my nice bright dress boots instead of my old hunting jacks. Very well! Early next morning while I was still on my back in bed, I heard a great barking and yelping in the garden below. 'What's the row?' I shouted. They told me the dogs had started a lynx out of the bushes. 'What! a lynx!' I cried, for a lynx, let me tell you, is a rare beast in these parts. I was out of bed in a twinkling, plunged into the nice dress boots, snatched my gun from the wall and was off into the thicket. I soon found the trail and after that lynx I went. The dogs led me further and further into the depths of the forest and the further I went the more fiery grew the pursuit. Once or twice I had a sort of feeling that I had forgotten something at home, and I felt myself all over, but no, powder horn, pipe case, tobacco pouch, flint, steel—everything was there. So on I went further and further. Again I felt bothered, but by this time the lynx quite carried me away with him and kept appearing and disappearing again in the most distracting fashion. Only towards evening did I hold its pelt in my hand and home with it I went straightway. And now, again, an oppressive feeling overcame me, just as if there was something wrong going on somewhere in the world which it was in my power to prevent. Only in the evening when I was pulling off my dress boots did it flash across me that I ought to have been present at my wedding that very day. And so matters remained as they were, for my bride was so angry with me for my forgetfulness that she went away and married a lawyer fellow. No doubt she got the right man, but since then I have had no desire for matrimony."

The company laughed heartily at this jest, and then attacked the patriarchal banquet with tremendous appetite, nor did they wait to be asked twice to fill their glasses. Henrietta, naturally, did not touch anything. Even at ordinary times she ate very little, but now there was nothing at all she fancied. Mr. Gerzson was in despair.

"My dear lady," said he, "you eat so little that if I were a day labourer I could easily support you on my wages."

The company laughed aloud at this. The idea of a day labourer with such hands and feet as that!

Then Gerzson proceeded to relate to them the exploits or misadventures in which his various limbs had more or less come to grief. "And now," concluded he, "I will tell your ladyship how I came by this scar on my forehead. A few years ago I was visiting our friend Leonard, your husband, my dear lady, at his castle at Hidvár, and whilst there we spent two weeks among the glaciers."

"Night and day?" enquired the astonished Henrietta.

"Well, at night we built ourselves huts out of the branches of fir trees. If, however, no rain fell we encamped in the open round our watch-fire snugly wrapped up in our *bundas**. Splendid fun I can tell you! For two days, when our stores gave out, we lived on nothing but bilberries and broiled bear's flesh."

"You were badly off then."

"No, on the contrary, the paws of a bear are great delicacies, only we had no salt to salt them with."

"Why did you not return home?"

"We could not, for four days together we had been on the track of a blood-bear. Do you know what a blood-bear is? A bear is a very mild, harmless sort of a beast in general, and is quite content with honey, berries, and roots; but let him once taste blood and he rages about like a lion, and more than that, he has a decided preference for human blood before all other kinds of blood. We had been pursuing one of these old malefactors four days running, as I have said; four times we got within range of him and four times he broke away. He carried a few bullets away with him beneath his hide, indeed, but a lot he cared about that! He gave one or two of our badly-aiming huntsmen a clout on the head which sent them flying, stripped the skin from the head of one of the beaters and then took refuge in the wilderness. Friend Leonard and the other gentlemen now wanted to abandon the chase, for they were frightfully hungry and the heavy rain and rock scrambling had pretty well torn our clothes from our

*Sheepskins.

bodies, yet I urged them to make another attempt on the morrow. I assured them that if they beat up the wood once more we should capture the bear. The whole lot of them were against me. Friend Leonard insisted that we should not catch him, as a bear never remains in the place where he has been wounded, but runs on and on night and day; by this time he would have got right across the border into Wallachia. 'Very well!' I said, 'What do you bet that he is not quite near and we shall come upon him to-morrow?' Leonard replied he would bet me two to one we shouldn't. 'All right!' said I. 'I'll pay you a hundred ducats if we don't find Bruin to-morrow.' 'And I'll pay you a thousand if we do,' said he. So the bet was clinched. Next morning in a thick mist we sent out the beaters while we ourselves stood on our guard. Leonard and I took up our post near a ravine waiting impatiently for the mist to disperse. Towards mid-day it began to clear. No end of stags and foxes ambled slowly past us, but we did not even aim at them; the bear was our watchword. The beaters had pretty nearly finished their work. We were standing only fifty paces or so apart, so we began to chat together. 'I begin to be sorry for your hundred ducats,' said Leonard. 'I am still sorrier for the lost bear's skin,' said I. 'It is in Wallachia by this time!' he replied. Behind my back, some ten yards off, was the opening of a narrow hole; there were hundreds such in the rocks all about. 'Come, now!' I cried, 'suppose my bear has stowed himself away in this hollow!'—and there and then, like a mischievous little boy, I poked the barrel of my gun into the hollow and fired off a couple of shots in quick succession. A frightful roar came from the depths of the cavern. The wild beast during all this noise, clamour and beating about the bush was actually behind my back holding his tongue,—and a splendid big beast he was, two heads taller than I and with tusks like a wild boar. In a moment he was upon me, and I had already discharged my two barrels. It is all over with me now, I thought! Why, it will be nothing at all to a magnificent beast like this to tear such a wretched creature as myself limb from limb! Erect on his hind legs he came straight at me, smashing my hunting-knife at a single blow, and, enfolding me in his terrible arms, he tried to mangle my features with his teeth. At the last moment I called to Leonard: 'Shoot between us, old chap! you will hit one of us anyhow!' I preferred being killed by a bullet to being torn to bits. The next instant a report sounded, and I was only just aware that the pair of us, still tightly embraced, were rolling backwards into the bottom of the ravine. There, however, the thick undergrowth held us up, and I perceived that my bear was quite done for. The bullet had gone clean through his ear. Yes, a masterly shot on Leonard's part it was, I must confess—at fifty paces at the very moment when the bear's head and mine were near enough for kissing. And I do think it was so nice of Leonard to risk a shot for me, when if he had simply allowed me to be torn to pieces he would have saved his thousand ducats, for he lost his bet, you see. Not only did he liberate me, but he paid a thousand ducats for doing so."

"He acted like a true gentleman!" they all cried. It was the general opinion.

"Your ladyship will see this splendid bear skin at Hidvár, it is a real treasure for a hunter, I can tell you. And in fact if I had had the choice I would much rather have had the bear skin than the thousand ducats, and the exchange would have been much better for me too in the long run, for I should have the skin to this day, whereas the thousand ducats were forcibly taken from me at Dévá by that villain, Fatia Negra."*

"Who is that?" enquired Henrietta curiously.

"A famous robber-chieftain in these mountains whom they can never lay hands upon."

Henrietta cast anxious glances around her.

But here Hàtszegi coolly interrupted him by striking his plate with his fork: "I won't have my wife frightened to death by your highwayman yarns," cried he, and changed the conversation. Shortly afterwards Henrietta went to her chamber, leaving her husband with Mr. Gerzson and his guests.

Such was Henrietta's first night after her marriage. She at least was so far fortunate as not to be obliged to see her husband. Towards morning

* Black face.

she dozed off, and when she awoke again she found that the whole company had long ago set off fox-hunting, nor did they return till late in the evening, tired out, wet through, and dripping with sweat. Henrietta meanwhile had discovered the remains of a dilapidated library in an old disused huntsman's hut, had ferretted out of it a few Latin books, and had amused herself with them,—at least so far as she was able, for many of the leaves had been torn out and used as tinder.

It is notorious that tired sportsmen are about the dullest dogs on earth; so Henrietta felt that she would not lose much when her husband told her she had better go to rest early, as they must be up betimes next morning. And, indeed, next morning they were off so early that, except their old host, not one of the hunting party was there to bid them God speed! But he again conducted his lady-guest to her carriage on his crippled arm and arranged her cushions comfortably for her with his three-fingered hand.

It was a very fine day for a journey, and the windows of the two carriages were let down so that Henrietta was able to view the landscape stretching out before her. She had never been here before, it was all new to her. She discovered from Clementina's lamentations that they had still a three days' journey before they reached home, and that they would spend the coming night at the castle of Count Kengyelesy. The coachmen had told Margari so, and he passed the news on to

Clementina. It also appeared that Count Kengyelesy was a very curious sort of man, who contradicted Baron Hátszegi in everything, yet for all that they were never angry with and always glad to see each other. The count was also said to have a young wife who did not love him. So ran the gossip of the servants. It was all one to Henrietta what they said about Count Kengyelesy and his consort.

Between five and six in the afternoon they reached the count's castle, which lay outside the village in the midst of rich tobacco and rapeseed fields. and enclosed on three sides by a splendid English garden; the place was arranged with taste and evidently well-cared for.

That the count expected the arrival of the Hátszegis was evident from the fact that dinner was awaiting them. Kengyelesy was a little puny bit of a man with very light bright hair, white eyelashes, and a pointed chin made still more pointed by a long goatish beard. It always pleased him very much when his friends confidentially assured him that he had a perfect satyr-like countenance.

His wife was a young, chubby, lively lady with smiling blue eyes unacquainted with sorrow, whom her husband on the occasion of a *bal paré* at Vienna had seen, fallen in love with, and carried off, although the girl's father, a retired Field-marshal, was quite ready to surrender her—they preferred, however, the romance of an elopement.

The countess received her lady-guest with the

most effusive heartiness, called her by her Christian name on the spot, and invited her to do that same with her. She told Henrietta she was to feel quite at home, dragged her all over the castle, and showed her in rapid succession her rare flowers, her Parisian furniture, her Japanese curiosities; played something for her on the piano, made her parrot talk to her and incontinently popped on her finger a large and beautiful opal ring, which she told her she was to keep as an eternal souvenir.

Then the countess seized the hand of the child-wife and led her into her bed-chamber. On the wall hung a fine large battle-piece, a splendid oil painting by a Viennese master.

"A magnificent picture, is it not?" enquired the countess with a broad smile.

"Yes," replied Henrietta absently.

"How do you like the central figure? I mean the hero on horseback with the standard in his hand?"

"He is handsome, but it seems to me that, situated as he is, he smiles too much."

The countess laughed loudly at this remark.

"That," said she, "is the portrait of a young hussar officer who for a long time paid his court to me. I could not, of course, keep his portrait in my room, for there everyone would know all about it, so I had a battle-piece painted in all round, and nobody suspects anything. Oh! my friend, if women were not so inventive, they would often be very unhappy. But that, mind! is a secret; not a soul must know about it."

Henrietta grew pensive. She also had her secret, but she would tell it to nobody, not even on her death-bed. She also had a portrait written in ineffaceable characters in her heart, yet between him and her stand two infinite obstacles, the one a betrayed star whose name is Mesarthim, the other that unbetrayable thing, whose name is—woman's honour!

"*Madame est servie!*" cried the epauletted lacquey, and the countess drawing her arm through Henrietta's, led her into the dining-room, where the gentlemen already awaited them.

After dinner the humorous young countess entertained Henrietta for a long time with her amusing chatter. She told her, at the very outset, things that young wives, as a rule, only confide to their most intimate friends. She told her, for instance, how very jealous her little Squirrel was (she called her husband by this pet name) and how he would never take her to Vienna or Pest, because he suspected that she might find someone there to interest her. Anything like correspondence on her part was of course impossible; a wise woman will always have sense enough never to part with a line of writing. Everything else, she witnesses, treacherous servants, for instance—can always be disowned; but there is no defence against a letter which has fallen into the wrong hands. Oh no! she knew a trick worth two of that. Whenever the Squirrel went to Vienna, she gave him a list of articles required by her from a modiste in the town, on this list are set down hats, head-dresses, muffs, and other similar articles. Squirrel always reads this list over ten times at least, but finds nothing in it to excite his suspicions. But it regularly escapes his attention what day is indicated by the date at the head of the list, for he can never tell for the life of him on what day of the month such or such a day will fall. Now at the head of this list stands, instead of the date on which the goods are to be sent, the date up to which the Squirrel intends to divert himself at Vienna. This list the Squirrel in person conveys to the modiste, who communicates with the person whom it most concerns, and the Kengyelesy *puszta** will not seem the end of the world to whomsoever has a magnet in his heart to draw him thither.

Henrietta was amazed and confounded by this new science, the very alphabet of which was unknown to her. Even when she lay in bed she ruminated for a long time how it was possible that certain things which break the hearts of some people are nevertheless regarded by other people as mere frolics all their lives.

The next morning everyone arose late. The gentlemen had been up till the small hours and were hard to wake. They all met together in the breakfast-room. Hátszegi and his host were preparing for the journey. The count asked the young wife what she had dreamt about, "for," added he,

---

* Heath. But also, as in this place, used to designate the unculterated land forming part of a nobleman's estate.

"whatever one dreams about the first night in a strange place is sure to come true."

Henrietta did not like to speak of her dreams; her waking thoughts were too often interwoven with them.

"And you, you great silly," said the countess to her husband in a bantering tone, "did you dream anything of me?"

"Yes, darling, I dreamt that we shall spend the coming winter in Vienna. Don't put so much sugar in my tea!"

"What! not for such a nice dream as that. Will it really come to pass?"

"Most certainly, pussy. We will go there together after the bathing season is over."

The countess possessed sufficient self-control to conceal her delight.

"By the bye," said Kengyelesy, turning to Henrietta, "how does your ladyship like the Kengyelesy *puszta?*"

"Very well."

"And the castle?"

"That is nice too."

"Don't you think it a good joke that yesterday your ladyship and your honoured husband were my guests, whilst to-day we are your ladyship's guests and that, too, without our having to move out of the house?"

"How?" enquired the astonished Henrietta.

"Why, we made an agreement this very morning whereby friend Leonard is going to take over the whole property and everything belonging to it —not you, my dear, of course," this to his wife, "I mean the nags and the cows—and henceforth this house belongs to you."

"Don't forget to invite the countess to Hidvár for the vintage festival," whispered Hátszegi to his wife.

Henrietta accordingly made the effort, and when they rose from the breakfast she timidly expressed the wish that the Kengyelesys would do them the honour to return their visit at Hidvár.

"Oh, we will be sure to come!" the fair countess hastened to reply, "Squirrel will bring me to you in the autumn and we will remain a whole month."

Kengyelesy also courteously accepted the invitation and then taking Henrietta's little hand between his own palms so that he could just manage to kiss the tips of her fingers, he said to her in a strange and piteous sort of voice: "But then you must promise to love our friend Leonard here a little better than you have done hitherto."

A shudder ran through Henrietta's body at these words. The very air of the room was all at once difficult to breathe, and she only felt better when she sat in the carriage again. But even there she was haunted by some unendurable, undefinable, torturing feeling which struck her still more unpleasantly when Clementina remarked: "Yes, there is nothing but good land on this *puszta.*"

Why, what could it matter to the honest creature whether the land was good or not, it was surely all one to her?

"Two thousand acres in one lot, nothing but first-class land."

"How do you know that?" asked Henrietta.

"Margari told me he drew up the agreement and witnessed it, and yet no money was paid down."

"What do you mean by that?"

"Did not your ladyship then understand the allusion the count made just now when he asked you to love your husband a little more than hitherto?"

"What has such nonsense to do with me?"

"He meant by that that he who is unlucky in love is lucky at play; for last night my lord baron played cards with my lord count and won from him the whole Kengyelesy estate straight off."

Henrietta felt like one who is in the embrace of the boa-constrictor and unable to defend himself. She had not expected this.

But Clementina was only too delighted to have something to chatter about. "And do you know, your ladyship," she continued, "the baron and the count have been rivals for a long time, and each has always been trying his hardest to ruin the other—in a friendly way, of course. The chambermaid told Margari, and Margari told me. "I will not be content, comrade,' my lord baron used to say to my lord count, 'till one of us is reduced to his last jacket, and as soon as one of us is absolutely beggared, the other will hold himself bound to maintain him, in a way befitting a gentleman till the day of his death.' Strange men these, madame, eh!"

Perceiving, however, from Henrietta's looks that there was something depressing to her young mistress in her narration, she tried to soften the effect of her words by intimating that the count had another property besides, although not such a nice castle, and also that it was open to him to buy back the former estate in thirty years' time if he could find the money.

"That will do, Clementina, my head aches badly!" said Henrietta. She wished to rid herself of this uncalled-for gabble, in order that she might devote herself to her own thoughts.

And what thoughts! She had had no idea that such things could be. How was it possible that two men who called themselves friends, could ruin one another thus in cold blood? How was it possible that a man could enter the house of an affectionate host as a welcome guest in the evening, and by next morning leave him not an inch of land on which to put his foot, or a roof to cover his head! "And one has to get accustomed to such things!" thought she.

All the day long their journey lay through that brain-wearying plain whose endless flatness oppressed soul and body with its monotony and soon drove her back to her own thoughts. Towards evening there were signs of rain. Clouds were rising and then, at least, there would be something new to point at in the eternal monotony of the sky. Unfortunately clouds have the bad habit of bringing tempests along with them, and tempests are evil travelling companions on the steppes of the *Alföld*.* The towers of the town they were trying to reach were still only dimly visible on the horizon. In ordinary weather it would not have mattered if they had arrived late, for they had reckoned upon the moonlight; but there could be no moon to-night, instead of her a storm full of angry lightnings was approaching. Already from afar they could hear it rumbling as it drove dust-clouds before it, could hear that peculiar, continuous, roar as of some giant hand playing uninterruptedly on the keys of some terrible organ. Whoever has been caught on the *Alföld* in a storm knows the meaning of that wind; it means that the tempest is bringing hail with it.

One thing was now certain: they must turn aside somewhere. All that Henrietta observed, however, was that her carriage stood still for a moment, and then Hátszegi's carriage went on in front, the baron himself seizing the horses' reins and shouting to the coachman behind him: "After me as hard as you can tear!" With that they left the road and plunged right across country through ditches and swamps and low, marshy ground till the water came up to the very axles of the wheels

---
* The great Hungarian plain.

and Clementina shrieked that they were perishing. But there was no need to be afraid. Hátszegi was a skilful coachman, who could ever find his way even where there was no way at all. About a four hours' journey off, a pump now became visible, and beyond it a little hut loomed white and high, there they must seek a refuge from the tempest as it passed over them. And indeed they had only just reached the small court-yard when the first lumps of ice as big as nuts, began bombarding the windows of the carriages.

"Quick, quick, into the house!" cried Hátszegi. The baron himself helped his wife and Clementina to descend and hurried them in beneath the verandah, which was made of crooked branches and hung over the kitchen door like a shade over the forehead of a weak-sighted man.

On their approach the woman of the house emerged from the kitchen with her head tied up in a red handkerchief. She was no longer young, but ruddy, robust, bright-eyed, and bustling, and as full of sparkle as if she had just sprung out of the fire.

On perceiving her guests she clapped her hands together.

"Lord deliver us, if it isn't his lordship! And only just married now, eh!—after all these years! But which is the bride, your lordship? Surely not this one (pointing to Clementina) for she is an old dear!—and yet the other is but a child!"

The baron hastened to interrupt this uncalled-for outburst.

"Come, come, my good woman! No chatter now, please, for the hail will be upon us in a moment; but take these ladies into a room and see that it is clean and comfortable. Henrietta! pray get out of the rain."

The *csárdá* woman kissed Henrietta's hand with great familiarity and kept on saying in a quavering voice: "Oh, thou tender little creature! to think of giving them to husbands so early!" cried she. But Clementina, who was always nervous in strange places, called the baron's attention to the fact that loud masculine voices were proceeding from somewhere within the *csárdá*.

"Have you anyone here now?" enquired the baron of the *csárdá* woman.

"Yes, three or four lads and *Ripa*. The old fellow has just been released from the prison at Arad. I don't know whether he served his full time. Pray walk in!"

"They are not robbers, are they?" asked Clementina hesitating.

"No, dear heart alive, there are no robbers in these parts, but only poor vagabonds. You will not find robbers nearer than the Bakony forest. These poor fellows hurt nobody, least of all ladies. I don't count old Ripa at all, but only the other three. It would be another thing if Blackey were here, for he is a fine gentleman and likes to amuse

---
* Inn.

himself with the ladies. But don't think, dear soul, that his features are black, oh, dear, no! I call him 'Blackey' because he always wears a mask of black velvet lest he should be recognized, only his eyes and mouth are ever visible."

And with such comforting assurances she escorted Henrietta and Clementina up the narrow staircase.

They had to pass through the long tap-room before they came to the inner parlour. At the guest table were sitting three hardy looking young fellows and an old pock-marked man, a foxey-eyed rascal who drank out of the others' glasses from time to time and kept the conversation going.

"Come! shut up, Ripa!" said the landlady to the old man. "This is no Jew-Madame, but the spouse of my lord, Baron Hátszegi. Show your manners if you have any and thank her for the honour."

The old rascal rose from his bench with cunning humility and twisting up both ends of his gray moustache, politely kissed Henrietta's hand, and would have paid the same compliment to Clementina if the landlady had not prevented him by shouting: "Leave her alone, she is only a sort of servant!"

With that she led the ladies into the inner room, where were two lofty bedsteads reaching to the beams above, covered with bright bedding and prettily painted over with tulips and roses. In the window screens were wide-spreading rosemary and musk plants. In front of one of the great chests stood a spinning wheel. From this the landlady, winter and summer, spun off that fine thread from which were woven those bright and gay handkerchiefs which could be seen bobbing about in the doorway of the inn from afar. One would never have expected to find such ease and comfort in a *csárdá* of the *puszta*.

The landlady very politely divested Henrietta of her travelling clothes, made a soft resting place for her with cushions in an arm-chair, put a stool beneath her feet, and in less time than it took to draw a breath, totted up ten different kinds of dishes that she might choose from them the one she liked best. Perhaps she would like some leaf-cake? It was just cooking and would be served up immediately, and she began spreading the table with a nice horse-cloth. Clementina whispered Henrietta to beware of poison, whereupon Henrietta told the landlady that she *would* have a bit of that nice dish, and when it came she really enjoyed it, though she did not know what it was, at which the landlady was infinitely pleased.

Meanwhile Hátszegi came in after seeing that the carriages were put into a dry place. He took no notice of the poor vagabonds, but hastily demanded a change of clothes, as his own were soaking, and was amazed to see Henrietta handling her knife and fork so well; it was the first time on the whole journey that she had eaten with appetite. Henrietta said that this peasant roast suited her taste.

"And now, Dame Kardos, will you put the ladies up for the night?" said Hátszegi to the woman of the *csárdá*.

"Certainly," returned the worthy woman, "I have feather mattresses enough and bedsteads enough for as many guests of quality as your lordship likes. This bed will be my lord baron's and this my lady's, and this the lady attendant's!"

"Not so quick, not so quick! I shall not lie here."

"Not lie here?" cried this child of the *puszta.* "Why, pray?"

"Oh! I'll find some place or other in the tap-room outside."

"It's a way great folks have, I suppose," murmured Dame Kardos, shrugging her shoulders, "but I never saw or heard the likes of it before."

"But, my lord," lisped Clementina, greatly agitated, "won't those wild vagabonds outside disturb you?"

"Me?" exclaimed Hátszegi, "how the devil can they disturb *me?*"

"They are such wicked men, surely?"

"I don't care what sort of men they are." And with that he went out with the utmost *sang froid;* nay, as Clementina herself noticed, he drew forth his pocket pistols and left them behind him on the table.

"His lordship has no need to fear such men,"

BRINGING HOME THE BRIDE

the landlady reassured the ladies, "for he can talk to them in their own lingo."

Henrietta did not understand. Did robbers then speak a dialect peculiar to themselves? She became quite curious to hear how Hátszegi would speak to the robbers in their own language.

But the landlady knew exactly what to do. She filled a *kulacs** for the baron and placed it on the table before him. Hátszegi took a good pull at it, dried the mouth of the *kulacs* and passed it on to the old pockmarked vagabond who, after raising his cap, took a little drop himself and then passed it on to the others.

"Well, old fellow, is the wine good?"

"Wine is always good."

"Have you had enough?"

"One can never have enough."

"Then God grant you plenty!—By the way, does the wind still blow through the crevices of the prison door at Arad?"

"It blows for him who lists to it. Let him who likes it not close his ears to it."

"Have many children been born to the governor of the jail lately?"†

"Yes, lots have been born there—and christened too."‡

"Has the daughter of the cord§ been married lately?"

---
* A wooden field-flask.
† Whenever a new convict arrives at the jail, the governor is said to have another son born to him.—*Jokai.*
‡ *i. e.*, with stripes.—*Jokai.*
§ A flowery expression for the gallows.—*Jokai.*

"Only Marczi Csendes has been elevated lately. He was a fool. He took the crime of two comrades on his shoulders in order to let them go free. They were caught in the act, but he swore he did the deed. They were young bloods, you see, and he had nobody to care for him. And yet it was they who presented the empty pistol at the Jew's head. The Jew himself pointed them out, but Marczi steadfastly maintained that it was he who frightened the fellow."

"So they made him cold against the winter time?"

"Yes, but he didn't very much care. The hour before his execution he took an affectionate leave of his comrades, and to me he bequeathed his warm old sheepskin. When the priest asked him whether he had anything upon his conscience, he merely said the only thing that grieved him was the thought that he would never again be able in this life to eat his fill of well peppered *gulyás** such as old Ripa knew how to cook. They humoured him, and I was sent into the kitchen to prepare it. My old friend ate with a good appetite and wanted me to take a bit too; but my throat felt as cramped as if they had already taken my measure round it with the gallows rope. He gave each of the two heydukes who accompanied him in the felon's car, one on his right, the other on his left, a silver coin apiece. The heydukes told us afterwards that when he got outside he rose up

---
* Hungarian pilau.

in the car and addressed the people. He was a tall, handsome fellow with red cheeks, long black hair and a fine sonorous voice like any chaplain's. His last words were: 'Well, I now look upon this fair world for the last time.'"

"Did he leave behind him any new songs," enquired Hátszegi. "He was always a famous singer."

"Yes, one he made in jail, and a splendid song it was too, I can tell you. Bandi! pipe it to his lordship on your *tilinka* as I have taught you." At these words one of the youths drew forth from his sleeve one of those flutes made of elder-wood, which in Hungarian goes by the name of a *tilinka*, and which with its poor six holes is able to give forth as many variations as the throat of a lark; then, without any virtuoso airs he simply piped the plaintive melody.

The baron was immensely pleased. "Margari," cried he, "go to the carriage, look for my fiddle and bring it hither!"

At this command poor Margari had a veritable ague fit of terror. All this time he had remained ducking down in the carriage firmly persuaded that the robbers in this lonely place would cut down every mother's son of them at nightfall. In such a case he was prepared to swear that he had never belonged to the party at all, but would pretend he was only a poor tramp, and so escape that way. And now the baron had ruined his little plan by ordering him to come forth! The robbers would now absolutely believe that he also was a swell. Oh, it is a frightful situation when a poor devil has managed to get a 100 gulden into his purse for the first time in his life and is obliged the very next evening to put up at an inn full of robbers! What the devil did the baron want with the fiddle at all? And then what sort of a thing *was* a fiddle? When a man is terrified he easily mistakes one thing for another and Margari's first experiment was to carry in to the baron a long leaden box containing the territorial chart of the Kengyelesy estate—was that what his lordship wanted?

"Have you lost your wits, Margari? How could you possibly get a fiddle into that? Or has the fellow never cast eyes on a fiddle? Bandi, you go and look in the carriage for the fiddle!"

But this was not at all to Margari's liking. What, send that vagabond to the carriage to ferret about there! His lordship must have clean taken leave of his senses. Why, in the carriage was Margari's own brand-new mantle, for which he had paid nine and twenty gulden. The vagabond would be sure to lay his hands upon it. No, he would rather go to look for the fiddle himself. So he found the violin case at last somehow, and handing it to the baron through the *csárdá* window (for he durst not trust himself inside), he retired again beneath the coach-house, although the rain was now splashing down upon it.

Baron Leonard took from its morocco case his splendid Straduarius, that relic of the greatest master of fiddle-making, for which he had paid a small fortune, and following the lead of the young vagabond's *tilinka* played the bitter-sweet melancholy air on the sonorous instrument, and at the third trial he enriched it with so many variations as to astonish everyone. Then Ripa became enthusiastic and chimed in with his hoarse old voice.

When the baron once had the violin in his hands, he was not content with playing a single song, one melody enticed another forth, and so, one after another, his fiddle-bow ran through all those rhapsodies of the last century, those compositions of the "Gipsy-Beethoven," Bihari, and other great popular masters, with the most classical variations. Princes listen not to such a concert as now resounded through that wretched, desolate *csárdá*. Even Henrietta arose from her couch the better to enjoy these melancholy airs. If ever in her life, it was at this moment that she beheld her husband in an aureole of dazzling light which irresistibly attracted, overpowered, subdued.

One thing, however, struck her as strange, incredible—how could a fashionable man brought up in the atmosphere of elegant saloons, find any pleasure in playing *bravoura* pieces in the tap room of a miserable *csárdá* to an audience of half-tipsy vagabonds? Was this an habitual diversion of these wealthy magnates, or was it only Hátszegi's bizarre humour?"

However, when "the lads" began to chime in a

little too vigourously, Hátszegi restored the violin to its case, took out his pocket-book, opened it before them all and nonchalantly displayed as he did so the bundles of thousand-gulden notes which it contained. Nay, he searched among them for stray ten-gulden notes and gave one to each of the four vagabonds "for the fine song they had taught him"—that was the way he put it—at the same time requesting them to quit the tap-room, as the ladies in the adjoining chamber wanted to sleep and must not be kept awake by any further noise. The vagabonds must seek a couch elsewhere.

The vagabonds, without the slightest objection, arose, drank up the dregs of the wine, pocketed the bank-notes without so much as a "thank you!" and settled down for the night on the roof of the coach-house—to the great terror of Margari, who was concealed in one of the coaches and did not have a wink of sleep all night, his teeth chattered so.

But Hátszegi, when the drinkers had withdrawn, spread out his hunting pelisse on the long table, laid down thereon and quietly fell asleep. He did not even shut the door, nor did he have his pistols by him.

In the adjoining chamber, meanwhile, the *csárdá*-woman had brought out her spindle, set all its many wheels a-working and began to tell her ladyship a lot of those wondrous tales that have neither beginning nor end, *puszta* adventures, the atrocities of vagabonds and their fellows, the sad love stories of poor deserted maidens and such like. And all the while the wheels of the spindle whirr-whirr-whirred monotonously, and Henrietta felt like a little child whose nurse sits beside her bed and lulls her to sleep with fairy tales. For weeks she had not enjoyed so quiet and dreamless a slumber as she had that night beneath the roof of the *csárdá* in the midst of the lonely *puszta*.

Next morning Clementina, after first making quite sure that nobody had had his or her throat cut during the night, was moved by curiosity to ask what sort of connection his lordship had with this *csárdá* since he seemed to know everybody in it. And then she learnt that not only this *csárdá* but the whole of the surrounding *puszta* also was the property of his lordship, for which the people who lived upon it paid very little rent, inasmuch as his lordship did not look upon it as a source of income but chiefly valued it on account of its numerous reedy lakes where he was wont every year to hunt water-fowl and beavers on a grand scale. Moreover, from this spot to his own house, a good two days' journey by foot, everything belonged to his lordship's estate. Nay, his lordship, if he liked, could traverse the whole kingdom from Deva to Pest, and be on his own property the whole time, it was only like moving from one of his houses to another.

The next day the Hungarian plain came to an

end and the Transylvanian Alps drew nearer and nearer. In the evening they descended into a little mining town whose forges and furnaces were all illuminated in honour of the arriving guests. Henrietta then learnt that this mining town also belonged to her husband.

On the third day, quite early in the morning, they crossed the Transylvanian frontier. The whole of that splendid region seemed to smile, but the faces of its inhabitants are sad and mysterious. Henrietta had a peculiar sense of anxiety during her stay among these angry looking people who spoke a language she had never heard before. At intervals of a mile all along the road a roughly carved cross shot up, covered with clumsily carved letters, which did not in the least resemble those we are accustomed to. Clementina once asked the coachman what these crosses might mean and repented doing so immediately afterwards, for he informed her that they marked the places where unlucky travellers had come by an untimely death; the inscriptions were the records of the tragic romances through the scene of which they were passing.

The valleys grew narrower and narrower, the road wound upward among precipices, and the loquacious coachman attached horrible stories to every rock and ruin. Each valley seemed to have its own particular ghost.

Here and there by the roadside stood silent houses not one of which had an inviting appearance, it would never have occurred to a human soul to knock at any of them, even at midnight, to ask for a night's lodging. They were all of them sooty dilapidated shanties, which might easily have been taken for stables, consisting of a single room in which the whole family lived, livestock and all. The church often lay far away from the settlement as if it belonged to two villages equally.

Then the road rose again between bare and barren cliffs, where only here and there a solitary bush seemed to cling to the rocky wall. There was no trace of a garden, but here and there was a fenced in space in which the Roumanians are wont to unload their hay, with a long pole sticking up in the midst of the hay ricks to prevent the wind from carrying it away, or else the hay was piled up on the branch of a living tree like a bird's nest.

Down-pouring mountain streams traversed the path at intervals, over which never a bridge is built, all cars and coaches must cross by the fords. From the depths of the wooded mountain slopes was reflected the blood-red glare of iron works and foundries, and the droaning monotonous din of the machinery scares away the stillness till it loses itself in the loud murmuring of the mountain torrents.

At every fresh mile, Henrietta felt how lonely she was in this strange world, whose giant mountains shut her out from the very prospect of the familiar places from which she had come and from every possibility of returning; and whose inhabitants would not even be able to answer her if she were to ask them: "Which is the way back to my native place?"

They travelled onwards till late at night by the light of the moon. Hidvár was now close at hand. As the prospect opened out on both sides, at the turn of a narrow defile, suddenly, like a picture in a black frame, between two mountain slopes, thickly covered with dark beech-trees, the castle of Hidvár came full in view, standing lonely and isolated on the summit of a hill. The mountain torrent shot swiftly down beneath a shaky bridge. The round moon stood straight over the tower of the castle, as if it had been impaled on the point of it, and painted everything with its silvery light, the tower, the bastions, the brook and the valley—only one thing it brightened not, the heart of the young wife.

CHAPTER VII

THE CAVERN OF LUCSIA

Not so very long ago there was in Transylvania a wide-spreading society of coiners which, it is now notorious, had carried on its nefarious business undetected for more than half a century. The science was an inheritance descending from father to son, people married and were born into it. Careful parents trained their children to follow it, and a very lucrative profession it proved to be. That it should have remained undiscovered for so long a time, that it should have been plied successfully for more than fifty years under the very noses of the authorities—all this was capable of a very simple explanation, *these men coined gold pieces.*

Yes, genuine ducats, of full weight, out of real three-and-twenty carat gold, without any admixture of baser metal, so that they absolutely could not be distinguished from the royal ducats of the authorized minting towns, Körmöcz and Gyulafehervár. If they fell into the hands of a goldsmith, and he melted them, he found that they did not contain half a grain more silver than the genuine ones. Indeed the public lost nothing by their fabrication, though the state treasury suffered considerably.

The whole region, in fact, from Zalathna to Verespatak abounded in that precious metal which some fool or other has called "a mere chimera," and the gold mining was farmed out to private individuals, the yearly output from the shafts being twelve hundredweights. These private diggers are bound to deliver the gold they obtain to the minting towns at Abradbanya or Gyulafehervár and there receive coined money in exchange. Nevertheless, during some fifty years, only about six hundredweights were delivered annually at these places; the rest disappeared, though at first nobody could suspect it. The State pays to the diggers 441 guldens for every pound of gold dust, which quantity when coined is worth 720 guldens. But it occurred to the mountaineers that they also might profitably engage in coining and circulate the money so coined. So they provided themselves with all the necessary implements and machinery (there were skilled workmen among them) and issued false ducats to their very great advantage. Their existence was not even suspected except by the parties interested in the concern, and they had every motive in the world for preserving the secret.

* * * * * * *

Travelling from Abradbanya up towards Bucsum, one might have seen two riders toiling up the mountain along the stream overshadowed by dark alders; one of them was a grey-haired, gigantic Roumanian, the other a proud-looking young woman. The old man wore a lambskin mantle, on his head he carried a tall pointed cap, also of lambs' wool, drawn down over his eyebrows, his body was carelessly girdled with a golden girdle. His rich grey locks were plaited into two thick pig-tails which reached down to his broad shoulders, and his snow-white moustache hung down from his mouth like two seamew's wings. A coarse sack lay in front of him across his saddle, both ends of which appeared to be full of something heavy; across the sack lay his fowling-piece.

The fair cavalier was sitting on a small, wild, shaggy horse, which constantly evinced a praiseworthy endeavour to overtake the rider in front of him; his mistress with difficulty held him in. She was one of those famous Roumanian beauties. Her features, the cut of her lips, her full chin could have stood as a model beside any antique statue. And then those sparkling eyes, that vividly red complexion, those coal-black eyebrows—they made an ideal beauty of her. And the picturesque Roumanian costume enhanced her charms. Her black hair, twisted into a double plait, was bound round with a flaming-red scarf, and on her head she wore a round hat, trimmed with pearls and garnished in front with a row of gold pieces which reached down to her marble-white forehead. Moreover, her fine cambric shirt embellished with bright flowers and gold ornaments fitted so closely as to betray the outlines of her harmonious figure. Wound ten times round her neck she wore a necklace of gold coins extending down to her bosom. As she rode along (and she sat astride her saddle like a man), every now and then one could catch glimpses beneath her variegated girdle of her red morocco boots and of a Turkish dagger, with a massive silver handle, gleaming forth from their shafts. On each side of her holsters peeped forth a double-barrelled pistol with an ivory handle.

When the old man stopped to water his horse at the spring gushing forth from the black slate rock, he said to the girl: "Anicza, when did you speak last with Fatia Negra?"

"Just a month ago. It was at the time of the full moon, like it is now. He then said that he was going away on a long journey."

"And yet he has already been at home these two days. I saw his sign over against my window."

"Impossible. It cannot be," cried the girl passionately.

"What cannot be? Do you think I am dreaming or lying?"

"If he were at home, he would have come to see me ere this."

The old man shrugged his shoulders.

"And yet he did not come. But the day before yesterday, about midnight, I found the three owl-feathers there in the window."

"The wind carried them thither."

"The wind did not carry them thither for they were stuck fast in putty. And only we three know what that means. Fatia Negra would speak with us and we are going to meet him in the Lucsia cavern."

"It cannot, cannot be—three days at home and never to come to me—to *me!*"

"Who knows?" said the old man coolly, tightening his saddle girth, "a whole month is a long while, long enough for the moon herself to change four times. There are many pretty wenches on the other side of the mountain."

"O no! such a one as I am he will not find there," said the girl proudly, glancing into the tremulous water-mirror which threw back a distorted likeness of her defiant face—"and besides he knows very well that I should murder him were such a woman to mock me."

"Ah, ah!" mocked the old man, "so Fatia Negra is afraid of you, eh?"—and with that he swung himself back into his saddle with youth-like agility. "Black Face fears nobody, I tell you. He is not even afraid of the commandant of Gyulafehervár, nor of the lord-lieutenant of Krasna, and they have no end of soldiers and heydukes. Nay, he fears not the devil himself."

And with that he urged on his horse which ambled forward meditatively, whilst the girl's little nag whinnied in the rear.

"He may not fear the great gentlemen, he may not fear the devil, but I tell you that he would be afraid of the girl he made to love him, if he proved false to her."

"So you really think he loves you violently?" said the old man casting a backward glance at her.

"He swore he did."

"To whom? the priest?"

"Go along with you! No, to me!"

At this the old man chuckled—"little fool!" said he.

"And if he breaks his oath now, the devil shall have him. I'll murder him."

"Very well, I suppose you know him. Yet you have never seen his face. If he were to tear the black velvet mask from his face you would never recognize him."

"But that he cannot do as to that mask he owes all his power."

"Well, you are a comical wench—to be enamoured of a man whose face you have never seen!"

"I recognize him by his voice, by the beating of his heart."

"Well, if I were a girl and had a lover, I would insist on seeing his face. He should not come to me in a mask anyhow."

"He cannot put off his mask, I tell you. His oath forbids him to. The moment he removes his mask from his face his power is gone, and neither the devil nor the good angels will obey him any longer."

"That is true," returned the old man solemnly.

"When he likes he can make himself invisible. I know it. He has always escaped pursuit even when the whole country was out after him, and when they thought they had him fast he always disappeared in the earth or in the air. Yet, for all that, if I were his love, see his face I would."

"He told me I should die of fright if I beheld it."

"Then I *would* die of fright—but I would see it."

"His eyes are very fine,—they glow like coals."

"Like coals? Perhaps he is the Dracu* himself. Have you ever tried to make him kiss the amulet on which is the image of St. George and the Dragon?"

"Yes he has kissed it and was none the worse."

"Have you tried to get him to lay his three fingers on a copper crucifix?"

"He laid his fingers thereon and yet they were not burnt."

"Can he say the prayer of condemnation without trembling?"

"He has said it hundreds of times."

"Nevertheless, I maintain he is no mortal man."

"If he should love another woman, I swear that he will very soon find out that he *is* mortal."

Talking thus the riders had descended into the depths of the valley, and when the mountain stream again crossed their path they quitted the usual footpath and followed the bed of the stream.

* Dracu-dragon, *i. e.*, devil.

And a very good road it is for such as do not wish to leave foot-marks behind them. The rapid current swiftly fills the traces of the horses' hoofs with leaves and pebbles.

The ravine grew ever deeper and narrower, and the stream at intervals formed small cataracts which the horses, who had been trained thereto, had to cross. Finally, at a sudden declivity, the water took an unexpected leap of four yards, and when the riders reined up at this very spot, it was plain that here a mill had been built into the hillside, whose wheel it was which drove the swiftly plunging water along.

If a stranger saw this mill he would certainly say: "What foolish man the miller must be who has built his mill here," (———) and that for three reasons. Firstly, because it was so concealed beneath the thick alders that even if one sees it one cannot get at it. Secondly, because it is built exactly under the water-fall which drives the wheel as rapidly as a spindle, so that the millstone must needs be red hot beneath it. Thirdly, because the way to this mill is so peculiar, passing right through the mountain torrent and then winding down to the door by way of a foot-path hewn in the naked rock, and inaccessible to horses. Well, such a miller will surely get but little grain to grind!

When the two riders reached this spot they sprang from their horses, led them into a little dry islet formed by the alders and tied them by their halters to the branches. Then the old man lifted the sack from the saddle.

"Give me a lift up, Anicza!" said he.

One would hardly have supposed that an old fellow of such a colossal build would have required any help at all in order to get this sack across his shoulders, nor would one have supposed from the size of the sack that it would have been so heavy to lift or that it would have weighed so heavily on the old man's shoulders that he had to plant his hand firmly on his hip in order to carry the load.

Then the girl drew both pistols forth from her holsters, stuck them into her girdle, threw the long fowling-piece across her shoulder and springing fearlessly across the stream from boulder to boulder followed behind the stooping old man along the narrow foot-path which led to the mill. In the doorway of the mill stood a youth clad in the usual coarse cloth "*guba*" and half concealed by the door post. In one hand he held a double-barrelled musket, an implement not absolutely necessary for a miller. The old man addressed him while still a good way off:

"*Che timpu?*"*

"*Luna plina.*"†

A strange sort of greeting, more like an exchange of pass-words.

Then both the new arrivals entered the mill in the midst of which a dilapidated grinding ma-

* What sort of weather?
† Full moon.

chine was revolving, the central wheel was minus a couple of teeth.

"Plenty of grinding going on, Paul?" asked the old man.

"Quite enough."

"Help me down with this sack."

"It is heavy certainly," said the other, panting beneath the strain, "how much does it hold?"

"A hundredweight and eighty pounds."

"No mere Turkish maize, eh?"

"Stop the wheel!"

The young man at once obeyed by driving an iron beam clean through the wheel which brought the machinery to a standstill. Then he raised the central revolving disc which was in connection with the millstone, hung in the hook of the millstone an iron chain which was wound round the beam and this done, laid the sack and its contents on the bolting-hutch. Then the old man himself, sat down on the hutch and extended his hand to the girl. "Jump on Anicza." And the girl jumped on without help for she was as agile as a chamois.

"Paul," said the old man to the young journeyman, "was not Fatia Negra here before us?"

"He has not been through here either to-day or yesterday. It has been my turn to watch these last two days."

"I am right you see; he is not here," said the girl.

"He *is* here, I tell you."

THE CAVERN OF LUCSIA

"Come Onucz," said the youth, "can Black Face make himself invisible then? He could not pass here without my knowing it!"

"What do you know about it?" answered the old man, adjusting himself on the bolting-hutch. "Let the mill go!"

As now the revolving disc or platform began to move, the machinery stood still, yet the millstone together with the bolting-hutch began slowly to sink downwards together with those sitting upon it, and after some moments, disappeared entirely into a dark gulf, the chain unwinding and rattling after it. Suddenly from the depths below resounded the old man's voice: "Halt!" Then Paul stopped the mill, hung the chain in an iron ring and the machinery once more set in motion, raised the millstone up, Paul fastened the revolving disc to it and it began to rattle round again so furiously that sparks flew out of it. Now whoever had any meal to grind might come, he was quite ready for them.

It was a huge subterraneous cavern into which Onucz and Anicza had descended. At the bottom of this hollow flowed a branch of the mountain stream which turned the mill and indeed was diverted thither by means of wooden pipes. Here, however, it flowed in its regular bed, glistening here and there in the light of two oil lamps which burnt on both sides of a small iron bridge that traversed the stream.

In the background of this hollow stood a peculiar, roofless, stone building, whose two round little windows, like the eternally watchful eyes of some underground worm, shone with a red glare which dazzled the eyes, while the slate-covered chimney belched forth a thick smoke filled with sparks into the subterranean midnight.

From the interior of the building resounded heavy thuds and the din of grinding as of machinery in perpetual motion which made the very foundations of the rocks quiver. On the bridge stood another armed man with whom the new arrivals exchanged watchwords and the same thing was done at the door of the stone building where the old man made the girl stop.

"Now Anicza," said he, "while I go in, you sit down on that stone bench and wait for me."

"Why cannot I go into the house as well?" enquired the girl, impatiently.

"No more of that. Once a year we come here and every time you ask again if you can come in, and every time I tell you that cannot be. And now I tell you once more: *it cannot be*—and there's an end on't."

"But why may others go in and I not?"

"Why—why! because you are a girl, of course. Leave me in peace. Women have no business in there, they are always so inquisitive, want to know everything and then blab it all out—it is their nature so."

"I'm not like that."

"And then whoever enters here has to swear a

THE CAVERN OF LUCSIA

frightful oath that he will divulge nothing that he sees. I myself shudder all over when I have to repeat it; it is not fit for the mouth of a woman."

"As if *I* were afraid of any oath!" cried the girl defiantly. "I would say any thing that a man might say."

"Don't be a fool, Anicza. A girl cannot come in here, because everyone has to strip himself stark naked before he goes out, before the watchman, and then dress himself again. So you see it won't do."

This difficulty appeared insuperable even to the iron will of Anicza. It was a test even she could not submit to. She stamped her foot with rage and uttered again and again the word Dracu, which in Roumanian means nothing less than his highness the devil himself.

Old Onucz and the watchman thereupon laughed heartily, and the same instant the iron door of the building opened and the girl exclaimed joyfully: "Fatia Negra!"

Onucz and the watchman immediately tore their caps from their heads. It was, indeed, Fatia Negra.

How could he get hither invisibly through all the ambushes set for him? Who could tell? Who had the courage to ask him? Not even Anicza. All she thought of at that moment was to rush forward, fall upon the neck of her mysterious lover and cover his eyes and mouth, which the mask left exposed, with kisses.

"Let Anicza come in!" said the black-masked man, "I'll answer for her, and she shall, like myself, be exempted from undressing."

"It is well, Domnule,"* said the watchman, "but let her at least take the oath which everyone here must swear."

"I am ready," cried the girl boldly.

"No, Anicza," replied Black Mask, "you shall swear to me a stronger oath even than that, you shall swear—by our eternal love."

The proud maiden, trembling with joy, fell at the feet of Fatia Negra at these words, and pressing one of her hands to her heart, raised the other aloft, and, raising her lovely eyes—which reflected the infernal glare of the windows—aloft, towards the smoking canopy above her head, she swore by her eternal love to her beloved that she would never, not even on the rack itself, betray a word, a syllable of what she was about to learn.

But old Onucz scratched his poll.

"Domnule, it is not wise of you to let women swear on such useless things. It is just as if one of us were to hold a penny in his hand and swear by that. It binds nobody."

"It is enough for me," replied the Mask, "and my head is no cheaper than yours. Let him who trusts me not keep away from here."

And holding the girl in his arms, he carried her with him into the building while old Onucz had to dress himself from head to foot in other clothes

---
* Master.

and leave those he had brought with him outside. He would have on his return to put on his own again and leave these others behind. Thus smuggling was impossible.

The first room was for the smelting.

Here there was nothing to be seen of the blazing fire which illuminated the dark hollow through the windows, in one corner of the room was a simple cylinder shaped iron furnace which radiated a burning heat, on the top of which stood a round graphite crucible covered in at the top and provided with a lateral pipe.

"Here the gold is remelted after it has come out of the purifying oven," said Fatia Negra to the girl who pressed close up to him. "Heretofore it required a whole apparatus of boilers and loads and loads of wood to bring it to smelting heat, but since I got that cylinder-stove, ten hundredweights of metal can be melted in ten minutes."

"But where does the fire come from?" enquired the girl.

"From the earth, my beloved."

The girl shrank back with horror, and yet Fatia Negra did not mean hell but that furnace whose powerful bellows drove the melting heat into the double cylinder.

He looked at his watch, the moment had come. At a single whistle a couple of workmen appeared, each of them stripped to the waist on account of the great heat; they held in their hands large iron moulds and stood facing each other opposite the crucible. Then by means of an iron tap Fatia Negra turned the pipe of the crucible and immediately a pale glare began to spread through the room—the liquid gold ran in a thin jet out of the crucible and that was the cause of the light. Actually genuine pure gold made liquid in the fire like wine in a glass and emitting on every side of it a glowing white radiance! Each of the two workmen held his mould beneath it and the girl surveyed the scene with bated breath.

When the operation was finished Black Face turned to the girl again and embraced her saying: "So you see, darling, that is how gold is melted." The girl smiled back at him; what a pity the Black Mask could not smile in return. And now old Onucz came up with his sack for the purifying furnace.

"How much have you in your sack?" asked Fatia Negra.

"A hundredweight and eighty pounds."

"Now we'll see into how much pure gold it will work out."

"The dross mixed with it is only a few pounds in weight."

"Of what quality is it?"

"Well, they purify it very incompletely you know. It is only two-and-twenty carat gold."

"It doesn't matter: we will coin Prussian ducats out of it."

"But where's the mould?"

"I brought it with me, to-day; we'll adjust that also to the machine. We shall gain a hundred florins in every thousand."

Old Onucz kissed Fatia Negra's hand. "Domnule," said he, "you are a man indeed. Domnule, since you became our chief our gains have doubled and the ducats are so good that one cannot distinguish them from the Imperial ones."

Meanwhile the girl felt her head going round to hear them talk of nothing but money, gold, gain!

"Come Onucz, let us look at the new machinery," said the Mask.

"When did you bring the new machinery here?"

"A long time ago; we have coined a great deal of money since it first came. The work is all the quicker and we need fewer men to work it."

They went into the next room through a low door, all three of them having to bow their heads as they entered, and there they saw a gigantic machine at work between whose revolving cylinders depended the long gold ingots which were gradually reduced to the proper thinness for making gold coins.

"Don't you see, Onucz? Hitherto we wasted too much time and labour in cutting the gold plates thin enough and the edges were always too thick to our great loss. Now the machine rolls them all out uniformly. It only cost 10,000 ducats."

"Very cheap indeed!" cried the old man, who

was wearing a ragged sheepskin and yet considered ten thousand ducats a moderate price for a rolling mill.

The Mask took up one of the little glistening plates.

"Do you know, my friend, the name of this?" said he.

"No."

"It's name is Zain. In order that you may not forget it I will wind it round your arm." And as if it were merely hard paper he lightly bent the gold plate round the girl's wrist and then pressed the ends of this improvised bracelet together with his steel-like fingers. "Don't forget that this is called Zain and that you got it from me."

The girl looked doubtfully at him as if she would have said: "Is it lawful for you to give away everything here as if it were your own."

But the old man could not look on at this in silence. "Alas! alas! Domnule, give not away uncoined gold. Rather squander coined gold in heaps. The other is of itself a witness against us and thereby we shall furnish a clue to our enemies."

"It is in a good place," replied Fatia Negra; "it is on Anicza's arm and there it will keep silence."

Anicza replied to this apology with ten kisses. And she calculated rightly. This necklace weighed exactly ten double ducats—but the kisses also were double ones.

Then Fatia Negra led them to another machine

which cut round gold pieces out of the rolled out "Zain." He showed the girl how every clipper, how every screw beneath the impulsion of the piston did its proper share of the work, and how the whole process was set going by steam power from without and could therefore be directed and controlled by one man with another man to relieve him at intervals.

"Dumnezu!"* sighed old Onucz, "when I think that fifty years ago we did all this with only our hammers and chisels! We sweated two whole days over a piece of work which this marvel can do in an hour. And how many hands we employed too!"

Then they went to another machine. This was a small table whose steel wheels notched the ducats before they passed beneath the stamping machine. Perpetually moving elastic springs pushed the gold pieces forward one after the other, turned them round and jerked them away. You saw no other motive power but a large wheel revolving under a broad strap; the strap disappeared through the floor, it was underneath there that the man who set it in motion lived.

Old Onucz sighed aloud. "What things they do invent now-a-days," said he.

But Anicza, full of superstitious fear, clung silently to the arm of Fatia Negra whom all these speechless marvels served and obeyed. Finally,

---
* My master.

descending six stone steps they entered the actual minting room.

A gigantic screw press stood in the midst of the low vaulted chamber. Through the head of the screw was driven a long moving bar, with leaden bullets at both ends and two strong fellows were pushing this bar backwards and forwards; the weight of the machine, as it turned, forced the screw sharply down and in a second it pressed the two round gold pieces laid in the steel matrix into the stamping dies, on one of which was the image of the Mother of God and on the other the cuirassed likeness of the reigning monarch. Immediately after the two matrices recoiled again of their own accord and the two powerful men repeated the pressure. Then a little steel ring shifted suddenly, flinging aside the coined ducat, and a fresh gold piece took its place. The coined ducats already lay in a heap in front of the machine and the workmen, now and then, kicked them away with their feet.

There was something impressive in the spectacle. Here were two poor men, working hard perhaps for their daily bread with little hillocks of seductive gold piled up all around them, gold of which everyone is enamoured in the earth above them, gold for which so many men gladly give up everything, even to their hope in Heaven!

Now and again a third man comes in and pitches the gold into a linen sack with a wooden shovel.

"Let us stamp a few ducats ourselves by way of souvenirs," said Fatia Negra. Anicza assenting, the workmen stepped aside, and Fatia Negra and the girl placed themselves on either side of the leaden bullets on the turning bar.

The Mask bade his sweetheart be careful to avoid the recoil of the machine for should the handle hit her the blow might prove fatal, whereupon the girl, burning to show off her great strength, did not wait for the end of the bar to recover its normal position, but seizing the iron rod when it was only half way round, tore it back again, with the result that the steel clapper did not cast the gold piece between the matrices in the usual way and it thus received a double impression, being stamped with a two-fold figure of the Mother of God on one side and a two-fold figure of the royal profile on the other.

Old Onucz rushed towards Anicza and angrily tore her away:

"You little fool, be off!" cried he, "you will spoil the machine, it is not for the likes of you."

But Fatia Negra now picked up the ducat which had fallen to the ground and showed it with a smile to Anicza: "Look," said he, "there is now a double picture on it."

The girl turned it curiously between her fingers.

"And what will happen to it now?"

"It will go into the smelting furnace again."

"Ah, don't destroy it, give it to me!"

At this the old man fairly lost his temper.

"Are you out of your mind to ask for such a thing? What! a ducat with a flaw in it, which, if seen in your hands would saddle us with the vengeance of the whole government! Domnule, be not so mad as to let her have that ducat! If she has no sense, you at least be sensible. You might ruin the whole lot of us with it."

"Well, Anicza will not wear it on her head, I suppose, or even on her neckerchief, but will fasten it to a little bit of thread and wear it next her heart, there nobody will find it but myself."

Onucz would very much have liked to say: "Neither have you any right to look there, Domnule, for you have not yet spoken to the priest about it"—but this was the one thing he durst not say.

But Anicza gratefully kissed Fatia Negra's hand like a child who has received a gift, not indeed for the ducat, but for the boundless confidence he had shown in giving it to her, which was the surest token of his love. Then she drew forth a little Turkish dagger, bored a hole with it through the ducat and fastened it to a little piece of thin black cord by the side of her little crucifix which she wore upon her bosom—and hid both of them away again.

"Well Domnule," remarked Onucz sulkily, "since we have placed our heads in the girl's hands we must beware of ever offending her."

But now the assayer came up, bringing with him a nice elaborate calculation on a black slate, showing exactly how much pure gold Onucz had handed in to the coining department, how much it would be worth when coined and deducting three per cent. for expenses, how much he was to receive in cash by way of exchange.

"And now go and let the cashier pay you what is due to you, Onucz," said Fatia Negra.

And so while he remained behind for the purpose of settling his account Anicza and Fatia Negra retired to a little adjoining chamber. There would be plenty of time for two lovers to talk over their love affairs while so many gold coins were being counted out.

"Where have you been? it's a whole month since I saw you?" asked Anicza sitting on the adventurer's knee. "Do you know how long a month is to me? First quarter, new moon, full moon, last quarter, all this have I watched through and never saw you once, where have you been?"

"I have been abroad for those new machines. That is a business one cannot entrust to another."

"Are there pretty girls abroad?—Might you not fall in love with them?"

"Hush! Those are not the questions that men should be asked."

"Why not?"

"Because men are not in the habit of answering them."

"But suppose a girl wants to know?"

"Then it will go badly with her. Besides, what do you want me to tell you? Would you like to know that I'm such a block, a clod, that no other eye but yours takes any pleasure in looking at me? Or would you like to hear that I am a sort of hermit who has wandered in disguise through seven kingdoms and casts down his eyes whenever he encounters a petticoat? Or that I cross myself and turn away whenever a woman looks at me? Or shall I tell you: in such and such a place I nipped the white cheeks of a pretty blonde, and in such and such a place the coquettrie of a pair of blue eyes made me forget myself, and in such another place I bedded my intoxicated head in the arms of a brunette?—and that after wandering through seven kingdoms I have found no lovelier girl than my own enchanting Anicza?"

The girl could neither reply nor scold, for her mouth was closed fast with kisses.

"You know I am very jealous," she said at last, when she was able to tear herself free. "I do not love as others love. I can only think of you and your love. I am neither hungry nor thirsty but only—in love. I am never weary, I scarcely know that I am working, for love makes me sing and sing all day. I dream only of you. I care not what is going on in the whole world so long as I only know what is happening to you. I know that you love me and that you are mine so long as you are here. But how often you are far away! How often I do not see you for weeks, for months at a time! Then I get nearly mad. I am determined to find out where you are and what you are doing, with whom you are speaking and then I say, I feel quite mad."

"Indeed! Then let me tell you, my dear girl, that it would do you no good to know where I am, for I am much more exposed to the fire of pointed rifles than to the fire of pretty eyes."

"Are you then a robber chieftain, a mountain smuggler?"

"I am a lot of things."

"Then take me with you into your band"—she spoke with heaving bosom.

But Fatia Negra stamped his foot.

"It cannot be, Anicza," said he; "think no more of it! I will never take you with me."

"Why not?" asked the girl and her eyes flashed like a wild cat's.

"Because then I should become jealous of you and that would be bad for us both. Remain in your father's house; there you are safe."

The girl drew from her bosom the defaced ducat she had just received together with the crucifix.

"Hearken, Fatia Negra! my father says that this badly coined piece of gold places your life in my hand. And know, besides, Fatia Negra, that I have sworn on this Crucified One here that if ever you betray me I will kill you in my fury without thinking twice about the how or where. It is not well that two such dangerous objects should repose on my heart. Look! I give them both to you."

"Wherefore, Anicza?"

"Take the things, I say, and keep them, for my guardian angel knows, I have told him, that with me they are not in a safe place. You do not know me yet."

The girl burst out crying, and Fatia Negra could no longer soothe her with kisses, and then old Onucz poked his gray shaggy head through the doorway and said: "I have been paid already, Domnule, have you?"

Fatia Negra stroked the girl's hair and face and whispered her not to take on so.

The stitches of the old Roumanian's patience now, at last, gave way altogether. "Domnule," said he, "would you not, if I earnestly besought you to do so, begin to think of the day on which you intend to become my daughter's husband?"

For a moment Fatia Negra seemed thunderstruck; then he recovered himself and replied in a calm but menacing voice: "If ever it occurs to you to put the question to me again, your head will reach home an hour earlier than yourself."

The old man made no reply, but he seized the girl by the hand and led her away with him, returning to the mill with her by the same way that he had come. They found their horses by the alder trees and remounted. It was a fine clear night, and Onucz told his daughter to ride in front. They had now divided the coined gold into two portions. When they had once more reached the ridge of the mountain the old man pronounced

Anicza's name in a low tone. The girl looked backwards and perceived that the old man's long-barrelled rifle was pointed directly at the back of her head. In her terror she covered her face with her hands. "What would you do?" cried she.

"Fear nothing, I only want that piece of gold which Fatia Negra gave you. I'll not stake *my* head on *your* whimsies!"

The girl had anticipated something much worse than this, so she quietly answered: "You can spare yourself the trouble, I have already returned it to Fatia Negra. I would not carry it about with me any longer."

"You have acted wisely," said the old man, lowering his musket. "Now you can ride on."

The early dawn was breaking as they reached home. When Anicza entered her room she found hanging up beneath the ikon that gleamed and shone over her bed both the damaged ducat and the little cross which she had given to Fatia Negra two hours before. He must indeed be in league with the devil—else how could he have got there, invisibly, so long before them?

Anicza said not a word about it to anybody, but she hid both the amulets safely away in her bosom again—and now she was right proud of her Fatia Negra!

CHAPTER VIII

STRONG JUON

HENRIETTA's married life was not a happy one. Her husband was polite, complaisant, and conventionally correct in his behaviour towards her, and that was all. And then she saw so little of him. He was frequently absent from Hidvár for weeks at a time, and when he returned he regularly brought in his train a merry company of comrades, in whose pastimes Henrietta could take no sort of pleasure.

During those long days when she had Hidvár all to herself and was left entirely to the company of her sad thoughts, she would sometimes walk about till late in the evening in the shady alleys of the home park, listening to the songs of the girls working in the fields. At the end of the park was a church, and in front of it a small clearing fenced around with stakes and looking like a cabbage garden. It surely belonged to some poor man or other. It did—and the poor man was the parish-priest.

Henrietta often saw him, a tall, grey-bearded man in a long black cassock, hastening to his little garden; there the reverend gentleman would divest himself of his long habit, produce a rake, and work till late in the evening. Henrietta fancied at first that was merely a dietetic diversion, but afterwards, when she found him there the next day and the day after that, and at every hour of the day; when she saw him wiping the sweat from his brow in the burning afternoons and leaning wearily at intervals on his rake to rest a while from his labour, then she was persuaded that this work was not a pastime, but a bitter toil for daily bread.

Often times she would very much have liked to ask him how this was, but she was a stranger in these parts and did not understand his language; at last, however, the priest, perceiving the lady one day, peered at her through the palings and wished her good-day in the purest Hungarian, thereby giving her to understand that the language of the gentry was well known to him.

Henrietta begged the old man to leave his labour and come to her.

"It cannot be, your ladyship; his lordship has forbidden me to appear in his courts."

"Why?"

"I am always a nuisance."

"How so?"

"Because I am always on some begging errand. At one time the wind carries off the roof of the church; at another, something is broken in the belfry. It is a year ago now since the school was burnt down, and since then the walls have become overgrown with thistles; the schoolmaster too has gone away, and there is nobody to teach the children, so that they grow up louts and robbers, to the great hurt and harm of the gentry."

"But why is not all this put to rights?"

"Because the poor folks are lazy and drunken, and his lordship is stingy."

Henrietta was astonished at the old man's words.

"Yes, stingy, that's the word," continued the priest. "I do not pick my words, for I am a priest and used to hunger. And he who is used to hunger is free from the yoke of servility. I told his lordship that to his face, and that was why he forbade me the castle."

Henrietta could not continue the conversation, so upset was she at the idea of Hátszegi's stinginess. What! the man who raked in hundreds of thousands at a time with the greatest ease, and no doubt scattered them as recklessly, could shut his door in the face of a poor priest who begged for the house of God and the education of the people! She hastily wished the priest good-night and returned to the castle.

The same evening she sought her husband, who had just come home wearied from the chase, "I have a favour to ask of you," said she. Hátszegi looked astonished: it was the first favour the wife had ever asked her husband.

"Command me!" said he. "Whatever you like to ask is as good as granted already."

"I should like to learn the language of the people in the midst of whom we dwell. I am like a deaf-mute among them at present."

"That will not be difficult. The Wallachian tongue is easily acquired, especially by anyone with a knowledge of French or Latin."

Henrietta blushed scarlet. Was there a covert allusion behind these words? Did Hátszegi know that she understood Latin?

"I should like to have a master who can put me in the way of it. The parish priest here would be a suitable person."

For an instant Hátszegi's eyebrows contracted.

"You shall have your way," he said at last. "It is true that he is the one man in the world who insults me to my face with impunity whenever he meets me, and even presumes to chalk upon the walls of my own castle denunciations against me from the book of the Prophet Nehemiah, so that I was obliged to forbid him ever to appear before me under pain of being thrown headlong out of the window; yet to show you what an obedient servant I am of yours, madame, I will not baulk you of your desire, or desire you to choose another master, but will send and invite him to come up here at once. Everyone shall see that in my house, my wife is the master." And with that Leonard kissed his wife's hand and withdrew.

Early next day the pastor arrived. Margari informed him of her ladyship's desire to learn the Roumanian language, and the words almost stuck in his throat when he added that his Reverence would receive a hundred florins every month for it. Fancy! a hundred florins a month for teaching a lingo only spoken by bumpkins.

Todor Rubán—that was the priest's name—was at once conducted to her ladyship. He was an elderly man, of an open, cheerful countenance; his fine, long white hair fell in thick locks on his simple black cassock, which showed considerable signs of wear.

Henrietta was not in time to prevent the old pastor from kissing her hand.

"This is no slavish obsequiousness towards a great lady," said he, "but the respect of a poor pastor for an angel whom Heaven by a peculiar act of grace has sent down to us. This is no empty compliment, your ladyship. I am not very lavish of such things myself, but I feel bound to address you thus because I am well aware that it is not merely to learn our poor language that you pay me so well for so little trouble. No, I recognize herein the good will which would do what it can to raise and help a poor neglected population: for I certainly shall not exchange my simple maize-bread for better, but will employ your ladyship's gift in the service of God and of our poorer brethren.

From that day Henrietta believed that a call from on high had summoned her to Hidvár to be the guardian angel, the visible providence of a poor, forsaken people, and her most pleasant occupation was now to go from village to village,—

often in the company of the priest, and at other times accompanied by a single groom or quite alone. Thus she visited one after the other all the surrounding parishes like any archdeacon, enquiring after and helping their necessities, distributing money for school-buildings and service books, collecting all manner of stray orphans and bringing them home with her to be fed and instructed; nay she erected a regular foundling hospital at Hidvár for the benefit of the sprouting urchins of the district, and had the liveliest debates with the priest as to the best method of managing it. Her benevolent enthusiasm cost Hátszegi a pretty penny.

"She is a child; let her play!" he would only say when Margari and Clementina represented to him that Henrietta had pawned her jewels at Fehervár in order to teach some more little Roumanian rag-a-muffins how to go about with gloves on like their betters. Nay the baron secretly instructed the tradesmen with whom Henrietta had pawned her jewels to advance her four times as much as they were worth, *he* would make it good again, he said—and then he would buy his wife fresh jewels. An admirable husband, truly!

One day, Henrietta had ridden out to the neighbouring Ravacsel in order to visit a poor Wallachian peasant woman, to whom she had sent some medicine a few days before. The woman, naturally, never drank the medicine, but instead of that got a village quack to rub her stomach with some wonder-working salve so vigorously that the poor patient died in consequence; in fact she was already at the last gasp when Henrietta arrived. Henrietta was beside herself with grief and anger. She felt like a doctor whose prescriptions have been interfered with by a competitor. She could not indeed help the woman, who expired soon after her arrival, but she had at least the satisfaction of making arrangements for a decent funeral. In the meantime it had grown so late that when she turned back toward Hidvár the moon was already pretty high in the heavens.

She was alone on horseback, for it was only a two hours' journey between the two places, and she had therefore not thought it worth while to bring an escort with her. Besides, whom had she to fear? Since she had lived in these parts, all the bad men had disappeared, and whoever she might meet in the roads or lanes would be ready to kiss her hand.

So she turned homewards again alone. The road wound in and out among the valleys and was therefore much longer than if it had gone in a straight direction across the mountains. She had, however, often heard from the peasants that there was a shorter way to Hidvár from Ravacsel on which mules and ponies could go, and she thought it better to look for this road lest night should surprise her among the mountains. But a road that is good enough for mules and ponies may not suit a thoroughbred English steed which does not care about putting its hoofs into the tracks of other beasts; and besides, a hundred paces on level ground is much shorter than twenty-five up hill. Henrietta vividly experienced the truth of this when she reached the summit of the hill, for her horse was sweating from every pore and trembling from the violent exertion. Such horses should not be used in hilly country: a shaggy, sturdy little pony would have treated the whole thing as a joke and not said a word about it.

But the real difficulties of the road only began during the descent, which was equally dangerous for horse and rider. The track, a mere channel washed out of the soft sandstone by the mountain torrents, descended abruptly, the stones giving way beneath the horse's hoofs and plunging after it. Frequently they had to cross very awkward places, and Henrietta could see from the way in which her horse pricked up his ears, snorted and shook his head, that he was as frightened as his mistress.

At last they came to a very bad spot indeed, where on one side of the road there was a sheer abyss, while the rocky mountain side rose perpendicularly on the other. The narrow path here ran so close to the rock that the rider had to bend her head aside so as not to knock it, and the horse could only go forward one foot at a time.

For an instant the horse stood still, as if weighing his chances on that narrow path; but, as there was no turning back now, he was obliged at last to go on.

Henrietta looked shudderingly down into the chasm below her, over which she seemed to hang suspended; and she thought to herself, with something very like a sob: what if we should stumble now!

The thought was scarcely in her mind when one of the horse's hind legs tripped, and the same instant horse and rider were precipitated into the abyss.

Henrietta never lost her head during the fall. She noticed everything that happened during the brief plunge, how the horse struggling desperately clattered down the mountain-side, how the saddle girth burst beneath the strain, how for a mere second some bush or shrub arrested the descent, and how the next instant the weight of the horse tore it down along with him. Finally, falling still lower and turning right round on its back the horse got wedged in between two rocks from which position he was fortunately unable to disengage himself, for had he fallen any further he would have been dashed to pieces.

Henrietta was quite conscious the whole time. Holding on with both hands to the roots of a bush with her left leg still in the stirrup (for saddle and stirrup also remained hanging in the bush) it occurred to her in this painful situation that she still had time to commend her soul to God and then face death more calmly. As to help, there was no hope of it, for the place was far away from all human dwellings; night would soon fall and the bush would presently yield beneath her feet—destruction was certain.

But while the lady neglected to call for assistance, the wedged-in horse did so all the more loudly. Supine and unable to free himself from his uncomfortable position, he repeatedly uttered that terrified scream which one never hears from this noble and reticent beast except in dire extremity. Whoever has heard such a cry will readily admit that it is far more terrible than any merely human appeal for assistance.

After a few moments it seemed to Henrietta as if a halloo were resounding from the depths below; looking down she perceived by the light of the moon a black shape leaping from rock to rock like a chamois, and gradually approaching the dangerous point where she hung.

Any efforts on this man's part seemed to her impossible. There was not a single visible gap or crevice in the face of the steep rock by means of which he could scramble up to her; and how could he help her, how could he liberate her, if he did manage to get at her?

Nevertheless the man drew nearer and nearer. She could by this time make out his goatskin cloak, his high broad cap, the clean shaved face peculiar to the mountain goatherds. His dexterity was as astonishing as the physical strength, with which he often raised himself on the tips of his toes in order to reach a cleft in the rocks, scarcely visible high above his head; often he could scarce hold on by the tips of his fingers, yet the next moment he would swing himself up with half a hand and, setting his foot in the cleft, look about for a fresh foothold.

About a yard below Henrietta was a projecting piece of rock just large enough for a man's foot to stand upon. The next moment Henrietta saw the herdsman mount to this place. He himself was a good fathom in height and his head reached up as far as Henrietta's hips. He looked up at her with a friendly smile, as if he had merely come there to help her down from her horse. Then he said to her in Roumanian: *"Noroc bun Domna!"* which means "Good luck to you, my lady!" So even in this perilous situation it occurred to him to say something pleasant.

"The horse took a false step, my lady," said he, "but all's well that ends well. Prithee, mount upon my shoulder, this bush will not hold fast much longer, it is only a juniper, its roots are weak." Henrietta's heart failed her. This man surely does not imagine that he will be able to carry her down on his shoulders.

"Come, my lady, don't be afraid, I can easily carry you down. Why I often roam about like this after my kids when they fall into the precipice; and you are no heavier than a young kid, I'm sure."

And then, with the hand that remained free, he plucked at the remainder of the damaged bush.

Henrietta perceived with astonishment that the roots which had not snapped asunder beneath his weight were loosened from the rock by the mere tug of the man's hand. But what was he going to do with them?

The herdsman bade the lady fear nothing; no further accident could happen, he said; then, sticking the torn out stump between his legs like a hobby-horse and pressing it against the rock with one hand, he himself turned his back to the mountain-side and suddenly, stretching his legs wide apart, let himself glide down the shelving rock.

Henrietta shrieked aloud, she thought she was lost, but the next moment the herdsman stood on solid ground and looked up at her with a smile: "We're all right, you see," he cried. "Oh, I have travelled like this many a time; it is rare fun,—sledging I call it."

Sledging indeed!—to plunge down a steep mountain side five fathoms deep with the aid of a juniper bush!

From where they now stood it was an easy matter to convey the lady to the bottom of the precipice, which was overgrown with bright grass, on which he deposited her.

"There you are, my lady," said he. "Don't be frightened; I will soon be back again."

And with that he scrambled up again towards the wedged-in horse. Henrietta gazed after him in amazement—whatever was he going to do there?

The fellow, on reaching the wriggling horse, first of all caught firm hold of its front legs and then tied all four legs tightly together with the stirrup-straps. Thereupon, he seized the beast by his fettered legs, pulled them over his shoulders, and with a violent jerk freed the animal from its uncomfortable position and carried it down into the valley likewise. There he untied its legs, helped it on to its hoofs again, and, turning with a smile to Henrietta, said: "A fine horse that; it would have been a shame to have let it come to grief!"

"And you were able to carry it on your shoulders?" gasped Henrietta.

"That isn't very much. It scarce weighs more than four hundredweight. The bear not long ago weighed five, and I had to beat it to death before I could take it home. Surely your ladyship knows that I am the strong Juon—Juon Tare?" And the goatherd said this with as much self-evident pride, as if everyone in the wide world had heard that strong Juon dwelt among these forests. Henrietta's look of surprise apprised him, however, that she, at least, had never heard of him.

"You do not know then, Domna, who I am? Yet I know who you are. I have often met the *Dumnye Barbatu** and he knows me well. He is the only man in the world who is as strong as I am. We have often wrestled together on this grass-plot for a wager. Neither of us has ever been

---
* My lord, your husband.

able to throw the other. His lordship can throw an axe deeper into a tree than I can, but I can put a greater weight. His lordship can kill an ox with a blow from his fist, but I can throttle a bear to death. But we cannot overcome each other, though we have often stood up together—only in joke, only in sport, of course, your ladyship. It would not be well if we encountered each other in our wrath—that would be terrible."

All the time he spoke Juon was skilfully mending the torn saddle-girths and the bridle; then he re-saddled the horse, which was still trembling in every limb, wiped the bloody foam from its mouth, washed its sores and encouraged the lady to remount. In a quarter of an hour, he said, they would meet the road again, and in half an hour they would be at Hidvár.

Then the goatherd, who was well acquainted with all the meanderings of the valley, took the horse's rein and conducted the lady to the mountain pass, where the beaten track began again. There he kissed her hand and parted from her.

"I must now go back," said he, "for they are waiting for me."

"Who?"

"My goats and my wife."

"Then you have a wife? Do you love her?"

"Love her?" cried the herdsman proudly,—and then he added in a lower voice: "She is as beautiful as your ladyship!—*Buna nopte, Domna!*"*

---
* Good night, my lady.

And without waiting for an answer, he plunged back into the forest, disappearing by leaps and bounds.

When Henrietta got home she said not a word to anyone about what had taken place, though the condition of the horse and his harness sufficed to show that an accident had happened. But she could scarce wait for the morrow to come, bringing along with it Todor Rubán, from whom she meant to find out everything relating to Juon Tare.*

---
* From the Roumanian *Taria*, strength, solidity.

CHAPTER IX

THE GEINA MAID-MARKET

"Would your ladyship believe,"— so Todor*
Rubán began his story of Juon the strong,—
"sitting here as you do by the fireside, accustomed
from your birth to every elegant luxury, with a
particular servant always ready to fly obediently
to accomplish each separate command, and with
different glasses and porcelain for each several
course at meals—would your ladyship believe, I
ask, that there are people in this world who know
not what it is to have a roof above their heads
when they go to sleep, who would not recognize a
bed or a dinner service if they saw them, nay, who
often are in want of bread—and yet, for all that,
are happy?

"And yet such people live quite close to us. We
need not think of the savage inhabitants of
Oceania,—we can see enough of them and to spare
in this very place. Your ladyship can hear from
your balcony the melancholy songs of their pastoral flutes, especially of an evening, when the
milch-goats are returning from the deep valleys.

"The herdsman here never sleeps beneath a roof
either summer or winter; every spring he counts
the goats of his master's herds and the half of

---
* Theodore.

every increase belongs to him; nobody enquires how he lives there among his herds in the lofty mountain-passes, how he defends himself against hurricanes and snow-storms, yes, and against the wild beasts of the forest, the bears and wolves—nobody troubles his head about all that.

"Such a goatherd is that same Juon whom your ladyship has learnt to know. Perhaps we shall hear something more about him some other time, for his life has been very romantic; now, however, I will only tell you of a single episode therein:

"There once lived near here in the district of Vlaskutza, a rich *pakular** who had scraped together a lot of gold out of a mining venture at Verespatak, and therefore went by the name of wealthy Misule.

"He had an only daughter, Mariora by name,—and has your ladyship any idea of what Roumanian beauties are? A sculptor could not devise a nobler model. So beautiful was she that her fame had spread through the Hungarian plain as far as Arad, and whenever great folks from foreign lands came to see Gyenstar and Brivadia they would make a long circuit and come to Vlaskucza in order to rest at the house of old Misule, where the finest prospect of all was a look into the eyes of Mariora.

"This wonderously beautiful maiden loved the poor goatherd Juon, who possessed nothing in the world but his sheepskin pelisse and his alpen-

---
*Roguish speculator.

stock; him she loved and him alone. Wealthy old Misule would naturally have nothing to say to such a match; he had in his eye an influential friend of his, a gentleman and village elder in the county of Féhervár, one Gligor Tobicza,—to him he meant to give his daughter. Reports were spread that Juon was a wizard. It was Misule's wife who fastened this suspicion upon him, because he had succeeded in bewitching her daughter. She said among other things, that he understood the language of the brute beasts, that he had often been seen speaking with wolves and bears, and that when he spread out his shaggy sheepskin, he sat down at one end of it and a bear at the other. There was this much of truth in the tale, that once when he was tending his flocks Juon heard a painful groaning in the hollow of a rock, and, venturing in, perceived lying in one corner a she-bear who, mortally injured in some distant hunt, had contrived to drag its lacerated body hither to die. Beside the old she-bear lay a little suckling cub. The mother dying before his very eyes, Juon had compassion on the desolate cub, took it under his protection, and carried it to a milch-goat, who suckled it. The little wild beast thrived upon the milk of the tame animal and, softened by human fellowship, grew up much attached to its master. Bears, I may tell your ladyship, are not bloodthirsty by nature. Henceforth the bear went forth with the herdsman and the herds, helped to drive the goats together of an evening, and enlivened the long dreary days by turning somersaults—an art at which bears excel. At night it slept by Juon's side and made itself cosey by burying its snout in his bosom. When meal-time came, the bear sat down beside Juon, for he knew that every second slice of cheese would be his. He also fetched fire-wood to put under the pot in which the maize-pottage was boiling. Then, too, he explored the woods in search of wild honey and brought back his booty to share it with Juon. When it was very hot he carried his pelisse after him, a pelt more or less made very little difference to him. Juon had nobody to speak to but the bear, and if a man speaks quite seriously to the beasts they get to understand him at last. Moreover, in moments of ill temper the bear had learnt to recognize that Juon's fists were no less vigorous than his own paws, so that he had no temptation to be ungrateful.

"This, then, was the man beloved by Mariora.

"In our part of the country, my lady, there is an original popular custom, the maiden-market.

"In the highlands of Bihar stands the rocky bluff of Geina, which grows green, like every other Transylvanian height, as soon as it is cleansed from snow. There I first met Juon, many years ago. He stood there on the mountain summit the live-long day, blowing on his alpenstock, while the bear was plucking strawberries in the valley below and guarding the goats, not from running away, but from other wild beasts. The prospect from this spot is really sublime. In one direction you can see the mountain-chain of Vulcani, in the other the environs of Klausenberg and the Gyalian Alps. But westwards stretches the great Hungarian plain, whose misty expanse loses itself against the horizon.

"On a certain day of the year things are very lively at Geina. In the evening of the first Sunday after St. John Baptist's day the ginger-bread-bakers come thither from Rezbanya and Topanfalu with their horses dragging loads of honey-cakes, and barrels full of meal and brandy, and pitch their tents in the forest-clearing. On that Sunday the highlands are full of merry folks, and the maiden-market is held there.

"From near and far repair thither the mothers and their marriageable daughters, all tricked out with their dowries ready in the shape of strings of gold and silver coins round their necks, with bright variegated garments at their horses' sides, and stuffed pillows and painted pitchers on the saddles in front of them. All these things they unpack and arrange in rows in front of the tents, just as at an ordinary fair; and then the purchasers come along, jaunty, connubially-inclined young fellows, who inspect the dowries, engage the wenches in conversation, and chaffer and haggle and go away again if they cannot come to terms. Many of the girls are kept back, others are given up to the first bidder, and when once a couple is mated they are escorted to the tune of lively flutes and bagpipes to the first Kalugye,* or pastor, who sanctifies the union according to the religion of the spouses.

"Your ladyship laughs at this custom, yet it is capable of a very natural explanation. The inhabitants of these Alpine regions live necessarily far away from one another—how else could they tend their herds?—even the nearest neighbours being a good stiff half hour's walk apart. So the young girls stay at home, and the young fellows only see them once a year—at the maiden-market of Geina.

"Now, of course such a famous beauty as Mariora had no need to go all the way to the Geina fair in search of a husband, especially as one had already been chosen for her who brought with him all the pride of riches. But her father Misule would not on any account have neglected the opportunity of exhibiting his daughter, during the pilgrimage to Geina, as the most lovely girl of the district; and his wife could not have lived unless she had hung out Mariora's gold-embroidered shift in front of the tent and haughtily sent at least ten suitors about their business.

"Gligor Tobicza, coming all the way from Rezpatak, appeared at the fair at the same time, with twelve high-backed horses and six Gipsy musicians, ribbons and coloured kerchiefs fluttering from every horse and every cap. The comrades drank together and then had a little rumpus also. Tobicza broke the heads of a few of the more up-

---

* Or rather, *Calugaru*, monk, not pastor.

roarious spirits, and then peace was restored again, and the general good humour was higher than ever—only the bride remained sad.

"Suddenly it occurred to Tobicza that it would be nice to get a kiss from Mariora. But the girl repulsed him: 'I am not your wife yet,' she cried.

"'Yet if Juon were to ask for you, I suppose you would not say no?'

"The girl honestly confessed that she would not.

"At this Tobicza was mad with rage. 'Let him come hither then, if he loves you,' cried he, 'let him tear you away from me if he be the better man. I will strike him dead with this—see!' And drawing a long goat-skin bag out of his girdle, the bottom of which was choke full of ducats, and whirling it round his head like a morning-star* he turned forestwards and roared: 'Come hither, tattered Juon, thou ragged dog! 'Tis now maiden-market day if you want to buy Mariora! Come forth thou cowardly hound and let me beat you to death! I'll fell you to the earth with my ducats. I'll break your head with my gold money.' And the whole crowd laughed at and loudly applauded these witticisms.

"But just as he was raging most furiously, a great roaring suddenly arose from the direction of the forest,—whereupon the crowd rushed away from their tents to their horses, overturning barrels and trunks as they went, the women screaming and the men cursing, and all with one voice

---
* A spiked club.

exclaiming: 'the bear is coming!' 'Juon is coming with his bear!'

"That was enough for every one. Only the most determined sportsmen care about tackling a bear in the open, for even when mortally wounded the beast is quite capable of taking his revenge. In an instant every soul rushed headlong from the summit of Geina into the roads below, leaving behind bride, dowry and drinking booth; so that when the bear and Juon leaped out of the juniper bushes there was nobody left on Geina. Nobody, that is, but Mariora, who did not fly with the fugitives, but hid herself in the tent.

"Tobicza had headed the race, but as his legs were heavy with the mead he had drunk, he threw away his big bag of gold to lighten his limbs and prevent Juon from overtaking him. But Juon, snatching it up, whirled it round like a sling and threw it with all his might after his rival, exclaiming: 'There's your money, big voice! take it and buy a wife with it. You are nothing at all without it. But I am still Juon, though I have only an axe in my hands.'

"Then he went up to Mariora, kissed and embraced her, and asked her if she would be his bride and go away and live with him in the forest. And when she said: 'Yes,' he kissed her again and took her with him into the free forest without once looking back at the dowry lying abandoned there with all its gold and glitter. In his eyes only Mariora was of gold, nothing else.

"The bear meanwhile made some little havoc in a mild sort of way, among the honey-cakes, but he did no other damage.

"And I can assure your ladyship that this wife who has nothing in the world but her husband, but that husband all her own—is even now very happy."

CHAPTER X

THE BLACK JEWELRY

It was during this time that Henrietta cherished the bizarre illusion that it was her vocation to cultivate the acquaintance of the honest but homely peasantry living around, in whose lowly circles a widowed protestant pastor's wife and a worn-out old miner were the principal personages. Her husband laughed good-humouredly at her vagaries, as he called them: "She is only a child," he cried, "let her play and cut out dolls' clothes for those who want them! When she has grown up, she will very soon look out for other diversions." "My dear child," he would sometimes say to her, "do exactly as you like. I only beg of you one thing: whenever you are tired of these innocent, well-meaning illusions and return to rough, prosaic, brutal reality; whenever you feel yourself deceived or wounded by those whom you may have implicitly trusted, pray recollect that you have a natural protector, a real friend—your husband!"

Thus it was that Hátszegi spoke to his child-wife on the rare occasions when they met together.

It was only rarely, for they saw nothing of each other for the greater part of the day. During the so-called honey-moon the husband and wife had scarcely spent half an hour a day in each other's company.

On one occasion the pastor went to Déva, and when he returned he had a lot to tell her ladyship of a fine young fellow, Szilard by name, who held the office of magistrate at Lippá. His other name he had forgotten, but Henrietta easily guessed it. Mr. Szilard had been very polite to him, the parson added, and had joyfully listened to all he had to tell him about Hidvár and its mistress; but when the priest had pressed him to pay a visit to that part of the country to see and admire its rare natural beauties, the young man had replied: "Anywhere in the world but there." What possible objection could he have against the district?

This piece of news gave Henrietta plenty to think about for days and nights together. So Szilard had not remained at Pest; he had followed her to the utmost confines of the realm; they were now quite close to each other and yet he would not see her. He seeks her out and avoids her at the same time. What a romantic dreamer!

And yet there was nothing romantic in it after all. Szilard had come to Arad county on a visit to Mr. Sipos's relations; he had been elected a magistrate there, and he did not approach Hidvár because he had no desire to run after a former sweetheart who was now another man's wife. As for Henrietta she had long ago earned from her husband's friends the name of the "little nun," the "little eremite" because nothing could entice her from her seclusion. If only they had known her thoughts!

One day, however, she surprised her husband by expressing a wish to go to the Charity Ball at a neighbouring mining town; it was for raising funds to build up again a burnt-down village.

Hátszegi, always courteous, bowed and consented.

Henrietta had made up her mind to go as simply dressed as possible. She wanted to be modest and humble, as it befitted a woman who, rich herself, envied everyone who was poor. While she was still in the midst of her preparations, she received through the post (Margari went to the nearest post-office once a week) a little sealed packet which, to judge from the postmark, must have been posted at Lippá. Before breaking it open, she locked herself in her room, like one about to commit a capital offence, and three times examined the seals which guarded it before she ventured to open it. The seal bore the impress not of a crest or an initial letter as usual, but of a single star. There could be no doubt whatever now as to who the sender was.

Then, very cautiously, she broke the seals and opened with a beating heart the lid of the box. Inside was a little morocco casket.

With a tremulous hand she opened it, and found inside it a pair of earrings and a brooch. Both earrings and brooch were of oxydized silver, dark blue in colour passing insensibly into black. The pendants of the earrings were in the shape of little fishes hanging upon little hooks and with mobile little scales, which at the slightest movement made them seem alive. Each of them had a pair of very tiny but very brilliant diamond eyes. The brooch on the other hand represented a butterfly, also with two sparkling diamond eyes; one of them was blue, a rare colour for a diamond.

Henrietta was indeed pleasantly surprised.

There was not a line of writing along with them, but was there any necessity for it? How simple, how nice it all was! How well he must know her taste who had selected it! Her husband could never have hit upon such an idea.

What should she say to her husband if he should notice them? But why should she show them to anybody? She would not even put them on till the last moment, just before she started on her journey. All day long she was as happy as a child who is going to its first party; even in her husband's presence she could not control her delight.

But Hátszegi never enquired why she was so joyous. On the day before the entertainment he went with his wife to the town in question, where he owned, not the castle, it is true, but a comfortable mansion of considerable extent, whose first floor was rented by a mining engineer and his family. These worthy people felt highly honoured at receiving the baron and his lady beneath their roof. They gave their distinguished guests their best rooms which looked out upon the street, and retired themselves to the back of the house. The mining engineer had a pretty young wife, with whom Henrietta immediately made friends. Ladies love the close companionship of their own sex best whenever something entirely different is occupying their thoughts.

On the morning of the great day the big-wigs of the little town hastened to pay their respects to the great lady who had arrived in their midst, and whose reputation for benevolence had spread far and wide. Amongst them was an aged woman whose hands and head were continually shaking, and who almost collapsed with terror every time anybody accosted her unexpectedly. She was the widow of a Unitarian pastor, well to do, people said, and a large mining proprietor. Her nervous affection was due to a painful episode in her life. One night Fatia Negra and his band had broken into her house and played havoc there, and ever since she had been tremulous and easily terror-stricken. The old woman was delighted to see Henrietta, whom she called the guardian angel of the county, and she would not be content till she had seized Henrietta's little hands in her own trembling ones and raised them painfully to her lips.

At last the joyous evening arrived. Henrietta put on a very simple ball-dress, compared with which the dress of the mining engineer's wife was really luxurious. The black ornaments well became her attire, but the engineer's wife was astounded at the simplicity of the great lady's costume. She had now only one anxious moment to go through, the moment when her husband first saw the new ornaments. But this moment sped away without any catastrophe, although with much of heart throbbing. Hátszegi observed the jewels in the ears and round the neck of his bride and paid her the compliment of saying that they contrasted admirably with the snowy whiteness of her alabaster neck.

So no ill came of it after all.

When the time came, the baron's carriage drove up to the door and the ladies entered it. The baron himself was to come afterwards with the mining engineer when the empty carriage returned. In the meantime the baroness was entrusted to the care of the mining engineer's wife, who was one of the notabilities of the little town.

The ball was to take place in the large room of the chief inn of the place, and the baroness, on entering it, was surrounded by a crowd of admirers. The young wife felt that she was being made much of. She felt in the midst of all this homage and devotion as if she had been lifted up to Heaven, and her heart was full of gratitude. If he be here (and he *must* be here somewhere, hiding in the crowd, no doubt, in order not to excite attention) then he will be able to see from his hiding-place how pale the face of his old love is from sorrow—and yet how radiant because of the honour now shown to her.

But Szilard did not see her face at that moment. He was far away, never dreaming that anybody still thought of him. A surprise of quite another sort awaited Henrietta.

After she had twice walked round the room—there was a pause just then between two dances—she perceived sitting on a corner seat the old lady already alluded to, whose head and hands were always shaking so, and hastened up to her as to an old acquaintance.

The old pastor's wife, perceiving Henrietta, rose at first from her seat in order to meet her half way, but the next moment she fell back horror-stricken, at the same time stretching out both hands in front of her with widely-outspread fingers as if to ward her off. Henrietta, unable to explain this odd gesture, remained rooted to the spot with astonishment.

The old lady, still continuing to stretch out her trembling hands, now advanced towards her with tottering footsteps indeed, yet with flaming eyes. Everyone regarded the two women with amazement. There was a dead silence, and in the midst of this astonishment, in the midst of this silence, the old woman shrieked with a voice full of horror that turned everybody's blood cold: "Madame!—those jewels—on your neck—that black butterfly—'tis the very same—which on that fearful night—that accursed Fatia Negra—tore from my

THE BLACK JEWELRY 173

neck—those black earrings which he tore from my ears—one eye of the butterfly is a blue diamond!"

Henrietta felt as if the floor were slipping away from beneath her feet. She was wearing stolen jewels on her neck, and their former owner had recognized them!

She heard a hissing and a murmuring all around her. She gazed about her, possibly for a protector, and she perceived that she was standing alone in the midst of the room and that everyone recoiled from her, even her companion, and all eyes were fixed upon her. She had a feeling of being branded with red-hot irons as she stood there, dishonoured and unprotected in the midst of so many strangers, and over against her a terrible accuser who had the horrible right to ask her: "Madame, where did you get those stolen jewels?"—and she had nought to say to such a question.

At that moment a manly voice, which she at once recognized, rang out close beside her.

"Madame, give me your arm!—I bought those jewels for you at Paris. I will be responsible for them."

It was her husband. And with that, he strode up to his wife, seized her hand and, casting a glance at the surrounding throng, cried in a threatening voice to those closest to him: "Whoever dares to cast a disrespectful glance upon my wife, will have to reckon with me. Make room there!"

Henrietta saw how the crowd made way, how everyone stepped aside at this word of command; she saw even the shaking widow sit down somewhere; but then everything began to grow black before her eyes and she sank swooning into the arms of the man whom, hitherto, she had hated so much, and who in this most awful moment had been her sole deliverer! When she came to again, she found herself in the carriage. Her husband had not stayed a single instant longer in that town, but was conveying her, though it was now night time, straight to Hidvár.

It is not very advisable to travel in pitch-black darkness along mountain roads. Henrietta could gather from the slow jolting of the coach that they were proceeding very cautiously. She opened the window and peeped out. She then saw her husband walking along by the side of the coach with a lantern in his hand picking his way. The coachman was sitting on the box and the heyduke was close to the carriage in order to steady it over the more difficult places.

A voice within her reproached her for hating this man so long—how could she have done it? He had always been delicacy itself towards her, he had never demanded anything of her, and no doubt the reason why he had held back from his young wife for a time was because he would not importune her with his presence—her who had now learnt to recognize him as her sole protector!

After a vast amount of jolting and tumbling

about, they got at last on to a regular road again. Here the baron halted the coach and looked inside it. When he saw that Henrietta was awake, he asked her if she wanted anything, and whether she would allow him to sit down beside her.

Henrietta had resolved to tell her husband everything at the very first question, everything, even to her most secret enthusiasms; nay, even that which God alone could read in her heart. But Hátszegi gave her no opportunity of doing so.

"My dear Henrietta," said he, "don't imagine for a moment that I shall trouble my head as to how you came into possession of that mysterious jewelry, or why you should have chosen them out of all your bijous to wear on this particular evening. I have charged myself with all the responsibility in the matter. I could not think of anything more appropriate to say at the moment. Only one thing I beg of you: tell me no lies. Act as if you had received the jewelry from me. I will so arrange the matter that nothing more will be heard about it. Such things may happen to anybody. The only awkwardness about the business is that the things were recognized in such a public place, and that the former possessor of the ornaments is so extremely nervous. Don't be afraid! Give me your hand! Why do you tremble so? I'll guarantee that there shall be no unpleasant consequences for you. In case, however, you did not receive this jewelry from your dear grandfather, I ought, I think, to write to the good old man and put his mind at ease by letting him know that I gave it you, as goodness only knows what Rumour may whisper in his ear."

Could any man have asked his wife for a confession more tenderly?

"Shall I write to him?"

"Yes, write," said Henrietta, and with that she fell upon her husband's bosom and began to sob bitterly—and a husband's breast is no bad place for a wife's flowing tears.

Henrietta was forced to confess to herself that her husband, at least so far as she was concerned, was a man of noble and tender sentiments. From henceforth she began to regard him through a glass of quite another colour; she began to believe that the faults she had noticed in him were only the usual bad habits of his sex, and began to discover all sorts of hidden good qualities in him. She began to love her husband.

When early next morning the carriage stood in the courtyard of Hidvár. Henrietta awoke in her husband's arms: there she had been sleeping for a long time. When she looked round and encountered Hátszegi's bright manly glances it almost seemed to her as if the dreadful scene of the night before was a mere dream, from which it was a joy to awake. When her husband kissed her hand before departing for his own room, Henrietta pressed *his* hand in return and gave him a grateful smile.

But what then was the key to this horrible mystery? Who could have hit upon the idea of sending this jewelry? There was not a gleam of light to go by. An enigma closed the way to every elucidation, and this enigma was—Fatia Negra. How did the jewelry get out of his hands into Henrietta's? What was the motive for such a transfer? And who was the man himself? This thought gave Henrietta no rest.

Why could they not seize this famous robber? First of all, she kept on asking her husband about it, and he replied that the whole story about Fatia Negra was only a Wallachian fable. It was true that robberies were committed by men who regularly wore black masks, but it was never one and the same man who was guilty of these misdeeds. Nevertheless the name had won a sort of nimbus of notoriety among the common people, many had made use of it as well as of the mask attaching to it, and though it was an undeniable fact that Fatia Negra had been caught and hanged more than once, yet he still continued to live and go about. The popular mythology had immortalized him.

The parson, however, had quite a different opinion of the matter; he seemed to be more particularly informed. Although he opined Fatia Negra wandered through every corner of the kingdom, his abiding nest was in this district; he had a sweetheart here to whom he appeared periodically.

"Why don't they seize him then?" asked Henrietta.

"Because a part of the common folks holds with him, and the other part thinks he is in league with the devil."

"I would set a high price on his head and give it to whomsoever caught him."

"Oh, my lady, the various counties have done that scores of times, and now and then a young fellow braver than the rest has tried to catch him; but they have all of them ended by losing their own heads instead of getting his."

"Never mind, I will not be satisfied till that man is in my power. Ah, the robber-chieftain little imagines what an enemy he has raised up against him in me, when he put this terrible riddle into my heart. And it is a riddle I mean to solve, too."

The priest shook his head as if he would have said: "Strong men have given up the task, what can a weak woman do?"

Henrietta told her husband not a word of all this, and the chatter about the black jewelry gradually died a natural death. Hátszegi sent back her property to the widow and told her where she could find the vendor—in Paris. We can readily imagine that she did not go all the way to Paris to make enquiries, being quite content with getting back her stolen property.

This incident made such an impression on Henrietta that she avoided all those circles in which she had been so ruthlessly exposed to insult. A blush of shame and anger suffused her face whenever she thought of it. She also abandoned all her work of benevolence among the people. She began to think that her husband was right after all when he said, as he did continually: "Let the gentry stick to the gentry, and the poor to the poor!" In fact she was now inclined to think him right in everything; the easiest thing a wife can do, she said to herself, is to trust her husband implicitly. Henceforth Henrietta adopted another mode of life; her motto now was: "Whatever my husband chooses, for at home he is my lord!"

So the halls of Hidvár overflowed with guests again, and balls, *soirées*, and picnics followed each other in quick succession. The young wife learnt to know the gentry and magnates of Transylvania face to face, and it was no wonder if she quickly accommodated herself to her new surroundings and began to be reconciled to her fate. She felt like one who, after seeing a landscape by moonlight and thinking it highly crude, sees it again by the light of day and finds it quite different.

And now the autumn came, the season when men prepare and congregate together for dangerous hunting expeditions. Bears and boars are now the only topics. For a week beforehand the women cannot get a word out of the gentlemen, they herd together in the armoury and talk of nothing but guns and dogs, firing each other by recounting their past exploits, making bets, and playing at cards. The ladies at such times are shelved altogether.

During the actual hunting season the men are not to be seen for whole weeks at a time, but off they go to the woods and stalk or lurk for their prey in the midst of water and ice, and the ladies think it nothing extraordinary if their husbands or lovers, as the case may be, come back, or are carried back, drenched with rain, invisible for mud, with their garments torn to shreds and their limbs mangled; for after all it is the only manly diversion—the only diversion really fit for a gentleman.

When the bear-hunting began, that heroic cripple, Squire Gezson, also appeared with Count Kengyelesy and numerous other familiar faces from distant counties, who had all met together on the day after Henrietta's wedding, and who regularly made Hidvár their autumn trysting-place.

Count Kengyelesy did not bring his wife with him: the little rogue on her husband's departure declared that she was ill and remained behind—*verbum sap!*

Henrietta was very much occupied by the duties of hospitality. She took a pride in anticipating the wants of all her guests, and at the evening *soirées* she played the part of hostess with becoming *aplomb*.

One day the gentlemen with their beaters, rangers, dogs, and carts, had all gone off to the forest as usual, and Henrietta was left alone in the castle with Clementina, Margari, and the domestics. As for Margari, he would not have gone to the woods for all the bears in the world.

Clementina, solemnly cackling gossip as usual, imparted to Henrietta that the night before, when the gentlemen played at cards, the luck had run dead against Hátszegi: Count Kengyelesy had won back from him the whole of the Kengyelesy estate. "Thank God!" sighed Henrietta at this glad intelligence. This was one of the things that had weighed down her heart like a nightmare, one of the partition-walls, so to speak, which had hitherto separated her from her husband. This, at any rate, had now disappeared.

Clementina went on to say that my lord baron had not cared a straw for this loss; nay, he had laughed and said that it only showed how lucky he was in love. Henrietta applied the saying to herself and began to be quite proud of it.

The count, however, pursued Clementina, had said that he durst not rejoice in his winnings or that accursed Fatia Negra might rob him of them again on the highroad as he had done once before.

A cold shudder ran through Henrietta's limbs at that accursed name. That Fatia Negra! She had already begun to forget him. And thus old memories began to revive, and at last her excited imagination began to fancy that there was some sort of connecting link between Szilard and Fatia Negra, between the dearest and the most terrible of beings! What if her rejected lover had avenged himself by publicly shaming her! It was with such anxieties as these that the young wife went to sleep in her lonely chamber.

Early next day she received a visit from the priest.

All the time the army of guests was going in and out of the castle gates, he never came near the place, but now he hastened to exchange a few words with the lady of the house. And Henrietta was very glad that he had come.

"I bring you news of Fatia Negra and of other things also," said the priest, as soon as he was alone with the lady.

Henrietta was instantly all attention.

"Yesterday the famous butterwoman who dwells at Dupe Piatra came to open her soul to me in a very difficult matter. This woman, as the whole country-side knows, is a famous quack and a preparer of such specifics as it is unlawful for one man to give to another. Formerly she was visited by multitudes of people suffering from every sort of ill—especially girls. More than once she has paid dearly for her quackery, for the county authorities apprehended her for poisoning, and clapped her into jail for some years. Since then she has grown more cautious and does not care about seeing everyone in her lonely little forest hut, especially since I impressed upon her severely what a heavy load she was burdening her conscience with by turning the secret healing forces which Nature had implanted in the herbs of the field, to the destruction of ignorant humanity. Yesterday, then, this woman came to me (and it is a very rare thing to see her among men) and informed me that last night Fatia Negra had visited her."

Henrietta shuddered all over. So he was as near as that!

"The medicine-woman said that the mask requested her to prepare poison for him that would be sure to kill. She said she would not as she had no wish to fall again into the hands of the county authorities. He promised her money, he showed her a lot of ducats. She told him it wouldn't do. Then he drew forth a pistol, pressed the barrel to her temples, and threatened instantly to blow her brains out if she did not comply with his request. 'Very well,' said she, 'fire away: I would rather be shot than hanged.' Perceiving he could do nothing with her by threats, he fell to entreating, and said it was not a man he wanted to poison but a wild beast. 'What sort of a beast do you want to kill?' she asked him. 'That is no business of yours,' said he. 'But it is my business,' she replied, 'for the poison that a wolf or a savage dog will eat, a bear will not even sniff at, and what makes one beast ill, on that will another beast thrive.' 'Then you must know that it is a bear.'—'Swear that you do not want the venom for a human being.' Fatia Negra swore with all sorts of subterranean oaths that it was really for a bear that he wanted the poison. The medicine-woman thereupon prepared for him a mortal concoction capable of killing the most vigorous beast in the world; then she kneaded honey-cakes, a delicacy to which bears are very partial as everyone knows, and mixed it well into them. Fatia Negra gave her ten ducats for the poison, but the old woman's conscience would not allow her to rest, and the next day she brought the ducats to me for the church's needs, as she put it,—and would I help her to relieve her soul of the heavy burden which oppressed it. And what now if Fatia Negra, contrary to his oath, were to make use of this poison against his fellow-men?"

"That would be horrible," said Henrietta apprehensively.

"I don't think he will," said the priest; "the poison is really meant for a beast."

"I suppose he wants to kill some animal who is a domestic guardian, in order that he may rob a rich man's house."

"No. He wants to kill a faithful animal in order that he may steal a poor man's only treasure —his wife."

"How so?"

"Listen, my lady, and I will tell you. After this had happened, Juon Tare's wife, Mariora, came to me at an unusual hour. Generally she only comes on a Sunday for prayers. What she said to me was not so much a confession made to a priest as a confidence reposed in a friend; I am therefore not committing sacrilege by retailing it to another person. That young woman is exposed to temptation."

"What! in the midst of the forest?"

"Yes, in the midst of the forest, where, for weeks at a stretch, the herdsman hears no other human voice than his own thrown back to him by the echoes. The seducer in this case is Fatia Negra."

"Then he must dwell hard by."

"None knows his abiding dwelling, but his temporary resting places among the high Alps are these herdsmen's lonely huts. For this reason he lives in good fellowship with the mountain goatherds, does them no harm, brings presents for them and their wives, pays handsomely for every bit of bread, and thus makes it pretty sure that they will never betray him. The place where Juon Tare's wife dwells is called the ice valley. They call it so because it is here that the first ice of the winter appears; as early as mid-September the stream is fringed with it. There, by the side of the stream, stands a little wooden hut, one of whose walls reposes on the ascending rock behind it. Here dwells the fair Mariora all alone. And yet I am wrong to say alone, for three of them dwell together there—herself, a little one-year-old child, and a tame bear. Her husband she sometimes does not see for a week at a time, especially in the autumn and winter when the freshly fallen snow has obliterated the pastures. At such times the goatherd encamps on the summit of the mountains and nourishes his kids by felling with his axe a growing beech-tree, on which the little creatures fall and gnaw off the juicy buds. Whenever a snowstorm overtakes him, the herdsman drives the goats into a glen, and lest the snow should bury them all by the morning while they sleep, he drives them continually up and down, thus making them trample down the falling flakes. Meanwhile Mariora sits at home and spins the wool from which she makes her own and her husband's clothes, or she pounds maize into meal in a stone mortar for household needs, playing at intervals with her child."

"And an evil hand would destroy their simple joys!"

"Hitherto the goatherd and his wife feared nothing. It is good to be in those solitudes. God dwells very near to them there. Then, too, Juon Tare is a strong man; no evil beast can harm him. Nor has he any fear of robbers. What can they deprive him of? Mariora is in a good place out of the reach of snow-storms. If a savage beast or a vagabond were to try to harm her, there is Ursu, the bear, with the terrible jaws,—he would tear them to pieces. So your ladyship will perceive that Juon Tare's castle is provided with a very strong guardian against thieves and wild beasts—but who can guard it against the wily and the insinuating? Fatia Negra is a guest of long-standing at the hut in the ice valley, and never goes thither empty handed. He brought the woman pearls and coral which she innocently hung about her person. How was she to know whether such trinkets were worth thousands or whether they could be bought in a pedler's booth for a few pence? She fancies it is but the thank-offering of a grateful guest. But now her eyes have been opened to the fact that these gifts *are* costly, very costly,—for the Black Mask demanded a price for them which all the treasures in the world could not outweigh, a price, the bare mention of which caused her to shut the door in his face. And when he, unable to obtain his desire by fair words, attempted to gain his object by force, a single cry for help from the woman caused Fatia Negra to feel Ursu's paws on his shoulders and so he knows that this lonely woman is right well defended. Only at Mariora's command did the bear release Black Mask who, attacked from behind, was unable to defend himself. Burning with rage, he quitted the hut and said, meaningly to the woman: 'You shall be mine nevertheless!' Mariora came to me next day, full of despair, telling me the whole story, and asking me whether she ought to tell her husband. I advised her to keep the secret in her own bosom and to close her door against Fatia Negra. Oh, I know the fellow! It is good to guard against him but it is not advisable to scratch him. He is no ordinary man. And now putting together all this with the confession of the Dupe Piatra milk-woman, I have a strong suspicion that Fatia Negra wants to poison the herdsman's bear."

"I will not allow it," interrupted the baroness emphatically.

"We shall scarcely be able to prevent it, my lady, for how can we warn the dwellers in the mountain hut of their danger? It is of no use sending a letter for they cannot read. We cannot entrust the secret to anyone, for no living soul in these parts would dare to convey any message to the disadvantage of the mysterious Fatia Negra. I myself dare not do it. I too am afraid of him. I am sure that if he found it out, and he is sure to do so, my days would be numbered."

"Yet I know someone who will take this message to the hut of Juon Tare."

"Not your ladyship, I hope?"

"No. Even if I knew my way among these mountains I would not venture to expose myself to the perils of such a journey after my last experience; since then I have grown timid and nervous. But I know of one who will hasten to take it, who will not be afraid, and who will show no mercy to him before whom everyone else trembles."

The priest did not guess to whom Henrietta alluded, yet he himself had once told her ladyship that Black Mask had a sweetheart to whom he had been married, not before a priest indeed, but in the sight of Heaven, and that this woman was very jealous and very brave. "But I beg of your ladyship," the priest had said on that occasion, "to leave my name out of the transaction if you repeat this secret, for otherwise, people will hear one fine morning that the worthy pastor of Hidvár has been found in his room with a split skull."

Scarcely had the priest quitted the castle than Henrietta had the horses put to the carriage, took Clementina with her in order to avoid all suspicion, and drove to Tökefalu. There, in front of the house of rich old Onucz she stopped and descended. The Wallachian Nabob was much pleased to have the honour of entertaining so distinguished a guest, and immediately spread his table and loaded it with preserves, honey, and fresh cheese. Clementina, who had a good appetite, remained with their host and made ready to talk scandal of her mistress and insinuate that the baroness wanted to get some money without her husband's knowledge, whilst Henrietta locked herself up with Anicza in the latter's bedroom and talked with her concerning things which had no relationship whatever with money.

CHAPTER XI

TWO TALES, OF WHICH ONLY ONE IS TRUE

AFTER a couple of days the whole hunting party returned from the mountains. This was much sooner than they had determined, and the cause was a very serious accident which had befallen Baron Hátszegi. They brought him home in an ambulance car to Henrietta's great consternation. The baroness, sitting by the bedside, heard from the doctor that her husband's wounds were serious, but that his life was not in danger, and that he might even be allowed to smoke a cigar if he liked. Then Mr. Gerszon related how it had happened: "Only imagine, your ladyship! This irrepressible friend of ours, not content with pursuing game all day through the thickets, learns, late in the evening, that a gigantic old bear was trotting towards the ice valley, and, without saying a word to anybody, must needs leave the company and set off alone, late at night, on the track, with only a double-barrelled musket and not so much as a dog to keep him company. The bear enticed Leonard further and further. At last down he squats before him in the bright moonlight and begins licking his paws; then suddenly quits the path and disappears. Leonard thought at first that the bear had returned within the deadly circle drawn for him by our beaters, till, all at once, on reaching a steep slope covered with reeds, he again heard a growling and perceived the savage beast trying to scale the slope. The place was too steep for a man to climb, but a bear with the help of his long strong claws can scale it like a fly climbing up a wall. Leonard soon saw that he would be unable to get a close shot at the bear, so he resolved to fire down from where he was at random. But the experienced old brute, guessing this good idea, instantly executed one of those surprising feats which only fall within the observation of veteran hunters. While Leonard was taking aim, the bear rolled rapidly down the steep incline by means of a series of clever somersaults and rushed upon Leonard with a sort of swift shamble. And a cursed bad manœuvre it is, I can tell you. The acrobatic beast, whether a man hits it or not inevitably bears down the hunter by his sheer weight, and as a man's bones are more brittle than a beast's, and he has no tough pelt to cover him withal, he will be infallibly crushed to pulp,—while the bear takes the whole thing as a mere joke and ambles on further. But the whole affair did not last half as long as I take to tell it. Leonard had just time enough to fling himself on the ground before the first rush came. Then he felt a heavy body fall prone upon him and then they began to roll over and over in company among all sorts of stones and bushes, till a benevolent rock interrupted their rapid descent. Fortunately the bear was underneath and lay stunned at full length upon the ground. Our friend Leonard naturally did not wait for his travelling companions to pick him up. He had lost his musket and it was a good job that his hunting-knife had snapped off close at the hilt instead of running into his body; then, too, his knees and elbows were badly crushed, yet he had sufficient strength and presence of mind to drag himself back to our hunting box, and his story was a very pleasant surprise for us, I can tell you. At first, indeed, we were much alarmed, and fancied that every bone in his body was out of joint, but now we can look on it merely as soldiers' luck. To-morrow he'll be up no doubt, and the day after to-morrow we shall all be dancing."

Henrietta had never removed her eyes from her husband's face during this narration, and it was plain from his looks that he was not proud of his adventure and did not want it talked about. "Why do you frighten my wife to death?" he said. "It is a mere trifle. Let me remain for a whole night in cold wet wraps, and to-morrow I shall be all right. And now, enough of the stupid business. And will you please, Henrietta, look after my guests while I lie here in swaddling bands? All I want is a couple of days of rest and then I shall be on my legs again."

Towards midnight Henrietta disappeared from among her guests and went to enquire after Leonard; but she found his chamber door locked, and received no answer to her gentle enquiries, from which she gathered that Leonard was still dozing. She did not want to disturb him, and as her husband's guests, judging by the noise they made, had evidently begun to amuse themselves in real earnest after her departure, she did not return to them, but hastened to her own chamber.

How amazed was she to find Anicza there closeted with Clementina!

The Roumanian girl had been awaiting Henrietta for some time, and Clementina thought it quite natural to conduct her into her mistress's sleeping-room, imagining that there was some monetary transaction between them, of which the baron and the domestics need know nothing. In order that she might not be bored by waiting, Clementina entertained her for a whole hour with a hair-raising account of the hunting accident, with which the whole castle was full. Anicza let the other talk on without so much as a hint that she had a still more hair-raising and terrific tale to tell of the night just past than ever Miss Clementina had.

As soon as Henrietta perceived Anicza, she politely requested Clementina to be so good as to leave them to themselves, a request which Clementina very naturally regarded as incomprehensible; and, of course, the instant she had crossed the threshold, she diligently took up her position before the keyhole. She was, however, furious to discover that Henrietta proceeded, more prudently than speakers on the stage who regularly allow themselves to be overheard by eaves-droppers, for she drew together the heavy damask curtains of the alcove and retired behind them with Anicza, so that neither prying eyes nor listening ears could find anything there to satisfy their inquisitiveness.

"It almost succeeded!" said the Roumanian girl impatiently, beginning her story at the end instead of at the begining.

"Only almost?" repeated the dissatisfied Henrietta.

"So far the game is neither over nor lost."

"Did Fatia Negra appear at the hut in the ice valley?"

"Pardon, my lady, but please never mention that name before me, for on hearing it everything I look upon grows red, and every limb of my body begins to tremble. You see, my hands are trembling now. Let us speak of him in future as the Unknown; so far as I am concerned he shall henceforth be the Unknown for ever more."

"Then you met him there?"

"Suffer me, my lady, to rally my scattered wits a bit. Oh! what a horrible night this has been! When I look back upon it, I feel giddy. But anger and despair sustain me. Oh! what have I not sacrificed for that man, for that devil, and oh! how I have been betrayed! But why should I worry your ladyship with my misery! Listen to what happened. When your ladyship left me the other night, I immediately saddled my horse and set off for the ice valley. The way thither is very bad, dangerous in fact, but fortunately the moon was high and bright and made it easier for me to find the path. The Pole star was already sinking when I reached the bottom of the valley, and I could see from afar that there was a light still burning in the goatherd's little hut. The night owls soon drove it out of my eyes, for in that valley dwells so many owls, and they are so bold that the tips of their wings brush against people's faces as they sweep past. I had known Mariora for a long time, while she still lived at home with her father, but since she became Juon Tare's wife we have only seen each other occasionally and at long intervals, and then too only when I visited her, for she, the poorly-married woman, never came to visit us—the rich people. On reaching the hut, I tied up my horse and tapped at the little window, through which one cannot peep as, instead of glass, the window-frames are filled with opaque mica which Juon Tare himself discovered amongst the hills. Mariora recognized my voice and hastened to unbar the door. She was much surprised and much delighted to see me at that hour. She embraced, kissed me, and burst into tears. At first I thought it was from pure joy,—then I thought she pitied me. 'Is there anything wrong?' I asked. Then she pulled herself together, dried her tears and said: 'I have an invalid on my hands.'—'Your child?'—'No, Ursu.'—It was just as if a viper had stung me.—'Ursu sick?' I cried.—'Yes, I don't know what ails him. Since yesterday he has been lying down shaking and trembling, while the day before he was skipping about and turning somersaults. Fatia Negra (Domne Zeu,* forgive my lips for uttering that name) was playing with him for a long time.' 'Did he come hither?' 'Yes, he said he was on his way to you.' 'He lied. Then it was he who poisoned the bear.'

"Mariora trembled at these words, and grew paler than ever.

"I seized her by the hand and drew her with me into the hut. I whispered in her ear that I knew all. 'The accursed wretch has been faithless to me because of your pretty eyes. He swore to me by sunlight and he swore to you by moonlight, but you would not listen to him. You love your husband and Black Mask relies on his strength now that fair words have failed. The coward has poisoned your faithful guardian like the wretched thief, the miserable house-breaker, that he is.'— Mariora's hut was lighted by the flame that flickered on the hearth. A bedstead of linden-wood covered with goat-skins, a table of slate and a few three-legged chairs were all the furniture. There was also a nicely carved and painted little cradle in which lay the little child, sleeping, with his plump little hands drawn up behind his head, like

---
* The Lord God.

an angel. In the extreme corner of the room the faithful beast lay all of a heap on a lair of soft moss,—at the last gasp. He groaned and shivered continually like one in a fever, and raised his failing eyes with such an eloquent appeal to his mistress, as if he would have spoken to her. Sometimes he pricked his ears as if he were listening and snuffed joyously. Perchance he expected his master, perhaps he wanted to lick his hands for the last time. Poor beast, how I pitied him! 'He will die,' I whispered to Mariora. I durst not say it aloud for I imagined the beast understood everything which men say to one another. 'And then will come the tempter, who knows that you are alone and defenceless.' I told her everything which your ladyship told me, and the woman trembled like an aspen-leaf.

" 'Where is Juon Tare encamping now?' I asked Mariora.

" 'Only a mile from here in the Vale Capra.'

"Hem! It is impossible to get there on horseback, but I can reach him by going on foot. Meanwhile you lock yourself in, put out the fire, and whatever noise you hear, do not open the door till we come back.

" 'Nay,' said Mariora, 'you must not go away. If Juon ought to come home, there is a sign between us. I have here an Alpine horn; he has taught me how to blow upon it, and has told me that if ever I should be in great danger I must blow it, and however distant he may be, he will hear it and hasten home.'

"'But it is night now; perhaps he is asleep.'

"'Juon never sleeps at night, he must be awake and protect his herds.'

"'And what then will become of his goats if he leaves them?'

"'Are not I and my child dearer to him than all his property?'

"Then I told Mariora that no time must be lost, and that she should blow the horn at once. It is a long tube made out of the bark of trees, with the end tilted upwards, and anyone who knows how to blow it can make its voice heard for miles. Mariora was too feeble with it. Perhaps at another time she would have been more up to it, but now she was upset, there was something which weighed down her bosom and hampered her breathing: the horn gave forth but a feeble and uncertain sound. We listened for the echoes and they scarce resounded from the sides of the adjacent hills. Juon would never hear that. 'Give it to me,' I said. 'I shall throw more force into it.' A moment after I had blown the horn, the woody heights repeated the sound just as if there was another hornblower there. Presently, from afar, right away among the hills, another horn replied, just as if there was another echo there. That was Juon's answer. He had heard the summons; we could now rest content. In half an hour he would have bounded across the mountains and through the glens and would be here. In the meantime we would barricade ourselves inside the hut. Mariora anxiously asked me what we should do if her husband were the last to arrive, for the robber had firearms. Acting on my advice, we closed the door with a heavy beam and put out the fire. The child began to cry, but Mariora took it in her arms and soothed it to sleep. A heavy groan sounded from a corner of the room: it was the faithful beast breathing forth his last breath. We exchanged not another word in order not to betray the fact that Mariora was not alone. Half an hour had nearly elapsed when we heard footsteps in the distance approaching. We listened. Who was coming? Which of us would recognize those footsteps first? I did. It was he! he for whose sake I had brought down a curse upon my head.

"For about as long a time as it would take one to repeat a Paternoster, he remained standing there before the door. Then he rapped lightly with his fingers and I heard the voice I knew so well: 'Mariora, are you asleep?'

"'I am awake. What do you want?' she replied.

"'Let me in, Mariora; open the door!'

"I whispered to her what she should say.

"'I cannot, my husband is not at home. I am alone.'

"'For that very reason open, so that we two may have it all to ourselves?'

"'There will be three of us, don't forget Ursu.'

"'It is all up with Ursu,' laughed the robber outside.

"'You have killed him, you villain!' cried Mariora though I never whispered this to her.

"'Not I, but the honey-cake.'

"'Why did you do so?'

"'Because he was in my way.'

"'Who will defend me now?'

"'I will defend you. I will take you away with me. I will take you to a beautiful city full of palaces. I will buy you a house and an estate and you shall be a great lady.'

"'It cannot be. I already have my lawful husband and you too have your lawful wife.'

"'Your lawful husband shall die when I choose, and you will then be a widow. As for Anicza, she only married a mask. I will tear it off and she will no longer know who I was.'

"Oh, my lady, can you not fancy how my heart broke at these words! Yet I did not weep.

"'You will deceive me as you deceived her,' replied Mariora.

"Then the robber began to swear that I had deceived him first. He lied concerning me, oh! the accursed wretch! Yet the game had to go on. Mariora was no longer the mistress of her own thoughts. She is a helpless creature. If I had not whispered in her ear what she was to say, she would have had no answer ready for him.

"'I fear you,' she said at my prompting, 'for

you are a robber; it is not love but money that you want. Why did it not occur to you to court me before? You have only come now because you have found out that my father has been here and offered me a hundred ducats that we may buy a little estate with it. You have only come here to rob me of that.'

"The tempter grew furious at so much gainsaying.

" 'Stupid wench!' he cried, 'what are your hundred ducats to me? I will give you ten times as much. Here! take them!' And with that he pitched through the little window—opening above the door a heavy purse which fell rattling at our feet. It was full of ducats. I kicked it aside with loathing.

" 'It is easy to talk,' replied Mariora. 'Now, you give and give, but if I were to let you in, you would take them back again to-morrow with my own.'

" 'I swear I will not.'

" 'No, I will not believe the oaths of a robber. You have firearms and I am therefore defenceless against you. Go and hang up your musket, your pistols, and your hunting-knife on that beech-tree, which is a hundred paces distant from the house; when you come back without your firearms I will believe that you do not want to kill me and will listen to what you have to say?'

"The robber fell into the snare and did as he

was bid. Then he returned. 'Here I am without weapons,' said he. 'Let me in!'

"We had to gain as much time as possible, so I whispered Mariora to say that she must first stir up the fire into a blaze for she could not let him in in the dark.

"These words inflamed the passion of the tempter still more.

" 'You will have time for that afterwards,' said he. 'I can see your beautiful eyes even in the dark, for then they shine all the more brightly.'

" 'Then I suppose I have eyes like a cat?' I made Mariora say.

" 'Silly fool!' growled the tempter to himself in Hungarian, which Mariora did not understand. 'No,' he then added in Roumanian, 'you have eyes like stars.'

" 'But confess now, do you really love me? Or do you only come hither with evil designs? Don't you want, now, to cut off the hands of my little child? for robbers covet the hacked off hands of babies,—they make them invisible.'

"At this the man's temper fairly gave way. He perceived that he was being trifled with and exclaimed roughly: 'Woman, open the door, or I'll bring it down about your ears!' And he gave the door such a blow with his clenched fist that it cracked from end to end. 'I tell you for the last time,' cried he, 'let me in peaceably. If you will come with me, I will take you, and your child also, to a pleasant place. I will make a gentleman of him and a lady of you. But if you gainsay me another moment, I'll batter in the door, dash the brains of your brat out against the wall and carry you off by force wherever I please.'

"Thereupon Mariora paid no more attention to me but began wringing her hands and I snatched up the child, who had been awakened by the noise and begun to cry. I drew my pistol from my bosom and planted myself beside the door. If there's nobody else, I thought, I must bear the brunt of it.

"The robber planted his shoulder against the door and pressed it inwards with tremendous force. The boards cracked and as the middle of the door was barricaded by a stout beam, there was soon a regular gap between the two folds of the door and the door inclined more and more inwards. Through the opening thus made, I held the pistol, pointed straight at his temples and only an inch away from him. He is a very strong man, I thought, but another effort of strength and he will be lying dead at my feet."

The girl was quite overcome by the narration of this scene. She paused for a moment to recover herself, during which Henrietta, as pale as a statue, gazed at her in silence.

Presently she resumed:

"At that critical moment, a cry like the howl of a wild beast resounded in front of the hut. The door fell back into its proper place and rushing to the little window, I saw that *two* men now stood in front of the hut.

"Juon Tare had arrived at last!

"It was neither speech nor language that he addressed to his antagonist in the first instant of their encounter, it was the savage roar of a wild beast rushing upon its prey.

"Juon Tare is a very strong man. Fortunately, he is also a peaceful, retiring creature, for if he were as passionate as he is strong and frequented the wine shops, every carouse would end with the death of a man. All the more horrible was it therefore to behold him at that moment like a ravening beast of prey.

"The detected seducer at once made a rush for his arms, but Juon Tare overtook him with an enormous bound and seized one of his hands. If Fatia Negra had been one of God's ordinary creatures, he must have been writhing the next moment with crushed limbs on the ground beneath Juon's knee; but at the very instant in which Juon caught hold of one hand, the robber faced about and seizing the herdsman round the body began to wrestle with him.

"The moon flooded the valley with its light; the whole course of the struggle was plainly visible.

"As soon as Juon Tare perceived that his antagonist was foolhardy enough to try a fall with him, he complacently allowed his body to be encircled and calmly murmured: 'Ho, ho! then you would wrestle with me, eh, Fatia Negra! Very well, be it so!'

"Then he also quietly encircled the trunk of his opponent with those terrible arms of his, which had shown themselves capable on one occasion of throttling a bear, and prepared to crush his adversary.

"And thus began an awful struggle, the mere remembrance of which is a horror.

"There is nothing more terrible than when two men struggle for life or death with their bare hands.

"Juon Tare's tremendous strength was unable to crush Fatia Negra. The herdsman might perhaps have been a little exhausted by his swift run, but the robber was skilful and opposed a steel-like elasticity to the herdsman's massive weight.

"Now the one, now the other was forced down upon his knee, only to bound instantly back again. The grass was rooted up by their stamping feet. Tightly embraced, with straining shoulders, with their fists tearing at each other's bodies, their faces were pressed so closely together that the two heads seemed but one.

"Now and then they would pause for an instant to take breath and at such times would gasp out short, fierce words.

"'Who are you?' growled Juon. 'Who are you that you can resist the arm of Juon Tare? Who are you that Juon Tare cannot put to silence?'

"'What is it you want, you fool?' the robber

gasped back. 'Has that two hundred ducats, the price set on my head, tempted you? Is that why you want to catch me? Let me go, and I will give you five hundred.'

" 'I will not let you go. I want neither your money, nor yet the money of the magistrates. Your destruction is all that I want. You should not escape from these hands if you were thrice a devil.'

" 'We will see.'

"And again the tussle began. Each of the two men put forth all his strength against his adversary. Fatia Negra's garments split into rags, the blood spouted from his shoulders where Juon had worried him with his sharp teeth like a wild beast. Not another word did they now speak, only their panting sobs were to be heard like the snorting of two wild boars as they dragged and dashed each other up and down on the sward.

"I was obliged to restrain Mariora violently from rushing to her husband's assistance. She would only have distracted his attention. And besides I would not have it so. Let the men fight it out, I thought. They are a well matched pair."

"Then you still love Fatia Negra?" enquired Henrietta sadly.

The girl blushed. —"I love him, yes,—and therefore he must die."

She went on:

"At that moment he was like a magician battling with a giant. The other was half a head taller than he, and the muscles of his arms stood out like the rugged bark of an oak's trunk. Black Mask was much the slimmer. But every muscle in his frame seemed made of steel. His gigantic adversary might pitch and toss him wherever he pleased, he always fell on his feet; nor was the other ever able, squeeze as he might, to disjoint his arms or free his own head from Fatia Negra's embrace, though again and again he ducked down to do it; and then they would struggle more fiercely than ever, on their knees, with their limbs interlaced like one single, inseparable quivering mass of flesh.

"'If I could only see your hidden face!' roared Juon, throwing himself with all his might on Black Mask. 'You devil, you, I'll tear your mummery off for you!'—and he gnashed at his opponent's face with his teeth, trying to snap his mask off.

"This attempt seemed to redouble Fatia Negra's fury. He too now began roaring like a wounded bear, struggling with a huntsman. It was no longer a struggle between men, but a ravening of two beasts. The combatants had now rolled far away from the hut. Their savage yells resounded through the still pastures. We, watching them from the hut, could see that they were drawing near the edge of a steep abyss with a sheer descent of many fathoms, at the bottom of which are the sources of the little mountain streams.

"'Take care, Juon!' cried Mariora despairingly.

But her voice was unheard. Both of them were deaf and blind. The next moment Juon gave his adversary a fierce shake and instantly the pair of them plunged head over heels into the gulf below.

"We both rushed after them, and on reaching the edge of the abyss perceived one shape lying motionless among the rocks of the stream, and another limping painfully towards the further shore. This second figure was Fatia Negra."

"Surely Juon was not dead?" cried Henrietta, horrified.

"No; only crippled by the fall. He fell undermost, the other on top. Yet the other must have suffered severely. We could see from his heavy movements that he had more than one limb damaged. Only with the utmost exertion did he manage to scale the opposite cliff.

"While he was clambering up the mountainside, Mariora sobbing and screaming, rushed down to her insensible husband, and taking his head into her bosom dragged his limp body out of the cold water of the brook, whilst I took down from the beech-tree Fatia Negra's double-barrelled musket and raised it to my cheek. Before me on the white rock, in the full light of the moon, a good mark for a marksman was that panting black object struggling upwards. I pointed the barrel straight at him. I took a long and careful aim. I am certain I should have hit him. And then I bethought me how much I had loved him once upon a time, and the weapon sank down. I flung it from me."

The girl ceased to speak and covered her face with both her hands. It was a long time before she took them away again.

At last she sprang up quickly, and turning her pale face towards Henrietta, said in a hard, dry voice: "It will be the last time, your ladyship. I am weak because I am a woman, folks would say. But they shall know that that is not true. Don't be afraid, my lady; what I have promised, that will I do. You have been very good to me in telling me that I was being deceived, and I will requite you for it. And now, God bless you, my lady. Farewell!"

"But surely you are not thinking of going home so late at night?"

"What care I about the night? No spectre can meet me anywhere that is worse than the horrible thing that dwells at the bottom of my heart. God bless your ladyship. You shall hear from me soon. Farewell!"

Then the girl gently kissed Henrietta's hand and left the room, throwing into her gait and bearing an energy and a self-confidence which she was far from feeling.

CHAPTER XII

THE SOIREES AT ARAD

DESPITE his misgivings, Count Kengyelesy succeeded in reaching his home at Arad without being robbed by Fatia Negra.

During the evenings of his visit at Hidvár he had won back everything which he had lost on the occasion of his friend Hátszegi's visit at Kengyelesy, and in the joy of his heart he gave his countess *carte blanche* in the matter of entertaining her friends and opened his halls freely to the elegant world of Arad.

For the society of Arad is distinctly elegant. Excepting Pest, there is no other place in Hungary where the aristocratic element is so strongly represented. Nay, it has this advantage over Pest that its society does not scatter as the seasons change. Such pleasure-resorts as Csákó, Ménes, Magyarát and Világos and the castles of the magnates residing on the circumjacent *puszta* are all of a heap, so to speak, around Arad; so that there is no occasion for acquaintances to separate in spring or autumn; wherefore to all those who would devote themselves uninterruptedly to social joys, Arad is a veritable Eldorado.

There was no need to offer the Countess Kengyelesy such an opportunity twice,—the very next day the round of visiting began. All the notabilities of the higher circles got themselves introduced to her ladyship by mutual friends, and the lesser fry, whom nobody knew, were introduced to her by the count himself. Amongst those who came from afar was a young man from Pest who had an official post in the county, a rare distinction in those days, who was much praised for his culture and who had spoken once or twice very sensibly at Quarter Sessions,—a certain Szilard Vamhidy. But what interested the ladies in the young man far more than his official orations was the rumour connecting his name with a romantic attachment he was said to have had with the daughter of a wealthy merchant of Pest. The young man, being disappointed in his love, had resolved to kill himself, and had persuaded the girl to do likewise at the same time. Only with difficulty had they been snatched from the threshold of death. Subsequently, on account of this very thing, the girl had been compelled to become the wife of the wealthy Hátszegi.

The countess quickly made up her mind that such a young man as this was an indispensable acquaintance. What! Henrietta's ideal, with whom she had been in love and who would have gladly embraced death with her! Here indeed was a rare species, especially in these modern days, which deserved to be exhibited; and she gave her husband no rest till he had promised to introduce the young man to her. To this end it was necessary that he should first of all make the young man's acquaintance himself, but this was an easy matter. The deputy Lord-lieutenant of the county knew them both and at his house they learnt to know each other. And Count Kengyelesy was one of those men whom it is impossible to avoid when once you have made his acquaintance. It was not very long, therefore, before he took his new friend, absolutely under his protection and hauled him off to his wife.

The usual stiffness of a first introduction was speedily broken down by the quaint conceits of the count.

The countess had donned a flowing antique *moiré* dress and wore her hair in long English curls to match.

"Come now, friend Szilard!" cried the count, "what do you say? this dress and that *coiffure* hardly suit the countess's style of face—eh?"

Many a worthy young man would have been plunged into confusion by such a silly question, but our Szilard's eternally composed countenance was not ruffled for an instant.

"Everything becomes the countess," he replied; "but I know of something which is still more charming and would make any fair woman still more beautiful."

"Really! You make me quite curious," said the countess.

"Why, Szilard, you a connoisseur!—you surprise me!" cried the count.

"I mean those blue stuff gowns with white spots, which lend quite a peculiar charm to our women, especially if you set it off with an old-fashioned *csipkeköto*."*

At the very next *soirée* the Countess Kengyelesy was attired in one of these blue stuff gowns with white spots, of home manufacture, and with a black lace head-dress—exactly as Szilard had described it to her.

"My dear friend, be so good as to look there!" said the count appropriating Szilard while he was still only half through the doorway. "There she is costumed from head to foot exactly as you advised. Ah! I pity you. You are already in the toils."

Szilard hastened at once to greet the countess, who treated the handsome young fellow with marked distinction all through the evening. Indeed she made no secret of it.

Three days later Szilard was bound by custom to pay a complimentary visit upon the Countess. He purposely chose an hour when he knew she would not be at home, and left his card, but the same evening he encountered her at the theatre. It was in the entrance hall, where she was waiting for her carriage, and till it drove up Szilard could not very well leave her.

"Ah, ah! my honoured friend," cried the countess archly, "this won't do. You wait till I

---

* A Hungarian headdress made of black lace. The dress suggested was also of native Hungarian manufacture worn at one time by the greatest ladies.

am not at home, and then you go and leave your card upon me as a token of respect. But I don't mean to let you off so easily. I have got a lot to say to you which I am determined you shall listen to. You must therefore promise to come to my house at twelve o'clock to-morrow, or else I shall astonish the world by inviting you to come along with me this instant in my carriage."

A man, in another mood, could scarcely have resisted the temptation of replying that he would be delighted if the countess put her threat into execution then and there, even at the risk of astonishing the world. Szilard merely looked grave and said that he would be happy to pay his respects to the countess at twelve on the morrow.

He went accordingly. His pulses beat no more quickly than usual as he entered the countess's private appartment, although she gave the footman to understand in a low voice that she would be at home to nobody else, and invited the young man to sit down close beside her, face to face.

The countess was a beautiful woman, and she possessed the art of dressing beautifully likewise. The countess had beautiful eyes and she could smile beautifully with them, too. The countess had an extremely pretty mouth, and when she spoke it was prettier still, for she had a witty way with her. The danger of the situation was very appreciable.

"My dear, good Szilard," began the countess, with that light, natural *naïveté* which so easily disarms the strongest of us, "do not take it ill of me if I speak to you confidentially. The world will very soon be saying that you are in love with me and I with you. I shall not believe the former and you will not believe the latter. Let the world say what it likes. I have a real blessing of a husband, whom it would be a shame to offend, and you have quite other ideas. I know what they are. Don't be angry, don't frown! I am not exacting. I don't want to fetch you away from other people. I will not ask where you have buried your treasures. I will merely say to you that I know you have treasures and that they are buried. Is it not so? You need not be afraid of me."

Szilard was a little taken aback by this unexpected turn. Could it be sheer curiosity, he thought?

"I have nothing to be afraid of, countess," remarked Szilard, smiling, "I have no buried secrets. I was a young man once, that is all. I have had my foolish illusions, like other people, and like other people I have cured myself of them."

"Nay, nay, sir, now you are not quite sticking to the truth; you are *not* cured of them. But before I go any further let me tell you that all this is not mere feminine curiosity on my part. I want you to trust me and I will trust you equally. Believe me when I say that if I love to make fun of empty-headed noodles, I can always respect a good heart because it is a rarity. The lady I want to speak to you about is my dear friend and she is very, very unhappy."

Szilard was bound to believe that this was true, for tear-drops sparkled in the countess's eyes.

"Is it my fault?" he asked bitterly.

"It is neither your fault nor her's. I know that as a fact. The cause of it all is money, the thirst for money. There is not a more miserable creature in the wide world than the daughter of a rich man. But that is the least of her misfortunes. They married her to a man who did not love her, who only took her because her grandfather was a millionaire. Her grandfather frightened her into the match by threatening her with his curse and now, when she has become the wife of this man who does not even feel friendship for her, I hear that this same old grandfather has made another will depriving her of everything."

Szilard's lips trembled at these words.

"You can imagine what will be the result. This young woman loves not and is not loved. They gave her away to an Oriental nabob who, imagining his wife to be wealthy, scatters his money like a prince. And now this man has suddenly been startled by the report that his wife has absolutely nothing!—do you know the meaning of the expression: bread of charity?"

"I have heard the expression, but the bread itself I have never tasted."

"Then you can have no idea what that sort of bread is like which a man gives to the wife whom

THE SOIRÉES AT ARAD 217

he finds to be poor, when he fancied her to be rich —oh! that sort of bread is very, very bitter!"

Ah! thought Szilard, the bread that *I* offered her was only dry—not bitter.

"I can tell you on very good authority," resumed the countess, "that the baron's conduct towards his wife has completely changed since he discovered that she has been disinherited. He had lost heavily at cards when the news first reached him, and he took no pains to conceal his ill-humour from his wife in consequence. The poor of the district had got to regard Henrietta as their ministering angel because of her labours of love among them, but now she can play the part of lady bountiful no longer. She has to shut her door in the faces of her poor petitioners, for her husband will not allow any unnecessary expense. Nay, more, they say that Hátszegi now keeps his wife's private jewels under lock and key to prevent her from pawning them and relieving the needs of the poor with the proceeds, as she was wont to do, and only brings them out on state occasions when he compels her to pile them all on her person. Isn't that a humiliation for a woman?"

"If only you had become mine," Szilard mentally apostrophized poor Henrietta, "you would now have had a cosey little chimney-corner, and a nice little room all to yourself; and though I could not have bought you jewels, the best of every morsel of food we shared together would always have been yours."

"And," pursued the countess, "most degrading experience of all, Hátszegi no longer attempts to conceal from his wife his outrageous *liaisons* with pretty peasant women. The thing has long been a byeword, though his wife knew nothing of it—but she knows it now. Nor is this all, my dear Vámhidy. Poor Henrietta's heart is suffering from another sorrow which she feels all the more keenly because it smarts unceasingly. Her young brother, Koloman, has suddenly disappeared from Pest and left no trace behind him. They say all sorts of things about him, which I do not care about telling you, but most of them are bad enough. On the news reaching Henrietta, she asked her husband to make enquiries as to the cause of Koloman's disappearance. Hátszegi wrote to his agent and received an answer which he will not show to Henrietta on any consideration; nay, more, he commanded his wife never to mention Koloman's name before him again. The poor woman is naturally in despair. She cannot conceive why the cause of her brother's disappearance should be hidden from her. And now I am coming to the end and aim of all this rigmarole. Henrietta believes, and I am likewise convinced of it, that if her brother be alive, there is only one person in the world whom he will try and seek out and that is yourself."

"Poor lad! he loved me much," sighed Szilard.

"And now you understand what I am driving at, don't you? If anybody can find out the whereabouts of Henrietta's brother and the real reason why he fled from his relations at Pest and took refuge neither with his aunt, Madame Langai, who, I hear, has taken his part all through, nor yet with his sister, it is most certainly you. This is no lawyer's business, for a lawyer would set about it too gingerly. Here sympathy and chivalry are before all other things necessary, and if the husband declines this noble task, we have nobody to turn to except—the man who has been sacrificed."

Szilard bit his lips to prevent the tears from coming. Who could ever have thought that so frivolous a woman would have had so much feeling for her friend? Then he rose, bowed and curtly informed the countess that he would undertake the commission.

The countess pressed his hand affectionately: "And keep me informed of everything," said she, "for I am the common post between you two."

Szilard thanked the countess and withdrew. He pondered the matter carefully till the evening, and by that time he had a plan all ready in his head.

For a whole week after this, nothing was to be seen of Vámhidy. Count Kengyelesy sought him everywhere and could find him nowhere. Every day he asked his countess what she had done with the young man.

Ten days after the first *soirée* the date for another had been fixed. Szilard did not appear even at this. Kengyelesy hunted for him from pillar to post, but could not discover what had become of him. Nobody had heard anything of him.

"He has poisoned himself," said Kengyelesy at last to a group of his sporting friends. "It is quite plain to me. When a fellow has got that sort of thing into his head once, he will try it again and again. I wash my hands of the business, it is all the fault of the countess. Why does she play her tricks with such people? No doubt he has swallowed poison and then crawled away into some nook or corner of a forest. In a month or two, I suppose, we shall come upon him unexpectedly."

"Whom shall we come upon unexpectedly?" cried a voice behind his back. He looked around and there was the long lost Szilard.

"Oh, there you are, eh? What have you been doing with yourself all this time? Come along with me—and Heaven help you!—I will take you to my wife. Poor young chap! I thought you had already had enough of it and made away with yourself in consequence."

Then he drew his arm through Szilard's and tripped off to the countess. "Here he is!" he cried. "We have found him, do not abandon yourself to despair on his account. Be so good as to sit down beside him!—here's a chair! I'll take care nobody disturbs you!"

The countess pressed Szilard's hand and made a sign to him to remain.

"I have just arrived from Pest," said Szilard.

"Really! Well?"

"I have found out everything, or rather, I should say, a good deal."

"Do pray tell me at once. All the people are dancing, they will take no notice of us."

"Ever since old Lapussa's death," began Szilard, "for he died soon after he had altered his will, all the members of his family have been at bitter variance. Madame Langai, the old man's widowed daughter, disputes the validity of the last will—whereby Mr. John Lapussa becomes heir to the exclusion of everybody else, and has instituted legal proceedings to upset it. Madame Langai seeks to prove that old Lapussa was *non compos mentis* when he disinherited the other members of his family, and she also maintains that the old fellow had no reason whatever for hating his grandchildren and reducing them to beggary as he has done. On the other hand, Mr. John maintains that his dear father had excellent reasons for detesting his grandchildren because the Baroness Hátszegi has never written a letter to her grandfather since her marriage and both she and her husband have expressed themselves, at home, in the most disrespectful terms imaginable concerning the old gentleman, even giving it to be understood that they would be very glad if they had not to wait too long for the curtain to fall on the fifth act of his life's drama. He calls as his witness one Margari, who was formerly old Lapussa's reader before the girl was married, and since then has been compelled to act as secretary to Hátszegi, or rather as a spy upon him. This fellow, who is now the mere tool of Mr. John, is quite prepared to retail all sorts of horrors about the Hátszegis. As to the other grandchild, the boy Koloman I mean, his uncle has saddled him with a terrible charge. He has produced a bill for 40,000 florins which he accuses the lad of forging in the name of his sister, the Baroness Hátszegi."

"Ah!" exclaimed the countess in an incredulous voice.

"The thing is ridiculously incredible, I know, yet there the bill is; I have seen it, for it has been sequestered by the Court. It is obviously in the youth's handwriting as also is the very bad imitation of his sister's signature. In connection therewith is the fact of the youth's sudden disappearance (and every attempt to trace his whereabouts has failed), for, on the very day when the subject of the bill was first broached, he vanished from his college, and apparently he had been preparing for flight some time before."

"But what could have induced a mere child to do such a thing, he is scarcely thirteen years old?"

"He was always somewhat flighty by nature, though that, of course, is not sufficient to explain how he came to forge his sister's name on a draft for 40,000 florins."

"But why will not the baron tell his wife all about it?"

"Does not your ladyship see?—It is quite plain

to me. Hàtszegi understands his wife thoroughly. He feels certain that as soon as the baroness hears of what her brother is accused, she would not hesitate a moment to acknowledge the forged signature as really her own."

"True, true. And then I suppose her brother could be saved."

"Completely."

"And then, I suppose, she would have to pay the money?"

"Either pay it or be sued for it."

"Poor woman! I know she has no money. A most awkward position, most awkward. But it does not matter; if her jewels are under lock and key, nobody guards mine."

At these words which came straight from the best of hearts, Szilard could not restrain himself from impressing a burning kiss on the countess's hand so affected was he by this outburst of generosity.

"Ah, ha!" cackled the count behind his back, "so we have got as far as that already, eh! Capital, capital, upon my word! Nay, nay, my young friend, don't be afraid of me. Do not put yourself out in the least on my account! God bless you, my boy!"

"To-morrow, we'll plan it all out, I'll be waiting for you at one o'clock," whispered the countess to Szilard, "now I must go, the cotillion is beginning."

"Don't you dance then?" enquired the count of

Szilard. "Nonsense! they'll say you are mourning somebody. Thank God, old Lapussa was not *your* father-in-law, but Hátszegi's. It is for him to pull a long face, but you go and dance!"

CHAPTER XIII

TIT FOR TAT

It may seem strange to us that the rumour of Fatia Negra's nocturnal adventure was not spread abroad in these parts, but as a matter of fact nobody did speak of it. It seemed as if everybody who knew anything about it, died out of the world before he could pass the news on to his neighbour.

The dwellers in the hut in the Ice Valley had vanished without leaving a trace behind them. The herd, untended by a shepherd, was scattered to the winds by wolves. Nobody could say what had become of Juon Tare and Mariora. The person who shewed least of all tell that she knew anything about this midnight adventure was Anicza herself. She had sobbed out the whole story before Henrietta, but after that she kept her own counsel and kept a good countenance also when folks looked at her. But there was venom at the bottom of her heart, and she nourished it there.

In a fortnight's time Fatia Negra visited her again. There was now nothing the matter with him, all traces of the life and death struggle had disappeared. Anicza was more affectionate towards him than ever. She did not even ask him where he had been all this time, nor did she notice the scar on his neck which had not been there before.

Fatia Negra came to her at night, as he always did. The famous adventurer was very cautious. Anicza knew for certain that whenever he came to visit her in a populous place like this, before him and behind him went faithful henchmen who stood on guard at the corners of the streets and gave a signal at the approach of any danger. Only amongst the snowy mountains was he wont to go alone. He was also very wary in other ways. Thus, he never drank wine: there was really no getting at him. And if once he had his weapons handy, then he could always cut his way through his enemies, even if he were completely surrounded.

"Fatia Negra," said the girl, throwing her arms round his neck, "last night I had an evil dream. I dreamt that the smallpox had ruined my face. Would you love me if I were pockmarked?"

"Yes, I would still love you," replied the adventurer.

"Well, as it happens I am not. Kiss me! Then I dreamt another dream. I dreamt that all our property was destroyed. I was a ragged wandering beggar with my head tied up. Would you love me if I were a ragged beggar?"

"Little fool, of course I should love you."

"Then embrace me nicely. After that I dreamt that some one had shut me up in prison for some great offence; they had condemned me to many years' imprisonment, condemned me to spend all my youth behind iron-barred windows and they would only let me free again when I had become a wrinkled old hag. Would you love me if I was in prison? Would you come and stand outside my iron bars and speak to me now and then?"

"Stop this foolish chatter! Who is able to answer such questions?" and in order that she should obey the more readily he closed her mouth with kisses.

But as soon as the kisses were over, she began to prattle again:

"But after that I went on dreaming again, and I dreamt what made me very angry with myself. I dreamt that I married someone else and forgot you. Would you still love me if I were to deceive you and wed another?"

"Yes, I would love you even then, Anicza,—and my love for you would make me shoot you through the heart."

How the girl laughed when he said this!

"Wait a bit," said she, "and you will see that it will all come to pass. I shall grow sick and ugly. I shall become a poor beggar. They will send me to prison and make a slave of me. I shall deceive you and wed another. Then we shall see whether you will love me; then we shall see whether you will kill me."

Anicza thought all this so amusing that she laughed aloud. The noise brought old Onucz into the room. His daughter turned towards him smilingly. "Isn't it true, father, that three suitors are courting me?" she asked. "I was asking Fatia Negra which of the three I should take."

Old Onucz scratched his nose pretty hard at this question. He would have liked to have said: "whichever you like, as long as it is the right one!" but he was afraid of offending Fatia Negra.

"Well, Domnule," said he at last, "truth is truth, after all. I'm getting an old man now, and what's the good of my scraping together and piling up all these ducats if nothing comes of it all? I have indeed an only daughter, a pretty girl and a good girl, too, but what's the use of that? You are not her husband. If I only knew of some corner of the world quite out of your reach, I would gather together all my belongings, seek it out and settle down there; but it would be of no avail, you would always find me out and befool my girl again, so I have to stay where I am."

"Don't grumble, old chap, there is a time for all things. This black mask shall not always cover my face; when I come to see you, my name shall not always be Fatia Negra. The day will come when a carriage and four shall drive into your courtyard, a sabre-tashed heyduke will then leap from the box and open the silver-plated coach and a cavalier in cloth of gold will step out who comes to you as a suitor. If you see this ring on his finger you will know that it is I, and there will no longer be a Fatia Negra in the wide world. We will go together to Bucharest, a true Roumanian city, where folks will respect us and then our happy days will begin."

"If only that could be soon! But you have been telling me this for a long, long time."

"That is because we cannot put an end to our work yet. There are very many people who still expect much from us. If I do not satisfy them they will remain a perpetual danger to us. That is why I am compelled to wear this mask a little longer. When once I have taken it off, he who used to wear it is dead and has nothing more in common with me."

"Then you really mean to break away from everything one day?"

"Yes, it is high time. My little finger whispers that someone wants to betray me. But say that to nobody. We must not frighten our own people. The Government is getting suspicious at the disappearance of so much gold. It is sniffing about, but at present it is on a wrong track. The Jews of Hungary are suspected and they happen to know nothing at all about it. But it is quite enough that suspicion *has* been aroused. So far they fancy that only about fifty to sixty pounds of gold a year are unlawfully made away with. They don't know yet that it amounts to five or six hundredweight, which is coined into ready money underneath the ground. This business must be put a stop to. This year the mines yielded a rich profit. Next Saturday there will be a last delivery of gold in the Lucsia cavern. As soon as the coins are struck, we shall divide the profits, wish one another 'buna nopte!'* and depart our respective ways. We shall destroy the machinery, blow up the smelting furnaces with gunpowder, break down the aqueducts and close up the mouth of the cavern. After that everyone can do as he likes with his gold. I shall wash my hands of it."

"Well said!" cried old Onucz, "that is as I would have it also. The whole lot of us who are partners in the concern will meet once more in the Lucsia cavern. There we will listen to what you say and swear to each other that we will not say a word of what has gone on down below there. Then everyone will do as you bid, for you are the most prudent of us all."

"Then I shall only have to wait another week?" enquired Anicza, winding the locks of Fatia Negra round her fingers.

"For what?" asked the adventurer.

"Nay, but surely you know?"

"Aha! of course!" said he smiling. "You mean you will only have to wait another week for me to cease to be your husband under a mask and become your real, true husband, eh? That is the end of all your thoughts, eh?"

"'Yes, yes!" said the girl, but she thought within herself: "I shall only have to wait a week to give

* Good night.

up your masked head into the hands of the hangman!"

So Fatia Negra unsuspiciously rocked the girl up and down on his knee and reflected complacently: "Girls are made in order that they may believe the lies which men choose to tell them."

But Anicza was a Wallachian girl and Wallachian girls are jealous, revengeful and artful.

*   *   *   *   *   *   *

That Saturday had arrived.

Seven hundred torches lit up the Lucsia Grotto. In between, from out of the corners of the cavern Bengal lights burst forth from time to time flooding for a few moments the whole of that gloomy palace with green, blue, white and rose-coloured flames to which the red flame of the pitch-torches with their black smoke formed a spectral contrast.

The great company of coiners had arranged for the last evening before their separation a sumptuous feast in this subterranean hall. The floor was strewn with white sand and all round about tents were erected in which roast and baked meats were piled up into veritable hillocks on broad beechwood dishes. In order to show the wealth at their command an ox was roasting whole on a flaming fire, revolving as it roasted, while two men, one on each side, basted it well with bacon fat held on iron forks. Close behind it was a gigantic vat of wine, everybody was free to drink out of it as much as he chose. Right in front of the smithy, too, was another gigantic vat holding about fifty firkins, filled to the brim with the finest eau de vié. A couple of young fellows lolled in front of the vat; they were already too lazy to dip their glasses into the fluid, they sucked it in from the brim of the vat itself.

The glare of the smelting oven no longer shone from the windows of the stone building in the midst of the cavern, the smoke intermingled with sparks no longer welled out of the flue, the subterranean hubbub no longer accompanied the stroke of the hammers, the machinery was silent, its work was done.

Two hundred and fifty thousand coined ducats await distribution; of these, fifty thousand belong to Fatia Negra and twenty thousand to old Onucz.

The smithy to-day is adorned with green twigs and bright ribbons, and on its massive chimneys all the requisites for a pyrotechnical display have been heaped up; it is from these that the rockets will ascend, it is here the blue and red Catherine wheels will revolve. The vaulted ceiling of the cavern is so high that the rockets in their highest flight will not graze it. An orchestral-like balustrade has been provided for the musicians. The shareholders themselves will do their best to enliven the festivities with fiddles, flutes and bagpipes. The guests are already appearing, singly and in groups, down through the machinery of the mill. The men are all accompanied by their womenkind in gala costumes.

Before the appearance of Fatia Negra, mirth and uproar have full swing. Everyone gives free course to his jollity till the chief comes whose black mask is sufficient to quiet everyone's good humour.

And to-day brings with it its own peculiar festivity. After the great distribution of money, Fatia Negra will take the daughter of Onucz by the hand and plight his troth to her in front of a crucifix placed on a high pedestal. The oath of betrothal will be an invention of Fatia Negra himself, filled with well assorted curses and promises. And he will swear to regard Anicza as his lawful bride from this day forth until such time as he can, without any mask or disguise, conduct her before a priest and solemnize his wedding in another place and before other people. For a long time this ceremony has been the pet idea of old Onucz and now Fatia Negra has agreed to it.

Gradually all the partners have assembled in the cavern. Amongst the last to arrive are old Onucz and his daughter with the bridesmaids. Anicza is dressed as usual with her girdle and embroidered bodice and a round hat on her head. The only difference is that now she sparkles all over with gold and jewels and her pig-tail is interwoven with real pearls. Amongst all the picked beauties who have gathered together here, she is still the most beautiful.

Only the bridegroom still keeps the good folks waiting. He is a long time coming, as becomes a great man. Nay, it is quite possible he may be there already without anyone seeing him. Perchance he is walking along there behind the bride in an invisible mantle and only when he throws it off, then only and not till then will the people see him.

Anicza screams aloud—perhaps with joy! Everyone is thunderstruck; they imagine their leader must be in league with the devil himself, for he comes up from out of the earth!

And with what splendour does he ascend! The purple robe that he wears is scarce discernible for gold lace; a long embroidered mantle, like the mantle of a prince, floats down from his shoulders and on his head he wears a golden helmet from which the mask depends.

The top of this helmet is set all round about with diamonds, and one of his comrades makes the remark that the spike of this helmet is somewhat muddy. He wore no weapon by his side, not even a dagger. Naturally,—one generally lays aside one's arms when one is about to swear solemnly before an altar. Onucz approached him obsequiously and kissed the hand of his mysterious leader with profound respect, whilst Anicza approached him with roguish archness, adroitly feigning a superstitious fear of her magician of a sweetheart.

"I am not afraid of you, Fatia Negra! though you come and go unseen. I fear you come not in God's name."

"That is true. We are nearer methinks to the Kingdom of the Devil."

"Hush! say not so!"

"Why not? If these men had imagined that I came down from Heaven, they would have betrayed me long ago. They would have carried me bound to Fehervár; but because they fancy I came from below and am acquainted with the devil, they fear me and are faithful. It is the same with you: you love me because you fear me."

"Ho, ho, ho! We shall see. I fear nobody, not even you. It was a joke when I said just now: I am afraid. You did not see that."

"Come now, I'll put you to the test at once. You see that crucifix on the altar? On that we will swear fidelity to each other and everyone here present will also swear to preserve eternal secrecy. As, however, we coiners cannot call God to witness, for by our trade we have rejected him, our oaths cannot ascend to Heaven but must descend elsewhere. In order then that our oath may be effectual, go if you have the courage, turn the crucifix and return it to its place—only upside down."

For an instant the girl grew pale and trembled, then she advanced boldly up to the altar, seized the crucifix and lifting it up, turned it round and thrust it upside down into a hole that happened to be on the altar, so that its pedestal stood up in the air.

All who were present looked on with wonder and horror.

As the girl raised the cross and put it down again reverse ways, a mechanical involuntary jolting motion of her arms was discernible, though her face betrayed nothing. An electrical machine hidden beneath the altar was the cause of this shock.

"Well?" enquired Fatia Negra as she returned to her place.

"The crucifix struck me when I seized it, and struck me again when I put it down," whispered the girl; and as she said these words she was very pale.

"And yet you did what I told you," said Fatia Negra, placing his hand on Anicza's shoulder. "You are a brave girl, and worthy of me."

"Comrades!" the leader of the adventurers now cried with a thundrous voice, "come and listen to me!"

Everyone thereupon abandoned his booth, his table or his diversion and stood in a circle round Black Mask.

"Ye know," he began, "the name of that place which is under the earth! Its name is the grave. Ye are all of you at this moment in the grave with me and if I wish it, dead men. Whoever would see once more the bright sunlight of the upper world where dawn is now breaking, he must swear that he will never at any time, drunk or sober, tell to any man what has happened, what he has seen or heard in this underground tomb, but will regard it all as a dream which he has forgotten on awakening. Swear this with me in this hour! I myself will first of all repeat the oath and ye must say whether ye are content therewith or not."

Thereupon he approached the altar whose basement formed the glass isolating "island" which all of us who have ever seen an electrical machine know so well. The electric machine itself, a battery of Leyden jars was hidden under the altar and connected by a piece of clockwork with that opening covered with metal in which the crucifix had been planted.

Black Mask stood silently for a moment on the basement of the altar after removing his helmet from his head, and those who stood nearest were horrified to observe that single hairs of his long flowing mane of hair rose slowly and remained stiffly suspended in the air. There was a deep silence, the silence that prevails under the earth—among the Dead.

And now Fatia Negra began to recite the words of the oath in a solemn ghostly voice: "I, the bearer of the Black Mask, Fatia Negra, as they call me, swear in the subterranean midnight by the living fire which falling like rain reduced Sodom and Gomorrah to ashes; by the flood which killed all the dwellers upon earth; by the gaping gulf which swallowed up the traitorous bands of Dathan and Abiram; by the spirit which announced the death of King Saul; by the Angel

Lucifer who by reason of his rebellion was cast down from Heaven; by the angel Malach Hamovesh who carries in his hands the sword of violent death; by the twelve plagues of Egypt with which Moses visited the land of the Pharaohs; by all these things and by the star under which I was born do I swear secresy—and may I perish in fire and water, may I be buried alive in the bowels of the earth, may I become a pillar of salt, may the wild beast of the forest tear me to pieces, may my own weapon turn against me in the evil hour, may I be terrified by midnight spectres and hag-ridden, may my body be smitten with leprosy, my eyes with blindness, my tongue with dumbness, my bones by rottenness, if ever I speak one syllable to anybody, be it priest, or child, or father, or condemning judge, or threatening headsman, of anything I have seen, heard or learnt in this place, or write it down with my hand or put anybody on the track of it! May every drop of my blood become curse-laden; may my remotest posterity anathematize me; may I awake in my grave and go about again as a spectre, if ever I act in anyway contrary to what I now swear! May all those who are under the earth and above the earth be the witnesses of this my oath!"

This drastic formula satisfied everybody. In those parts the people much prefer such unmeaning self-objurgation to our legal oaths as taken in the presence of the judges and they are considered a hundred times more binding. Meanwhile numerous single hairs had seemed to detach themselves from Black Mask's long locks and now stood upright all around his head like some spectral crown. Those who stood around regarded him with deep horror. Many believed that a supernatural marvellous power was in his words; only the girl did not believe in him at all.

In order to increase still further this terrified respect the adventurer beckoned towards him the old men of the assembly.

"Come hither, that ye may see for yourselves how well acquainted with the words of the oath are those in that other place where knowledge needs must be; stretch out your hands towards me, touch me with the tips of your fingers and ye will discover there is something else present here besides yourselves."

Old Onucz tremblingly stretched out his hand in the direction of Fatia Negra and the next moment collapsed with fear when he perceived sparks crackle forth from his leader's garments which burnt his finger tips. More than one elder was afraid at first to put out his hand till curiosity made him venture everything. Several wanted to convince themselves personally of this miracle, which they could not credit from the hearsay of others and the juggler himself encouraged those standing near him to touch him wherever they chose and fire would spring from his body. Sparks sometimes leaped forth from his neck and sometimes from the tips of his ears and everyone was persuaded that the curse had already made its way into every drop of his blood.

Anicza alone did not draw near him.

"Are you afraid of me, then?" enquired the imposter.

"No."

"Come and kiss me then!"

Anicza approached and allowed herself to be kissed.

Immediately afterwards a shudder ran through her.

"Well? What did you feel?"

"Your mouth burnt my mouth," replied the girl, and Fatia Negra happening to look aside just then, she furtively crossed herself.

Fatia Negra was completely satisfied with the success of this comedy. Their awe of the mysterious and the unintelligible had made his comrades his slaves; he need have no more scruples concerning them.

"Give me your right hand, Anicza," said he, "and give your other hand to your next neighbour, and let everyone take the hand of the person next to him."

Thus he made them form a long chain, the extreme end of which was brought up by old Onucz in whose hand he placed a slender conducting rod which hung down from the altar. Then he recited the fantastic oath before them all once more, whilst they repeated every syllable of it after him.

The comedy was concluded by a violent electric shock which instantly sent a spasm of pain through the muscles and sinews of every member of the living chain. The poor untaught creatures all imagined that the devil himself was flying through their limbs and with tears and groans they begged Black Mask not to put them to any further test.

"And now, Fatia Negra," said old Onucz respectfully, "the moment has come in which you also must keep your word. Will you really take my daughter to wife?"

"I will not see the light of day again until I have done so."

"Will you swear to be her husband in the way you promised to swear?"

"You shall hear me."

"Then have I something else to say to you. Over there, as you see, stands the great weighing machine, in one of the scales I will place Anicza and in the other as many piles of ducats as will make her kick the beam. I will give my girl as many gold ducats as she weighs."

Thereupon the two bridesmen produced a large wooden platter, placed the bride on it, raised it high in the air and carried it to the huge weighing machine. Onucz bade them place both bride and platter in the scale that it might weigh the heavier. Then they piled up into the other scale as many of the sacks of ducats sealed with the seal of Onucz as were necessary to establish an absolute equipoise between the two scales, and then while both the girl and the gold, balancing each other were floating in the air, old Onucz, his face beaming with triumph, poked Fatia Negra in the side with his elbows and said: "And now all that is yours."

The adventurer rushed to the weighing-machine, not indeed to the scale on which the gold was, but to where the girl stood and lifted her down on his arm as if she were a child. The other scale, losing its balance, rushed earthwards and the sacks filled with gold ducats toppled off it left and right.

At this the company was delighted. Fatia Negra's manly tenderness was appreciated by everyone and old Onucz, radiant with joy, turned towards his cronies: "You see it is not my money but my daughter that he is after!"

And yet if Fatia Negra had only been able to foresee what was about to happen the next instant, if only he had been able to guess what would happen during the first few moments of the first approaching quarter of an hour, could he but have heard one step, one bump which might have told him what was going on just then above his head, instead of extending his hands towards the girl, he would have done much more wisely if he had grasped in each hand one of the sacks lying on the other scale and made off with it somewhere through that dark corridor which nobody knew of but he himself, under the special protection of the devil. Just now, however, the devil was evidently not looking after him as carefully as usual, for he returned to the altar with the girl in his arms and deposited his load on the altar steps. The girl knelt down.

"Strew over her corn moistened with honey!" whispered old Onucz to the bridesmaids;—he considered this old custom as of the highest importance. Possibly it was a symbol of fruitfulness.

Anicza wanted Fatia Negra to bend down to her. She had something to whisper in his ear. He leant over her as she desired, drew her pretty face close up to his, and the girl timidly whispered:

"Are you going to take me away under the earth?"

"Are you afraid I shall do so?"

"With you I will go wherever you choose and will fear nothing."

"I take you at your word."

"I don't care. Whither lies the way, to the right or to the left?"

"To the left. Everything which brings luck must be done lefthandedly."

"Is the door underneath the coining-shop?" asked the girl carelessly.

"Yes, if you must know."

"I am ready. Say the oath that I may hear it!"

Fatia Negra repeated his hocus-pocus, kneeling down beside Anicza on the steps of the altar, and raising his eyes towards the black vault of the cavern as he recited the words of a new oath, which kept all the listeners spellbound, so full it was of grisly images and hellish fancies. So deep indeed was the general attention that nobody observed in the meantime that, in the dark background formed by the distant walls of the cavern, a multitude of strange faces were popping up. First two men descended through the machinery of the mill and then two others until, gradually, a hundred of them had assembled. They were all armed and dressed in uniform, but their arms were concealed beneath their mantles, that they might not glimmer through the darkness. And then they quietly formed into ranks like supernumeraries on the stage of a theatre whilst the chief comedian is ending his monologue in front of the footlights. Only Anicza had observed them. During the whole course of the oath, she had not once looked at Fatia Negra's cursing lips, but at the groups forming in the darkness above his head.

The oath over, Fatia Negra seized the reversed crucifix and an electric shock again jolted the hand of the girl which he held fast in his own right hand. "Now, you swear it also!" cried he.

The only reply the girl gave was to passionately tear her hand out of the adventurer's. Rising from her knees, and with her handsome face full of rage, scorn and hatred, she turned upon him, who knelt at her feet, gnashing her pearly teeth as she spoke: "Wretched play-actor! masked imposter! You have deceived everybody, but nobody so much as me. Do you remember that night in the ice valley and how shamefully you betrayed me there? Know then that I was present in that hut, that it was I who blew the horn and brought back the jealous husband from the forest. I saw the tussle that followed and I swore, there and then, that I would be your ruin. Just now you swore that if ever you betrayed me, thus might you yourself be betrayed by whomsoever you trusted most. You said: 'Let water pursue; let fire seize me, let the axe of the headsman descend upon me and the dogs drink up my blood!' Be it so, then—here is fire in front of you and water behind you and the headsman's sword above your head! The dogs that are to lick your blood are already barking for it. I have betrayed you. Look behind you!"

The armed band of soldiers, moving forward in line, like a piece of machinery, suddenly disclosed a row of bayonets glittering in the light of the torches. "We are lost!" howled the mob, whilst the voice of the officer in command (it had a strong foreign accent), rose above the din: "Down with your arms! no resistance!"

Onucz rushed roaring towards his sacks of ducats, the women scattered screaming among the tents. For an instant Fatia Negra stood petrified before Anicza, like a devil caught in a trap, and gazed vacantly at the girl's flaming face.

Anicza now turned quickly towards the armed

soldiers and cried with a piercing voice: "Hasten Juon Tare! Seize the smelting-oven entrance, else this devil will still escape us!"

That was why she wanted to know from Fatia Negra which way they would go underground.

At these words, however, the adventurer recovered himself. He saw a pitiless enemy and a troop of armed men hastening to the door of the smelting-furnace and that way of refuge was consequently closed. The same instant an infernal idea occurred to him.

Hastily snatching up a burning torch from the altar with a couple of vigorous bounds he approached the smelting-furnace. Twenty bayonets and a long axe in the hands of Juon Tare were raised against him—and he was unarmed.

But it was not to the door he wished to get. With a spring sideways he reached the huge vat filled with brandy, threw the burning torch down in front of it and placing his muscular shoulders against the vat, with a desperate exertion of strength scattered its contents on to the floor of the cavern from end to end.

In an instant the whole cavern was in flames!

The floor was of stone so that it could not absorb the spirit as it leaked out and it flashed up as it caught the flame of the torch close at hand. It spread rapidly like a lake of fire that has burst its dams.

The blue spirit-flame filled the whole of the empty cavern with a pale, ghastly glare, the air, the empty space itself seemed to burst into flame. Hundreds of torches, burnt down to their very roots, flickered luridly in the midst of this blue fire of hell, and the heaped-up fire works,—the Bengali pyramids and the rockets and crackers—flamed, fizzled and banged about in the midst of the terrible heat. And in the thick of this infernal blaze black figures, like the souls of the Accursed, were running frantically about, howling, shrieking and toppling over one another and seeking a refuge on the higher rocks whither the flames, spreading through the air, leaped after them. Juon Tare lost his eyesight in the flames. The others tried to find a refuge in the aqueduct running through the cavern, but the pursuing alcohol rushed after them like a living cataract of fire. Everyone seemed bound to perish at this hellish marriage feast.

Only two people did not lose their presence of mind; only two knew what ought to be done, and one of these was Fatia Negra. When the armed soldiers scattered from before the door of the smelting-furnace, he had boldly waded through the burning spirit; he knew very well that it could not set fire to clothing immediately and he took care to hold his hands in front of his eyes to save himself from being blinded. He tore the door open and hastily vanished through it.

The other was Anicza, who, when she saw that in the hundred-fold confusion everyone had lost his head and was running desperately to certain death, quickly snatched up an axe, rushed to the gigantic beer vats and staved in their bottoms. The neutral fluid streamed down upon the floor like a water fall and, gradually gaining ground, forced the flaming *palinka** back further and further, till at last the infernal blue light was gradually extinguished.

By that time, however, the beautiful bride was a sight of horror, her face was burnt out of all recognition.

Every member of the party had received injuries from the fire. Some of them, already blinded, writhed in agony on the ground and dipped their faces in the cool puddles formed by the flowing beer. Old Onucz had not a hair of his head left, but for all that he was still sitting on a heap of ducats, which were rolling in every direction out of the half charred sacks. His scorched hands he dug down deep among his ducats, and thought, perhaps, that they would assuage his pangs.

Both of Juon Tare's eyes had been burnt out by an explosion of gunpowder, and two of the soldiers had also received serious injuries.

Only after the general terror had subsided a little, did it occur to someone that now that the fire had been brought under, Fatia Negra might be pursued. This someone was the bride.

It was she who seized a new torch, it was she who cried to the soldiers: "After me!" and was

---
* Hungarian brandy.

the first to tear open the door of the smelting-furnace. Within was darkness. By torchlight they explored every corner of that underground world—but Fatia Negra was nowhere to be found.

CHAPTER XIV

THE MIKALAI CSARDA

From Hidvár to Gyula Fehervár is a good day's journey, even with the best horses and in the best weather; in the rainy season the mountain streams make the journey still longer. Fortunately, exactly half-way lies the Mikalai *csárdá*, in which dwells a good honest Wallachian gentleman who also follows the profession of innkeeper. In these mining regions there are no Jews, all the inns and *csárdás* are in the hands of the Armenians and Wallachs: the people are content with them and the Hungarian gentry like them.

Young Makkabesku had built up his den in a most picturesque situation beside a stream gushing down from among the mountains and forming a waterfall close to the very house. This stream possessed the peculiar property of turning to stone every leaf and twig which fell into it, even the branches of the trees hanging over it were turned into pretty white petrifactions so far as the water was able to reach them.

Domnul Makkabesku did not carry on the business of inn-keeper for the sake of gain (he would not have been able to make a living out of it if he had tried), but from sheer goodheartedness and good-fellowship. His charges therefore were extremely moderate. A traveller on foot who asked for a night's lodging, had to pay twopence, a traveller on horseback a shilling; if he required wine and brandy for supper as well, still he was only charged a shilling. Who would go to the trouble of totting up extra figures for trifles of that sort? A carriage and four was not taxed at all, those who came in it paid what they chose. If anybody did not ask what he had to pay but simply shook hands and went on his way, mine host simply wished him a happy journey and never said a word about his account.

For Makkabesku was a proud man in his way and thought a great deal of his gentility. He expected to be addressed as "Domnule!* and was delighted when his guests took notice of his coat of arms hanging up in the guest chamber,—to-wit, a black bear with three darts in its heel—and enquired as to its meaning; when he would explain that that black bear with the three darts which was also painted on a sheet of lead and swung backwards and forwards in front of the house between two iron rods was not a sign-board, but his family crest.

Late one afternoon Baron Leonard Hátszegi might have been seen on foot crossing the bridge which led to the Mikalai *csárdá* and entering its courtyard. He came on foot with a small box under his arm and his double-barrelled gun across his

---
* Sir.

shoulder. Makkabesku greeted him from the verandah while he was still a long way off.

"God be with your lordship! Is anything amiss that your lordship comes on foot?"

"Yes, at that cursed *tyira lupului** the axle of my coach gave way. I have always said that that bad bit of road ought to be seen to, this is at least the sixth time that this accident has befallen me."

"God is the cause thereof, your lordship. Whenever the stream overflows it damages the road."

"That is no consolation for me. My fellows are struggling with the coach yonder and cannot set it upright again, so badly damaged it is. It is a good job I was driving my own horses, for otherwise my neck might have been broken. As it is one of my heydukes has sprained his hand. Send help to them at once, or they are likely to remain there all night. Where's your little girl?"

"Ah, my lord! your lordship will always be having your little joke.—Flora, come hither!"

A pretty little maid came out of the inn at these words, and smiled upon the nobleman with a face toasted red by the kitchen fire.

"Take his lordship's gun and little box and carry them into the guest-room!"

"Well, my little girl! how are you? not married yet, eh?" said the baron, pinching her round red cheeks whilst the wench took his box.

"Heh, but 'tis heavy!" she gasped, as if she

---
* Wolf-corner.

were quite frightened at the weight of the box. Won't the gun go off?"

"Don't turn your fiery eyes upon it, or else it might—eh, grandpapa, what do you say?"

"Come, Flora, go in, go in! His lordship is always in such capital spirits. Even when his carriage comes to grief he will have his joke all the same."

The point of the joke was that Makkabesku was a man not much beyond forty though there were flecks of grey on the back of his head here and there. The girl, on the other hand, was scarcely sixteen when the Roumanian gentleman took her to wife. Leonard therefore always made a point of aggravating the innkeeper by pretending to believe that his wife was his daughter and by regularly asking him, as if he were her grandfather, when he intended to get his granddaughter married."

"You need not send help to my carriage, after all," said Hátszegi, after due reflection; "for, by and by I'll see to that myself. I am going back that way. But I should like you to place that little box in some safe place for the time being. It contains 4,000 ducats and that is no trifle."

"Huh! my lord!" cried the innkeeper clapping the back of his head with both hands, as if he feared it was already about to fall off backwards. "Your lordship dares to carry so much gold about with you and stroll so carelessly about in these parts!"

"Carelessly!—what do you mean? I cannot wheel them in front of me on a barrow can I? I want to pay them into my account at Fehervár the day after to-morrow; I have payments to make. That is why I carry them about with me."

"I only meant to say that it is dangerous to go about alone with so much money."

"I am not in the habit of going about with an escort."

"The more's the pity, Domnule. These parts are panic-stricken, since Anicza betrayed the coiners in the Lucsia Cavern, we have been saddled with a whole heap of calamities. A lot of poor fools and a heap of treasure were captured, but the head of the band, Fatia Negra, was suffered to escape. And now, furious at his loss of treasure, he blackmails the whole region. Nobody is safe here now,—only the day before yesterday he stopped and robbed the royal mails on the King's highroad."

"Ho, ho! If he takes to those games, he'll soon get his teeth broken. He won't venture to touch me though, I'll be bound."

"I don't know about that Domnule. He wears a mask and therefore has no need to blush or blanch at anything."

"Does he ever look in here, or has he ever lodged with you?"

"No, my lord, I can safely say that he has never been here, to my great astonishment I must confess. For a great many gentlemen call here and many paths lead hitherward."

"Don't you keep arms in your house?"

"Why should I? I have not enough money to make it worth Fatia Negra's while to rob me. Besides, it is a great mistake to resist him. Juon Tare actually had him in his hands, yet what was the result? He goes about now a blind beggar. Anicza betrayed him and brought down the soldiers upon him, yet what did *she* get by it? *He* vanished under the earth, but she reduced her old father to poverty and is now sitting with all her acquaintances in the dungeons of Gyula Fehervár!"

"Fear nothing! At any rate no ill can befall you while I go to my coachman and come back again. Lock this casket in your wall-cupboard in the meantime, and keep the key yourself."

"Nay, let your lordship keep it rather. I don't want it to be said that I knew anything about it."

So Makkabesku locked up the casket in the huge wall-closet which greatly resembled a large standing clock case and in which were his diploma of nobility and all his domestic treasures. The key of the locked closet he returned to his guest. Then by way of extra precaution, he locked the room as well and forced that key also upon the Baron.

"Domnule," he added, when he saw that Hátszegi was determined to return to his wrecked coach. "I can only say that I should be very glad if your lordship would not go. The servants will be quite able to bring the carriage along."

"That they cannot: the whole lot of them are mere boors who have never seen a carriage with an iron axle."

"Let me go then, and your lordship remain here."

"I suppose you want me, then, to show your daughter how to cook?"

The innkeeper's eyebrows contracted at these words; his desire to go visibly subsided.

"But suppose I am afraid of being left alone in the house with so much money?"

"Come, come, wretched man!" cried Hátszegi at last losing all patience, "you don't suppose that your blockhead of a bandit is lying in wait for me, do you? Look you now! I'll leave you my gun. Take it in your hand and plant yourself there before the door. Bring out a chair, if you like, and sit down on it. Pull down the hammers of both barrels and hold your thumb on them and your index finger on the trigger. The left barrel is filled with ten buckshot and you can be quite sure that whoever approaches you from the lower end of this passage will inevitably get five in his body,—and five of them is enough for anybody. The second barrel, the right one I mean, is loaded with a bullet which we generally keep in reserve for a wild beast, at the last moment, at six paces; at that distance any child could kill a giant. Don't be afraid, if he wore a coat of mail, it would go through it, for that bullet has a steel point and would perforate a leaden door. Come, you are not afraid now, surely?"

Makkabesku certainly felt a great stream of courage flow into his heart at the knowledge that he held in his hand a weapon which could kill the most terrible of men twice over.

"But what about your lordship?" he enquired.

"Oh, I've got two revolvers in my pocket."

And with that, gaily whistling, Hátszegi strode down the long passage and peeped into the kitchen, on his way out, to exchange a word or two with the fair young cook.

"Look ye, my daughter, have supper ready by my return, and take care not to over-salt the soup!" and then with the nonchalance becoming his station he sauntered across the bridge again into the highroad, followed all the way by the eyes of Makkabesku.—"What a gallant fellow it is!" reflected the Roumanian.

The innkeeper did not count courage among his virtues. He was a peace-loving soul who detested the very idea of a brawl. Even when he sat down to drink, it was always inside a room with a locked door, for on one occasion, when he had got drunk in public, the wine had instilled within him such unwonted audacity that he had got his skull broken in two places in consequence. After that he avoided all such occasions of heroism.

For such folks who have nothing to do with

firearms as a rule, there is a peculiar charm in suddenly holding a loaded weapon in their hands. Valour and a sudden access of pugnacity combine to put them in a condition of perpetual fever. A strange longing arises within them to make use of their weapon. Once or twice Makkabesku raised his gun to his cheek and made a target of a fly on the wall. At the end of the vestibule facing him was an old Roman image, the head and bust of an Emperor, which had been unearthed in the neighbourhood of the house when the foundations had been laid, and had been adopted forthwith as a family relic. If this old imperial figurehead had been an enemy, let us say the famous robber of the district, our marksman felt that he could easily have shattered his skull for him.

The sun was now slowly descending from the sky, and the lower it sank, the less golden and the more purple grew the light which it threw upon the ancient monument opposite, till the shadow of an adjacent column fell softly across it and hid it half from view.

Suddenly it seemed to Makkabesku as if he saw the shadow of a human head moving beside the shadow of the column.

The breath died away on his lips—someone was lurking there!

"Who is there?" he cried, in a voice half choked with terror. The same instant there stood before him at the opposite end of the corridor—Fatia Negra!

Yes, there the figure was just as it had been described to him, enfolded in a black atlas mantle, with a black mask across its face.

"Stay where you are, don't come here!" cried the armed Makkabesku, in an agony of terror, "or I'll shoot you through," and as the mask continued to advance, he hurriedly fired off the left barrel of the gun.

The smoke of the powder cleared away, Fatia Negra stood there unwounded, he was coming nearer and nearer!

Ah, those little shots could not hurt him, of course—but now he shall have the bullet with the steel point.

As the first shot was fired, Makkabesku's wife came running out of the kitchen and came face to face with the robber. He immediately seized her arm with his muscular hand and flung her back into the kitchen the door of which he locked upon her.

Mr. Makkabesku permitted all this to go on before his very eyes, but he had raised the gun and held it firmly pressed against his cheek, he wanted the robber to draw nearer still that he might make quite sure of him.

When there were only three yards between them he aimed right at the middle of the intruder, pressed the trigger of the gun and the right barrel also exploded.

Yet the report was followed by no death cry— and Fatia Negra still stood in front of him unscathed.

Paralyzed with terror Makkabesku continued to hold the discharged gun in front of him as if he expected it to go off again of its own accord; but Fatia Negra, catching hold of the end of the gun with one hand, wrenched it out of the innkeeper's grasp and brought down the butt of it so violently on the top of his head that he collapsed in a senseless condition.

After that nobody knew what happened.

When Hátszegi and his servants arrived with the patched-up carriage, Makkabesku was still lying on the ground unconscious, his wife was thundering at the locked door, the door of the guest chamber was smashed and the cupboard in the wall had been broken into and pillaged. Curiously enough, while not one of the innkeeper's relics was missing, Hátszegi's box with the 4,000 ducats had disappeared. A little later it was found in the bed of the stream—empty of course.

Makkabesku was a very long time coming to, but he contrived at last, in a very tremulous voice, to tell Hátszegi the somnambulistic case of the double shots, nay he called Heaven to witness that Fatia Negra had caught the bullets in his hands as if they were flies.

"You're a fool," cried Hátszegi angrily. "I suppose you fired above his head on both occasions."

"But then you ought to see the marks of the bullets on the opposite wall."

And it was a fact that, look as they might, they found no trace of a bullet on the walls or anywhere else.

CHAPTER XV

WHO IT WAS THAT RECOGNISED FATIA NEGRA

THE events at the Mikalai *csárdá* considerably upset Hátszegi. He returned home very sulky and was unusually ungracious towards Henrietta. There were several violent scenes between them, in the course of which the baron twitted his wife with having betrayed him and hinted that it was all in consequence of her own and her brother's bad conduct that she had been disinherited by her grandfather. He revealed to her that he knew everything. He was well aware, he said, that in her girlhood she had had a rascally young attorney as a lover and had thereby incurred her grandfather's anger.

Henrietta, poor thing, had not the spirit to answer him back: "If you knew this, why did you marry me? Why did you not leave me then to him with whom I should have been happy if poor?" She could only reply with tears. She trembled before him while she loathed him.

And yet how dependent she was on him.

She was well aware now of what her brother was accused, and never doubted for a moment what she ought to do. She ought to atone for his fault by an act of self-sacrifice. She must recognize the forgery as her real signature. But what then? The recognition of the signature must needs have consequences. What would be the result of her action?

She could see she had no help to expect from her husband. At every step she perceived that he eagerly sought occasion to quarrel with her and seized every pretext for avoiding her. And now to add to her embarrassment, there was this unlucky Mikalai accident. It seemed just to have come in the nick of time so far as he was concerned, just as if he had actually agreed with Fatia Negra that the latter should rob him on the high road in the most artful manner so that she might not have the slightest hope left of being relieved from her anxieties by the assistance of her husband. The baron, now could always end every *tête-à-tête* by remarking that that rogue Fatia Negra had relieved him of all his money, and he knew not how to make good his loss.

One day, while away from home hunting at Csáko, Baron Leonard learnt that the Countess Kengyelesy's latest ideal was Szilard Vámhidy and when chance soon afterwards brought him also to Arad, he could see for himself that the countess really did load the young man with distinction in society.

The circumstance began to irritate him.

This pale-faced youth with the big burning eyes had turned the head of his own consort once upon a time, and now he was making other enviable conquests. The idea occurred to Hátszegi to knock this "student chap" out of his saddle a second time. Heretofore he had never regarded the countess as a particularly pretty woman, but now he very readily persuaded himself that he was over head and ears in love with her.

He began to pay his court to her—and he was lucky. At least everybody believed it—himself included.

The countess always seemed pleased to see him, and the oftener he paid his visits, the less frequent grew the visits of Szilard. Occasionally they met at the countess's and then Szilard would hastily step aside, as vanquished rivals are wont to do when their conquerors appear. At last Leonard was a daily institution at the countess's, while Szilard only appeared there occasionally.

Yet one day, while Hátszegi was in the drawing room of the countess, paying his court to her most assiduously, Vámhidy entered *sans gêne;* whereupon the countess hastily springing up from her *causeuse* asked leave of the baron to withdraw for a moment and there and then conducted Vámhidy into her private boudoir and remained closeted with him for a good quarter of an hour, whilst Hátszegi, yellow with jealousy, was left alone with the countess's French companion, who could answer nothing but "oui" and "non" to all his remarks.

When the countess emerged from her room, she seemed to be in a very good humour. She accompanied Szilard all the way to the drawing-room door, pressed his hand, and when they parted at the door exchanged a significant look with him, at the same time touching her lips with her index finger—a very confidential piece of pantomime as any connoisseur will tell you.

And all this Hátszegi saw reflected in the mirror, opposite to which he sat.

As soon as the countess sat down, her companion, as if at a given signal, arose and left the room.

Scarcely were they alone when the baron petulantly remarked: "It appears as if your ladyship and our young friend rejoiced in very intimate mutual relations."

"Oh, very intimate. I assure you he is a most worthy, honourable man."

"So I observe."

"I am quite in earnest. I find him quite a treasure, and he is extraordinarily attached to me."

"Very nice of him, I'm sure."

"Oh, you gentlemen, what mockers you are. There are men, I can tell you, who for all that they are poor are more capable of self-sacrifice than the haughtiest nabobs who make such a fuss over us till we are in trouble and then snatch up their hats and fly from the house. You also belong to that class, my lord!"

"I don't understand you."

"Suppose, for instance, I were to say to you: my dear friend, I have fallen into quite an awkward predicament and to-day or to-morrow they will distrain upon me for 40,000 florins."

The baron burst out laughing.

"Don't laugh, for so it really is. That need cause *you* no anxiety, however, I only ask you to tell nobody, especially my husband. He would be capable of making an end of me if he knew it."

"But seriously, countess, who could ever have lent you 40,000 florins?"

"Nobody, and yet I am indebted to that amount. You must know that once upon a time, many years ago, when we lived at Vienna, I was given to card playing. We played for high stakes in those days. One evening not only did I lose all my cash, but had to give I.O.U.'s for 1,000 florins besides. Debts contracted at play cannot remain unpaid for more than a couple of days. It was absolutely indispensable that I should procure these thousand florins somehow. I would not ask my husband for them and that was very foolish of me. I got the amount at last from a wretched usurer at an enormous rate of interest. When the amount plus interest became due again, I was still more afraid to tell my husband, and so kept on giving fresh bills, with the result that the amount of my indebtedness grew and grew as the years rolled on, till it resembled the egg of the widow in the nursery tale—out of which came first two cocks, then a bristling boar, then a camel, and finally a carriage and four, for at last my original poor little debt of one thousand florins swelled into forty thousand and the usurers became importunate and would allow me no more credit. Once when I was in a very bad humour, I let out my secret before Szilard, and the worthy young man undertook to relieve me of my burden. I don't know whether he detected a technical flaw in my bonds or whether he found out some other means of frightening my creditor; anyway, he assured me I only need pay the original sum with interest upon it at the legal rate. Moreover, he undertook to procure me an honourable loan on easy conditions, which to me was a veritable godsend. And so now you know, my dear friend, why Vámhidy is so welcome a guest at my house that I leave even you all alone with my companion when he comes. But you can see for yourself how dear and necessary he is to me and how much I owe to him."

Hátszegi remained in a brown study for several moments, and began biting his lips. The countess sat down at the piano with the most amiable nonchalance as if she gave not another thought to what she had been speaking about.

"If only I had not had the misfortune to be robbed!" cried Hátszegi at last.

"Do you know what, my dear friend," said the countess, at the same time letting her fingers glide lightly over the ivory keys of the piano, "I consider the whole of that affair as simply incredible. Two shots so close to a man and no result!—why it borders a little upon the fabulous!"

"Then I suppose you think it was the innkeeper himself who robbed me?"

The countess shrugged her round shoulders slightly and went on playing.

"That is not possible," resumed the baron, answering his own query, "for I myself saw the blow which Makkabesku received on the head from the butt of the musket, and I can tell your ladyship that there are no four thousand ducats in the world for the sake of which I could lend my head to such a blow."

The countess interrupted her *roulades* for a moment:

"You saw it, eh? And did anybody else see it?"

Hátszegi was strangely surprised by this question.

"What is in your mind, Countess?" he asked.

"I am thinking, my dear friend, that you have some particular reason for playing the injured man, and I have read the whole tale of the Maccabees in some history or other of the Jews which you would now palm off upon the world as something new."

"Your jests are most unmerciful, Countess; but may I beg of you to give that piano a little rest, especially as it wants tuning. I should like to speak seriously to you for a moment or two."

"About the Maccabees, eh?" enquired the countess, laughing.

"No. About myself. I am quite serious when

I say I have had losses. Your ladyship need not know how. But for all that I know what a gentleman ought to do after such a revelation as that with which the countess has just honoured me and which I accept as a most flattering mark of confidence."

"Impossible."

"What I say is never impossible; but what that student fellow has chosen to palm off on your ladyship that *is* impossible. He will not be able to help your ladyship without a great scandal. Naturally a mere attorney looks upon that as a matter of course. He does not understand that there are cases in which a person would rather spring into a well than risk her reputation in the eyes of the world by appealing to the courts for redress. I make your ladyship another proposal: I will exchange a bond of my own against the bond of the countess to an equal amount. I feel confident that the usurers will lend readily on my paper and will jump at the exchange."

"Oh, many thanks, many thanks! But, first of all, I should like to know what interest you mean to charge me; for I am not going to pay anything usurious again."

"Legal and Christian interest, I assure you. But I must impose one condition: your ladyship's doors must henceforth be closed against this lawyer fellow."

"Are you serious, Baron?"

"Perfectly so."

"Are you not afraid I shall take you at your word?"

"By doing so you will satisfy my desires. Look, Countess! I consider myself as one of your most sincere admirers and it wounds me to hear all this tittle-tattle circulating in our set which links your ladyship's name with that of young Vámhidy."

"But will it not injure the respect you entertain for me if your name takes the place of Vámhidy's in the gossip you complain of?"

"All that I desire is that a certain man shall be excluded from this house, and if the countess desires it I will then keep away likewise."

The countess hastened to press Hátszegi's hand as a sign that *she* did not desire *that*.

"Very well, then, to prove to you that my relations with Vámhidy were purely professional, I will break off all further intercourse with him."

"Then we'll clinch your ladyship's determination at once. May I make use of your writing table? Have you any other ink than this rose-coloured ink, with which to be sure, your ladyship generally writes your letters, but which is a little unusual in official documents?"

"Everything you desire, sealing-wax included."

"That is not necessary for bills. What a fortunate thing that I have a blank form with me."

The baron discovered in his pocket a blank form, without which no gentleman ever goes about, and filled it up in the usual way. The countess, with her elbows on the back of the armchair, looked over the baron's shoulder while he signed the precious document, and thought to herself: what an odd thing it is when a rich and influential man refuses, with a heart of iron, to give his wife a little assistance which would make her happy and save her brother from dishonour, and yet lightly pitches the very sum required out of the window for the sake of a pretty speech from another woman who is almost a stranger to him!

After signing the document Leonard did not linger another instant, but snatched up his hat and hastened off so as to avoid the suspicion that he was expecting some little gratification on account.

The pressure of the hand which the countess exchanged with him at parting assured him that this conquering manœuver on his part was a complete success.

Subsequently, however, as, stretched at full length on his sofa, he was smoking his first pipe of tobacco, he grew suspicious, and speedily felt convinced that the countess's tale of the usurers was a fable from beginning to end and that Vámhidy was some broker or other who lent money privately; and he began to be not quite so proud at having ousted the fellow from her ladyship's drawing room.

But a still greater surprise awaited him.

He had a shrewd suspicion that the Countess Kengyelesy did not require the bill he had signed to discharge any debt to usurers; but not even in his dreams would it ever have occurred to him that Madame Kengyelesy, at the very moment when he had gone out into the street, had sat down on the very same chair from which the baron had arisen, taken into her hand the very same pen in which the ink he had used was not yet dry, and selecting a sheet of letter paper, written a few lines of her long pointed pot-hooks to her friend, the Baroness Hátszegi: informing her in a most friendly manner that she had succeeded in persuading Hátszegi to exchange the bill that Koloman was suspected of forging for one of his own in order to give his wife the opportunity of acknowledging the signature as her own and putting a stop to all further legal proceedings. All this was set forth with far greater elaboration than it is here, but was nevertheless perfectly intelligible. The original bill was appended to the letter and the letter was posted. Henrietta was bound to receive it next day.

Imagine then the surprise of Hátszegi, who for the last three days had been pacing impatiently up and down his room, naturally expecting every moment that the countess would surrender at discretion and send for him out of sheer gratitude, when the door was suddenly opened with considerable impetuosity and in came—Henrietta. Before he could sufficiently recover from his amazement to ask her what she was looking for there, his wife fell on his neck, and, sobbing with emotion, came out with some long rigamarole about delicacy,—gratitude—a delightful surprise—and only half suspected kindness of heart—and a lot more of unintelligible nonsense, winding up by begging his pardon if ever she had unwittingly offended him and promising him that *after this* she would ever be his faithful slave!

After this!—after *what?*

It was only when his wife told him that she was alluding to that bill for 40,000 florins which he had been so kind as to send her through the countess, that some inkling of the truth burst upon him.

"Oh, that eh! It quite escaped my memory and is not worth mentioning," he cried, hiding his astonishment beneath the affectation of a magnanimity which scorned even to remember such trifles.

Oh, if the countess had been able to see him at that moment, how she would have laughed!

Every drop of Leonard's blood seemed to turn to gall. How ridiculous he had been made to appear by a woman's nobility, and the consciousness thereof was still further embittered by the artless and innocent gratitude of that other woman—his own wife. He could have torn the pair of them to pieces. What a pretty fool he had made of himself. He had purchased the love of his wife for 40,000 florins. He could not demand back the bill from her, nor could he explain to her the compromising origin of that document. And in addition to that, he must play the part of dignified pater familias which his wife had assigned to him in this domestic drama, instead of that of first lover which was so much more to his liking.

"All right, Henrietta," said he, assuming a calmness he was far from feeling. "If you like to give me the bill, I'll see that it is posted to your lawyer at Pest, Mr. Sipos."

Henrietta thanked him sincerely, but said she would rather take it to Pest herself in order that she might have a long confidential talk with Mr. Sipos personally about her poor brother.

"Then wait, Henrietta, till the Arad races are over. You know I am greatly interested in them. If I am not there myself they are quite capable of striking my horses out."

"My dear Leonard, I don't want you to interrupt any of your business or pleasure on my account. I can easily go by myself. But I don't want to postpone the matter a single day. You know how anxious I am about my poor brother."

"Well, but you know that the roads are very dangerous just now. You know what happened to myself a little while ago."

"Oh, I have my plan all cut and dried. I am prepared for the very worst. If robbers attack me I will give up to them, at the first challenge, all the cash I have about me. What I am most afraid of is the bill, but I will hide that so that nobody can find it."

"My dear, these men are very artful."

"Oh, they won't find it, I can tell you. The insides of my upper-sleeves consist of steel rings which fasten close to the arms, and I will roll up my bill, insert it within my sleeve and draw a steel ring over it. They will never guess that, will they?"

"A good idea, certainly."

Yet, good idea as he thought it, Hátszegi nevertheless complained to his friend Gerzson, whom he met at the club the same evening, how anxious he was about his wife, who was going all the way to Pest next day, and how glad he would be, since he was unable to accompany her himself, if someone would persuade her not to go.

Naturally Mr. Gerzson at once offered to dissuade the baroness, as Hátsezegi had anticipated, and was invited to tea by him the same day with that express purpose, but, talk as he might, he could not prevail with Henrietta. In reply to all his arguments, she pleaded for her poor brother, whose fate, she added, with tears, depended upon her instant action.

Now, Mr. Gerzson was a gentleman—every inch of him. He was also kind-hearted to a fault, and when he beheld the poor woman in despair, he put an end to the difficulty by saying: "Very well, my lady, then I will escort you to Pest myself."

At this Hátszegi fairly lost all patience. "Why, what can you be thinking of?" cried he.

"Your pardon, Leonard, but I suppose you may regard me as old enough and honourable enough to fill the place of a father to your wife on an occasion like this! It appears to me that it will never enter anybody's head to speak slightingly of a lady because she travelled alone with me."

Good, worthy old man, he was quite proud that no woman could look at his face without a shudder.

"And then I fancy that there's still quite enough of me left to defend a woman against anybody, even though it were the devil himself. And I should advise that worthy Fatia Negra not to show his mug to me, for my stunted hand does not fire guns as our friend Makkabesku is in the habit of doing, nor will my bullets be caught like flies, I warrant."

"You will be done out of the horse-racing, all through me," remarked Henrietta sadly.

"Oh, it does not interest me much. I don't care much about it."

This was not true, but it was all the nicer of the old man to say so.

"Then you really mean to escort my wife to Pest?" said Hátszegi, at last.

"With the greatest of pleasure."

"Very well. At any rate, I will see to all the travelling arrangements that there may be no delay at any of the stages. Which way do you prefer to go *via* Csongrad or *via* *Szeged*?

"By way of Csongrad."

"Well, 'tis the shorter of the two certainly, but at this season of the year the road is as hard as steel. It will be as well to provide my horses with fresh shoes."

"It is now ten o'clock. By midnight your coachman will have managed to do all that. The baroness would do well if she had a little sleep now. Meanwhile I will go home for my luggage and my weapons; at two o'clock in the morning I shall be here again, and at three we can start."

"I will be awake and watching for you, and I thank you with all my heart."

Mr. Gerzson drank up his tea and hastened home. Leonard advised Henrietta to go and sleep—and she really was very sleepy—while he went to the stables to see to the horses.

It was about midnight when he returned. He looked very tired, like one who has had a great deal of bustling about. He was alone in the drawing room, so he stirred up the fire, lit a cigar and waited in silence.

At half past two Mr. Gerzson rang the gate-bell; he entered the drawing-room very boisterously like one resolved to wake up the whole house. A little coffer hung upon his stunted arm, in the other hand he carried a double-barrelled gun, and from a pouch, fastened by straps to his shoulder, peeped forth two four-barrelled pistols.

"Why, plague take it!" laughed Hátszegi, "you are armed for a whole guerilla warfare."

"No more than Fatia Negra deserves," replied Mr. Gerzson with a sombre grimace. "Is your wife up and dressed?"

"I fancy she lay down ready dressed."

"All the better. It'll be as well if we start early."

"I hear the opening and closing of doors in her apartments, no doubt your ringing disturbed her. She will be here in an instant, for she is very impatient."

"That is only natural."

"And in the meantime, let us have something to strengthen the heart," said Hátszegi producing a flask of *szilvapalinka** and filling his own and his guest's glass. "If you have a chance of shooting Fatia Negra, you must give me one half of the thousand ducats set upon his head, because I have abandoned this fine opportunity to you."

At this Mr. Gerzson coughed.

"I have also provided you with a good wooden flask of *Hegyalja*,"† said Leonard, taking from the sideboard a handsome flask bound in foal-skin.

"Therein you acted wisely."

"All this side of the Theiss you will get no drinkable water, and Henrietta always gets ague at once if the water is bad. Although but a child, she will never take any wine unless you force her to do so. I earnestly beg of you to take great care of her. I don't like this journey a bit. A letter would have done the business just as well; but I make it a rule never to thwart her when she gets these ideas into her head. All I say is: take care of her."

---

* Hungarian cherry brandy.
† A species of Tokay.

"I'll watch over her as if she were my own child."

In a quarter of an hour Henrietta appeared in full travelling costume. The lacquey brought in breakfast. The gentlemen also sat down to it lest the lady should breakfast alone.

We shall have splendid weather, Baroness," observed Mr. Gerzson, dipping his cake into his black coffee. "The sky is full of stars, we could not wish for better travelling weather."

"The sky is nice enough, but the ground is a little stumbly," put in Hátszegi. "Around Dombhegyhaza in particular the roads will spill you if you don't look out."

"I don't care a bit, for I mean to drive the horses myself."

"Oh, that I will not allow," said Henrietta. "It is no joke to hold the reins, for hours at a stretch, on bad roads."

"I do it because I like it, your ladyship. You know I love my pipe, and how can I smoke it in a covered carriage?"

Shortly afterwards Mr. Gerzson asked leave to go out and inspect the coach and the coachman, and after closely investigating everything and wrangling a little with the coachman, purely from traditional habit, just to show the fellow that he understood all about it, he ascended to the drawing-room again and announced that the horses had been put to.

Hátszegi helped his wife to adjust her mantle

WHO RECOGNIZED FATIA NEGRA

over her shoulders, and impressed a cold kiss upon her forehead. Henrietta once more thanked him warmly for being so good to her and allowed Mr. Gerzson to escort her down the steps. The old gentleman, however, would not allow himself to be persuaded to take his place in the carriage by her side. His hands itched to hold the reins and he would, he said, be sure to go to sleep and make himself a nuisance if he sat inside. So he had his way, and indeed in all the Hungarian plain a more adroit and careful driver could not have been found.

Gradually the night began to die away and the sky began to grow lighter behind the mountains of Bihar, which they had now left behind them. The smaller stars vanished in groups before the brightening twilight; only the larger constellations still sparkled through the dawn. Presently a hue of burning pink lit up the sky and long straight strips of cloud swam, like golden ribbons, before the rising sun whose increasing radiance already lit up the broad cupolas of the dark mountains. Before the travellers extended the endless plain of the *Alföld*,* like a bridge rising from her bed to greet her beloved Lord, the Sun.

On Mr. Gerzson, however, the romantic spectacle of sunrise on the *puszta* produced no romantic impression whatsoever. He neither observed the golden clouds in the sky, nor the dappled shadows flitting across the dewy fields, nor

---
* The great Hungarian plain.

the lilac-coloured nebulous horizon. He saw none of these things, I say, but he saw something else which did not please him at all.

"I say, Joska, the right leader is limping."

"Yes, it certainly is," replied the coachman.

"Get down and see what's the matter."

The coachman got down, lifted the horse's leg, brushed away the dust from around the hoof and said with the air of a connoisseur: "This horse's hoof has been pricked."

"What the devil . . . !" rang out Mr. Gerzson, but there he stopped, for it is not becoming to curse and swear when a lady is in the carriage behind you, even if she does not hear.

Meanwhile the coachman mounted up beside him and they drove on again.

"Well we cannot drive that horse much further," grumbled Mr. Gerzson, "the other three must pull the carriage. At Csongrad we must get another to take its place and leave it behind there."

A long discussion thereupon ensued between him and the coachman as to the clumsiness of smiths in general, who when they pare away a horse's hoofs in order to shoe it, so often cut into the living flesh, which is very dangerous, and is technically known as "pricking."

They had scarce proceeded for more than another half hour when Mr. Gerzson again began to cast suspicious glances down from the box-seat.

"I say, Joska," he cried at last, "it seems to me the left leader, the whip horse, is also limping."

Down leaped the coachman, examined the horse's foot and pronounced that the hoof of the left leader had also been pricked.

"Devil take ... !" cried Mr. Gerzson, but once more he did not enlighten the devil as to the particular individual he was desirous of drawing his attention to.

"Well, I suppose we must go on as best we can with two horses now, for the first two are good for nothing." And in the spirit of a true driver he stuck his whip beneath him, as being a thing for which there was now no further use, and resumed his argument with the coachman about the inefficiency of smiths in general.

"As soon as we reach Oroshaza, we'll get two fresh horses; we ought to be getting there now."

Yet the steeple of Oroshaza was, as yet, scarcely visible and midday was already approaching. There was no intermediate station where they could change horses.

Half an hour later Mr. Gerzson dashed his clay pipe against the wheel of the coach and swore that he would be damned if ever such a silly-fool thing had ever befallen him before, for now the thill horse also began to limp.

Naturally, that also was found to have been pricked.

"May the devil take all those scamps of smiths who look after the poor beasts so badly! A pretty fix we are in now. We may thank our stars if we are able to crawl into Oroshaza before nightfall. A pretty amble we shall have now, I'll be bound."

And indeed ambling was about all they could do. As for the Oroshaza steeple, so far from drawing any nearer, it seemed to be travelling away from them, and with very much better horses than they had. It seemed to get further off every moment.

"Well, all we want now is for the saddle horse also to throw up the sponge and we shall be complete."

If that were Mr. Gerzson's one remaining wish, Fate very speedily granted it to him, for they had not gone another quarter of an hour when all four horses began to limp together, one with the right foot, another with the left, the third with the fore and the fourth with the hind leg, till it was positively frightful to look at them.

Mr. Gerzson leaped from the box, and in his rage and fury dashed his pipe-stem into a thousand pieces.

"What can the smith have been about!" whined the coachman shaking his head, " and yet his lordship had a look at them too!"

"Devil take your smith, and his lordship also for the matter of that. The whole lot of you deserves hanging." And it was a good thing for the coachman that he happened to be standing on the other side of the horses, as otherwise he would certainly have had a taste of Squire Gerzson's riding whip.

Henrietta, who had hitherto been sleeping quietly in the carriage, aroused by the loud voices, put her head out of the window and timidly inquired what was the matter. At the first sound of her voice, Squire Gerzson grew as mild as a lamb.

"Nothing much," said he. "I have only been trying to put together again my broken pipe-stem, the carriage-wheel has gone over my pipe, that is all."

"But where are we now?" asked Henrietta, peeping curiously out of the carriage. Then of course they had to tell her the truth.

"We are three leagues from the station in front of us, and about four from the one behind us, and there is no prospect of our getting on any further. All four horses are lame, they have been damaged during the shoeing."

"What steeple is that in front of us?"

"Oroshaza, I fancy, but with these four lame horses I don't believe we shall get there before midnight."

Henrietta perceived the confusion of the old gentleman, who for sheer rage and worry could not keep his hat on his burning head, so she tried to comfort him.

"Never mind, dear papa Gerzson, not far from here must lie Leonard's *csárdá*. You and I, papa Gerzson, might go on there with the horses while the coachman makes the best of his way on foot to Oroshaza, where he can get fresh horses and join us early in the morning at the *csárdá*.

Squire Gerzson jerked his head significantly.

"I don't want to alarm you, my dear Baroness," said he, "but that *csárdá* lies in the beat of the "poor vagabonds"—you may have heard of them."

"Oh, I have spent a night there already. I know the innkeeper's wife. She is a very good sort of woman, who told us tales all night long while she worked her distaff at my bedside. I should very much like to see her again. Besides, I know the "poor vagabonds" also. All of them kissed my hand in turn when I was there. If, however, anybody should be rude to me, have I not papa Gerzson?—when he is by I fear nobody."

"Noble heart!—very well, be it so! If your ladyship fears nothing, I think I may very well say the same."

Whereupon Squire Gerzson gave the coachman two florins to speed him on to Oroshaza, where he was to get fresh horses and come on the same night to the *csárdá*, so that they might be able to set off again before dawn on the morrow. He himself then quitted the highroad in the direction of the well-known *csárdá* which, with sound horses, he might have reached in about an hour, but which with lame ones he only got up to towards evening, having repeatedly to rest on the

WHO RECOGNIZED FATIA NEGRA 285

way. Squire Gerzson kept on asking Henrietta whether she was hungry or thirsty and offered her his flask again and again; but she always gently declined it, the old man feeling in honour bound to follow her example. He comforted her, however, with the assurance that the *csárdá*-woman was a dab hand at turning out all sorts of good old savoury Hungarian dishes.

At last, after a weary journey, when evening was already closing upon them, Henrietta perceived the *csárdá* gleaming white behind the acacia trees. When they stumbled into the courtyard they found nobody, and nobody came out of the door to meet them.

"All the better, nobody will see these game-legged nags," growled Squire Gerzson as he helped Henrietta out of the carriage.

"It is odd that the woman of the inn does not come out to meet me," said Henrietta. "She liked me so. How pleased she will be to see me."

Nevertheless no one came. Squire Gerzson grew impatient. He could not leave the coach and horses all by themselves.

"Hie! somebody! Who's at home? Landlady, wenches, or whoever you are, can't you creep out of your hole?"

In reply to his hallooing, a hoarse voice resounded from the taproom: "Who is it? Can't you come inside instead of standing and bawling there?"

"What, you scoundrel! Come out this instant,

Sirrah, do you hear, or do you want me to come and fetch you?"

At this categorical command, the speaker inside made his appearance. Henrietta recognized him at once, though Squire Gerzson saw him now for the first time. It was old Ripa.

"I am a guest here myself," said he.

"Thou blockhead! by the soul of thy father I charge thee—where is the hostess?"

"She is outside in the cool air."

"What is she doing there?"

"She is guarding the moles"—which means in the flowery language of the *puszta:* "she is dead."

"Surely she is not dead?"

"Yes—she did away with herself."

"When?"

"The day before yesterday."

"What was the matter with her?"

"She drank too much water."

"Where?"

"In the hurdle well."

"Why?"

"Because her feet did not reach the bottom."

"She leaped in then?"

"It looks something like it."

"But why did she do so?"

"She was much upset about her lover."

"Did he leave her?"

"The rope-girl* took him."

Henrietta listened with a sort of stupefaction

---

* *I. e.,* the gallows.

to the cynical answers of the old scoundrel, and her heart grew heavy within her. To think that that merry, rosy cheeked young woman should have killed herself out of grief for her lover.

"Then who is carrying on the house?" enquired Squire Gerzson.

"Nobody. All the servants bolted after the funeral, in order that they might not appear as witnesses."

"Then why do you remain here all alone?"

"Because if I went on my way, everyone would be sure to say that I had murdered the hostess, I mean to remain here till they come for me."

"Yes, you old swine, and drink up every drop of wine that remains in the meantime."

"Your pardon, sir, but it all turned to vinegar when the landlady killed herself. That is always the case."

"None of your nonsense, Sirrah, but listen to me. There's a shilling for you, forget for the time that you are a guest here. Take out the horses, put them into the stable, give them hay at once and water them in about an hour's time. Don't steal them for they are lame and you would be caught at once. We shall remain here till our coachman returns with four fresh horses. Should any troublesome person look in, you may tell him that the consort of Baron Hátszegi is here and that Gerzson of Satrakovics is mounting guard before her door."

Old Ripa kissed her ladyship's hand without

so much as thanking Squire Gerzson for his tip, but he quietly unyoked the horses and brought into the house some of the things he found in the coach.

And Henrietta stood once more in the landlady's room and gazed pensively out of the window. Her meditations were presently disturbed by Squire Gerzson.

"My dear good lady," he began, "fate has certainly sworn to be our enemy in every possible way to-day. I would not have believed it myself if I had not actually experienced it. First of all, all our four horses fall lame on the road. Then, at the very place where we decide to take up our quarters, we find that the landlady has jumped down the well. Truly fate pursues us with a vengeance. But we'll defy it, won't we my lady? Fate is very much mistaken if it fancies it will get the better of us, eh? It does not know with whom it has to deal, I'll be bound. For our hearts are in the right place and we'll pretty soon show that we have not lost our heads. Our greatest misfortune is that the fine supper we promised ourselves has vanished to dust beneath our very noses. Never mind. We have brought with us in our knapsack, after the custom of our ancestors, some good ham, some hung beef and some white loaves, to say nothing of a flask of prime wine; we don't mean to starve ourselves do we, my lady?"

The good old gentleman then took out of his knapsack all these good things and piled them up on the table, then he fetched the carriage lamp to light up the room a bit and politely invited Henrietta to partake of his simple banquet.

The young lady smilingly took her place on the bench.

"We really cannot drink the water here, your ladyship," said Gerzson, handing her his flask; "to all appearance nobody will ever drink the water out of the well of this shanty again. Such wells are generally walled up."

Merely to oblige the old man, Henrietta raised the flask to her lips and pretended to drink out of it so as not to spoil her companion's good humour, but really she drank not a drop. She never used to drink wine and wiped off the drops that remained on her lips with her pocket handkerchief. Nor did she eat anything except an apple which was just sufficient to keep the pangs of hunger off.

Mr. Gerzson, however, fell to like a man. He had generally a good appetite, and the lack of a dinner, the worry and trouble of the journey, and the labour of driving had made him hungrier than ever. He cut such whacking slices off the loaf and off the good red ham beside him that it was a joy to watch him; after he had raised the cluck-clucker* to his lips, his conversation became so entertaining that Henrietta listened to him with delight.

"But now I am not going to drink any more," said Mr. Gerzson at last, "for it is apt to make me

---
* *I. e.*, the wine-flask.

sleepy and I don't want to sleep to-night. About midnight the coachman will arrive with the fresh relay of horses. Won't your ladyship rest a little in the adjoining room?"

Henrietta shook her head.

"Well, I suppose you are right. How indeed could you remain all alone in the room of a suicide? Let us stay together then and tell each other tales."

"Yes, that will be nice, and I'll begin by telling papa Gerzson something."

"I could go on listening to you till morning, it will be like the angels singing in my ears."

So Henrietta began to tell him all about the dead hostess and about her love, and also the story of the robber who was hanged for his companion.

Mr. Gerzson, with his head supported by his hand, listened religiously and struck himself violently on the mouth when he was seized by an involuntary fit of gaping.

"I cannot understand why I am so sleepy,—my eyes seem to be closing in spite of me."

"Why don't you have a pipe then? Come light up!"

"What, light up? Your ladyship will really allow me? You are sure you don't mind tobacco smoke? You are indeed a blessed creature. But are you sure it won't make your head ache?"

"On the contrary, I like tobacco smoke."

Squire Gerzson half drew out his cigar case, but he immediately shoved it back again.

"No, I won't smoke a cigar. One ought not to abuse one's good fortune. I shall get on well enough."

Then Henrietta began to tell him of Fatia Negra's Transylvanian exploits, of the Lucsia Cavern, of the capture of the coiners—and then she observed that Mr. Gerzson's eyelids were sinking lower and lower and he was nodding his head violently.

"Now you really must light up, papa Gerzson," she cried, "or you'll never be able to keep awake."

On being thus accosted, Mr. Gerzson bobbed up his head with a frightened air and rubbed his eyes, like one who has been suddenly aroused from slumber and knows not what is going on under his very nose.

"I am not asleep, 'pon my word I'm not. I was only nodding a little."

"Light a cigar."

"No I won't. I prefer to go out and have a turn in the open air and get the cobwebs out of my head. I'll have a look round outside a bit."

And with that he planted both his arms on the table, laid his head upon them and fell fast asleep.

Henrietta could not help smiling. Poor old gentleman, he had had a good deal of exertion and no doubt that wine was uncommonly strong. Let him rest a bit. He had had no sleep the night before. It would be quite sufficient if one of them kept awake.

Then she took up the lamp and went out into the hall observing to her great satisfaction that the door thereof was provided with a good lock. So she locked and fastened it. With timid curiosity she then explored every corner with the lamp and came upon nothing suspicious. Finally she returned to the guest room, locked the door of that also and placed the carriage lamp on the table, turning its shade towards the sleeping old man so that he might not be awakened by the glare of the lamp; and there she remained all alone, watching in the *csárdá* of the desolate *puszta,* patiently waiting for the night to pass over her homeless head.

So patient was she that only once did she take her watch from her bosom to see what the time was.

* * * * * * *

It was now past midnight.

She began to calculate how long it would take the coachman to get to Oroshaza and how much time he would require to reach this place. If he had got horses at once he ought to be near now.

A short time afterwards she heard the tread of horses' feet in the courtyard. Those must be our horses, thought she, and hastening to the window looking out upon the courtyard, she pulled the blind a little to one side and looked out.

The night was so light outside that she could

see the four horses quite plainly in the courtyard—but she observed that a man was sitting on *each* of them.

"This is very curious," thought she, "*two* men would have been quite sufficient to bring along the relay."

Three of the four men dismounted from their horses and a fifth came out of the stable and had a short consultation with them; then the three approached the *csárdá* door and tried to open it.

This struck Henrietta as suspicious and she thought it was now high time to awake Mr. Gerzson.

"Pardon, papa Gerzson, but four men have arrived here."

Still Mr. Gerzson did not awake.

Henrietta approached, bent over him and gently insisted:

"My dear papa Gerzson, just wake up for a moment, somebody wants to come in."

Even then Mr. Gerzson did not awake.

Henrietta listened. Outside, the hall door was beginning to groan and rock. They were forcing it.

Full of terror now, she seized Mr. Gerzson's arm.

"Sir, sir! robbers are upon us. Awake, awake. This is no time for slumber."

But Mr. Gerzson still slumbered on—he might have been dead. In vain she tore him away from the table, he fell back again all of a heap and went on slumbering.

The strangers were now in the hall, and a heavy hand was trying the latch of the guest chamber.

"My God, my God!" moaned Henrietta, wringing her hands and rushing up and down the room, terrorstricken, not knowing where to look now for refuge.

A violent thud resounded against the door. Someone had placed his shoulder against it. Henrietta clung to the table to save herself from falling.

At last the lock burst, the door flew open, and Fatia Negra with two masked companions stood before the lady. The same instant Henrietta recovered her presence of mind. At a pace's distance from danger she ceased to tremble and calmly addressed them: "What do you want?"

"Why are you not asleep now like your companion?" enquired Fatia Negra in a low voice.

One of his comrades approached the sleeper and held the barrel of his pistol to his temples. In Fatia Negra's hand there was only a dagger.

"Don't wake him," he whispered to Henrietta, "for if he should but raise his head his brains will be blown out."

"Do him no harm!" implored the lady. "I will give you everything you want. Here is my pocketbook, here are my jewels, and you shall have my watch too. See, I will draw off my rings, only don't touch me. But if possible let me keep this round ring for it is my wedding ring."

"All that is nothing," whispered Fatia Negra, "nor do we want these things. Your ladyship has received a bill for 40,000 florins from your husband; give up that and swear that you will not say anything about it to anyone for three days so that we may have time to turn it into cash."

At the mention of the bill Henrietta felt her head reel, the blood stood still in her veins, she could scarce keep her feet. Her voice trembled as she lied to the robber denying that she had any such thing.

"We will search you, my lady, if you do not give it up voluntarily."

Henrietta persisted in her falsehood: "I have nothing upon me. I posted it in order that it might get to its destination more safely."

"My lady, you are only wasting our time. Turn round, take that steel netting out of your puffed sleeves and hand it over to us."

At these words, all the blood flew to Henrietta's head. It was no longer fear but the fury of despair that possessed her. It suddenly occurred to her that here was the man whom nobody had ever recognized; the man who had made so many people unhappy; who had robbed her husband and would now stifle her last hope of saving her brother from disgrace. Who could this terrible man, this accursed wretch, be? And so, as Black Mask drew near to her, flashing his dagger before her eyes, she, the weakest, the most timid of women, made a sudden snatch at the mask and tore it off

She saw his face and recognized him. . . .

For an instant her eyes gazed upon him and then she collapsed on the ground in a swoon.

* * * * * * *

It was pretty late next morning when Mr. Gerzson raised his muddled head from the table. The sun was shining brightly through the blinds.

He looked around him. He was quite alone.

He looked for Henrietta, he called her by name. She was nowhere to be seen. Their luggage had also disappeared. He went into the courtyard and looked for the carriage. That also was nowhere to be seen. Only the four horses were in the stable, and they were neighing for water; nobody had watered them.

After that Mr. Gerzson's head grew more muddled than ever.

What had become of the lady? What had happened during the night? How was it that he remembered nothing about it, he who generally used to sleep so lightly that the humming of a midge was sufficient to awake him?

Gradually he bethought him that the evening before he had drunk some wine with an unusual flavour. Even now he was conscious of a peculiar taste in his mouth. Yet no wine in the world had ever been able to do him harm. He returned to the room to examine the contents of his flask.

But even the flask was now nowhere to be seen. There was not a single forgotten object, not a single indication to give him a clue in this obscure confusion. What could have happened here?—he had not the faintest idea.

He went and stood in front of the *csárdá*. He gazed out upon the desolate *puszta* stretching around him in every direction. From every point of the compass wagon tracks, some old, some still fresh, zig-zagged to and from the *csárdá* and he could not make up his mind which of them to take in order to reach the world beyond.

CHAPTER XVI

LEANDER BABEROSSY

WHENEVER one carts away a heap of stones which have been lying undisturbed for years, or whenever one removes the shingle-roof of an ancient tenement, or drains off the water from a marshy place, one generally stumbles upon all sorts of hitherto undiscovered, curious beetles, odd looking moths and spiral-shaped, creeping things in these routed out lurking places, which nobody ever saw before or read of in the natural history books; and at such times a man bethinks him how wonderful it is of Mother Nature to provide even such holes and corners as these with living inhabitants which never see the light of day at all.

Once, while on circuit, Vamhidy was obliged to lie one night at a village within his jurisdiction whose inhabitants were a strong mixture of Hungarian, Servian and Wallachian ingredients. Arriving late, it was a long time before he could go to sleep, and he was awakened rather late next morning by an unusual hubbub. His bedchamber was only separated from the large drinking room by a door and through this door broke every now and then very peculiar sounds the meaning of which, on a first hearing, it was very difficult to explain.

It sounded as if a couple of women and a couple of men were roundly abusing one another, sometimes in a low tone and sometimes in a loud, and the most peculiar thing about the whole business was that two of them never spoke at once but each one of them allowed each of the others to have his say out to the end. All at once the noise grew more alarming and broken outbursts plainly suggested that someone in the adjoining room wanted to murder somebody else. Vamhidy leaped from his bed and was about to intervene when in came the landlord with his coffee.

"What is that row going on next door?" enquired Szilard irritably.

"Oh, I cry your honour's pardon," replied the innkeeper with a proud smile, "it is only our actors. They are rehearsing a new piece which they are going to act this evening. I hope your honour will condescend to go and see it—it will be real fine."

"What, actors in this village?" cried Szilard in amazement. "Why, where do they come from?"

"Nobody knows where they came from or whither they mean to go, your honour."

"How many of them are there then, and who is their manager?"

"Well, it seems that there is only one man among them and he is half a child; all the others are women and girls, even to the ticket taker and the prompter."

"And what sort of pieces do they act?"

"Oh, all sorts, your honour. Those of the women who have the deepest voices dress up as men, stick on beards and mustaches and act much better than men would, because they don't get drunk."

"And they are able to make a living here? Who goes to the theatre then?"

"Well, the rustics about here come if there is anything to grin at. They don't give money because they have none themselves; but they bring corn, potatoes, sausages and hams and the actors live upon the proceeds as best they can. When they have made any debts they cannot pay they simply bolt on the first fine night and go somewhere else."

"But don't they leave their decorations or their wardrobe in pledge behind them?"

At this the landlord laughed aloud as if it were a capital joke.

"Decorations, wardrobes, indeed! Why their stage curtain consists of a large piece of threadbare sackcloth pasted over with tricolored paper on which they have painted the national coat of arms. Their wardrobe too is of the very simplest description. When they play a piece in which kings and queens appear, they borrow the gold bespangled dresses of the rich Servian women of the district to serve them as royal mantles. All they require besides is a little tinsel, some spangles and some pasteboard—and there you are! The manager, as I have said, is still but a child, but so ingenious is he that he can make moonshine out of a yellow gourd and produce thunder and lightning,—but that is a professional secret. It is true they have only six pieces in all, and when they have played these through they begin them all over again. The public, naturally, does not like to see the same piece twice, so the manager gives the piece another title, changes the titles of all the characters and represents the piece over again as a brand new one."

"I should like to see to-day's representation," said Szilard, whose curiosity had been excited by this peculiar description.

"I'll fetch your honour a play bill immediately," said the innkeeper.

Off went mine host returning in a few moments with a MS. play bill on which was written in large red letters: "Hernáni or Castilian Honour," followed by the names of the personages. Hernáni was naturally the manager himself, Leander Babérossy,* Elvira was to be played by Miss Palmira, the other gentlemen were simply indicated by N. N., X. X. or * *. "They are all women you know," explained the innkeeper, "who don't want to advertise their names. The charge for the front seats is 2½d, for the second-class places, a penny.

* *I. e.*, Laurel bearer.

"The gentry can sit where they please, I presume?"

"I suggested to the manager that he should write that on the play bill, but he replied that that would be an impertinence. I also advised him to take the play bill to your honour himself and was almost kicked out of the room for my pains. Did I take him for a bill poster? he said."

"This manager of yours seems to have a pretty good opinion of himself."

"Oh, he is frightfully proud, your honour. He will play no other pieces but sword pieces because, says he, they are classical. The poor fellow is so very young you know. When he grows a little older and learns to starve a bit he will soon lower his crest."

"I like him none the less for holding up his head. I will come to the play."

"But you must be there at seven o'clock sharp. He always begins punctually; whether there is any audience or not."

"The lad has character, I see; pray give him this"—and he handed the innkeeper half a sovereign. He quickly returned with the reply that the manager could not for the moment give change.

"But I meant him to keep the whole of it as an admittance fee."

"Ah, yes."

A short time afterwards, the innkeeper reappeared with a whole bundle of admission tickets for Szilard, saying that the manager thanked him for his sympathy, but as he was not in the habit of accepting presents from anyone, he assumed that his honour meant to engage the whole house for himself that evening and he, the manager, would therefore give a representation for his honour's sole benefit.

Szilard laughed heartily at this comical conscientiousness, and after dressing, he went about his official business with as much dispatch as possible in order to arrive at the play at seven o'clock sharp, for he was now the whole public and the public ought always to be punctual.

When he got to the room set apart for the performance he found that, despite the provisional *abonnement suspendu* arrangement, the place was not quite empty, for the gratis public, the lenders of the theatrical requisites and their families, the letters of lodgings to the actors and other peaceful creditors, occupied a couple of benches, so that Szilard had the opportunity of effacing himself and thus avoiding confusing the *troupe* by his solitary and imposing personality.

No sooner had the innkeeper's cuckoo clock struck seven than the ring of the prompter's bell resounded behind the curtain (it sounded suspiciously like a glass struck smartly with the back of a knife) and by means of a highly ingenious piece of machinery the drop-curtain, stuck over with the tricolored cardboard representing the national flag, was hoisted up to the ceiling-beam, and the open stage was revealed.

The background was formed by a collapsible screen which was painted to represent a room; in the foreground on one side was a paper window painted black and white, and on the other side the cellar door, metamorphosed into the portal of a Gothic palace. Through this entry the whole of the *dramatis personae* came and went, for it was the only one.

The piece acted was, naturally, not "Hernáni or Castilian Honour," but Schiller's "Robbers." Szilard recognized it at the very first three words. He also noticed that the characters of Karl and Franz Moor were acted by one and the same person (the manager himself, as he was informed) with a simple change of voice and mask, and despite the different disguises employed, it constantly seemed to Szilard as if he had seen that caricature of a face somewhere else and the voice, parodied as it now was, nevertheless seemed familiar to him. No less familiar appeared the violent gestures of the young actor which frequently endangered the side scenes.

Now as early as Scene 2 the noble public began to be aware of the unheard of fraud practiced upon it; a murmuring, an agitation, a whispering and a wagging of heads, and finally an impatient thumping of sticks began to mingle with the bustle of the drama, till at last a worthy cobbler, who had lent the *troupe* three wooden benches and received in return a free pass every day, suddenly bawled out: "Halloh there, Mr. Manager! we have seen this piece once before. There's politics in it."

Franz Moor, disturbed in his artistic interpretation by this sudden onslaught, suddenly forgot himself, lost his cue and answering the interpellator in his natural, everyday voice (he knew he had only a free list public to deal with) exclaimed: "Whoever has seen this piece before and does not wish to see it again, will have his money returned to him on applying at the ticket office."

These words were no sooner uttered than Vamhidy leaped from his seat, rushed upon the stage, caught Franz Moor in his arms and kissed his painted face crying with a voice trembling with joy: "Coloman!"

Franz Moor hesitated for an instant, then tore off his Spanish beard, dropped his red wig, wiped the painted wrinkles from his forehead and Szilard saw before him a pale, melancholy, childish countenance.

Leander Babérossy was young Coloman, Henrietta's brother.

The representation naturally ceased at once. Szilard hustled the rediscovered "prodigal son" off the boards and never let him stop for an instant till he had got him safe and sound into his own private room. There he embraced him again, held him at arms' length and had a good look at him. The lad seemed to be twenty years old at the very least, yet really he was but fifteen. Play acting, want and premature shaving soon make a youth look old. Moreover, in his whole bearing, in all his movements, there was something precocious, a resolute, bold expression which made one forget that he was a mere child—a sort of cynicism not pleasant to behold.

Szilard soon had a good supper ready for him, which the youth fell to work upon without ceremony.

"My dear Leander," said Vamhidy when the meal was over, "no doubt it is a very fine thing when one can say that he is his own master, nor is it so difficult to attain to such a position after all. All that is wanted is a strength of character always true to itself. But you, my friend, have committed follies which might easily make of you something very different."

Coloman shrugged his shoulders.

"I have committed many follies no doubt, but I do not call to mind any which I should be afraid to confess."

Szilard began to fancy that his suspicions were groundless.

"People are talking of a certain *bill* which you have given in your sister's name?"

At these words Coloman cast down his eyes upon his plate and his whole face grew blood-red. In a scarcely audible voice he enquired: "And has Henrietta refused to honour that bill?"

Vamhidy sighed deeply. Then it was really true that this thoughtless child had committed the crime!

"My dear Coloman," said he, dropping the Leander now, "your sister is the martyr of her own devotion. She was most certainly ready to acknowledge the bill as her own; but you ought to have thought what sacrifices she will have to make now that her grandfather has cut her off with a shilling and her husband refuses to place such a considerable amount at her disposal."

"Good gracious!" cried the itinerant actor, thrusting his hands deep down into his empty pockets, "what then do these big wigs call considerable amounts. Very well, sir. I had no idea that the Baroness Hátszegi was *so very poor*. I will try to recover the bill, and it shall be the first thing I will pay off with my benefit money."

Szilard could not help being struck by the terrible comicality of the idea.

"But, my dear young friend," said he, "if you had two benefits every year and got a clear forty florins at every one of them, it would take you at least a hundred years from to-day to discharge the amount."

"What?" cried Coloman with wide open eyes, and in his amazement seizing the candlestick instead of his fork.

"Why, don't you know that the bill is for 40,000 florins?"

"What?" thundered the young vagabond. And kicking aside his chair, he snatched up a knife lying by the side of his plate and, bareheaded as he was, rushed towards the door. Szilard had need of all his dexterity to catch him before he reached it and prevent him from rushing into the street like a madman.

"Let me murder him, let me murder that villain," he cried.

Szilard was a strong man so he easily disarmed the youth.

Then Coloman began to weep and fling himself on the ground. Szilard seized him by the arm and hoisted him on to a chair again.

"Be a man!" he cried. "Of whom do you speak?—whom do you want to kill?"

"That villain Margari."

"Then it was he who persuaded you to take this step?"

"I will tell you all about it, sir, and you shall judge me. When I left my grandfather's house, that Satan sought me out, affected sympathy for me and asked me what I meant to do. I told him I intended to go on the stage and he said I did well not to remain there. I had only a florin which I borrowed from one of the lacqueys, and I told this devil that I should require 20 florins at the very least. He promised to get them for me from a usurer but told me I should have to give a bill for forty. Do you think I cared what I signed then? Not long afterwards he came back again and said the usurer would give nothing on the strength of my signature, because I was a minor, but that if my sister's name stood upon the bill he would advance upon that because she was a married woman. Margari persuaded me to sign the bill in her name. What was forty florins to Henrietta? he said, a mere trifle. If I were to ask her, she would give me twice as much. Surely she would not proclaim me, whom she loved so much, a forger for the sake of a paltry 40 florins? But 40,000 florins, 40,000!—that is a frightful, a horrible villainy. I only made it forty."

And with that he began to dash his head against the wall like a madman.

"My dear Coloman, do pull yourself together," said Szilard, "what you have just told me is of the very greatest importance. Be quiet and don't tear out your hair! Are you aware that your infinitely good sister has honoured the 40,000 florin bill also in order to save you?"

The poor youth was thunderstruck at these words.

"And now you can imagine the embarrassment of the baroness, who has been disinherited and is nevertheless responsible for this very considerable sum without being at all sure that her husband will pay it for her."

"I will hang myself."

"That would be the most gigantic piece of folly you could commit. You must make good your fault. And now for a time we cease to be friends and I am simply an examining magistrate, and you are an accused prisoner who is about to make a voluntary confession before me. Pray sit right opposite to me and answer all my questions clearly and accurately—in fact tell me exactly what happened."

And Vamhidy produced paper and writing requisites, lit a pair of candles which he placed by his side and began the examination of the youth sitting in front of him.

By midnight the confession was duly written down.

When, however, Vamhidy proposed that Coloman should now come back to Pest and be reconciled to his relations, the youth hesitated: "We will see," said he.

"At any rate remain here with me then," continued Szilard. "Sleep in my room and take till to-morrow to think it over. I won't lock the door but you must give me your word of honour that you will not go out of that door without my knowledge."

"I give you my word upon it."

Then Szilard made the youth lie down and only went to rest himself when he was sure that Coloman was asleep.

Nevertheless on awaking next morning and looking round the room he could see no trace of Coloman, but there was a letter from him on the table as follows: "Dear old friend, I thank you for your extreme kindness to me, but I don't want to see my relations any more, not because I fear to meet them, but because I have a holy horror of the very atmosphere they breathe. My confession will suffice to rectify my fault. I am going on the tramp again. The linen tent is my home. And then—there are obligations in respect to the discharge whereof I am not my sister's brother. I have taken nothing with me but four cigar ends from the table, a liberty I hope you will pardon me. As I have given you my word that I would not go out of the door without your knowledge, I have been obliged to make my exit through the window. Adieu! Till death thy faithful admirer. COLOMAN."

A couple of hours later Vamhidy learnt from the innkeeper that the manager, without any previous leave-taking, had decamped leaving behind him his decorations and theatrical wardrobe as some compensation for his trifling debts. All he had taken away with him was what he actually had on his person—and Miss Palmira.

And now Szilard understood the meaning of the passage "there are obligations in respect to the discharge whereof I am not my sister's brother."

This vagabond comedian had an equally vagabond childish ideal, and when he had to make his choice, he flung his arm around her and fled away with her—into the wide, wide world.

CHAPTER XVII

MR. MARGARI

MR. MARGARI had got on in the world. He was now a real gentleman who had a four-roomed domicile, paid house-rent, and had even gone the length of marrying. And can you guess the lady of his choice?—why it was no other than Miss Clementina. That worthy virgin was of just the proper age for him, moreover a cosy little bit of cash might safely be assumed to go with her, which exercised a strong attraction upon Mr. Margari—and goes to prove that iron is not the only metal susceptible of the influence of the magnet. The worthy maiden had persuaded her respected swain to abduct her from Hidvár, an enterprise which he had nobly performed while the lady of the house was travelling with her husband to Arad. It is true there was no necessity whatever for an elopement, for the baroness was very far from being one of those dragons in feminine shape who love to tear asunder hearts that are burning for each other. If Mr. Margari had respectfully solicited the hand of her lady-companion, there is no reason to suppose he would have sued in vain; but Clementina was far too romantic for anything so humdrum as that. She insisted that he should abduct her, at night too and through a window, although she had the key of every door close at hand.

So Margari had managed to set up as a gentleman and become his own master. Clementina's money bought the furniture and they even sported a musical clock.

Mr. Margari had a smoking-room all to himself, in which he did nothing all day but smoke his pipe. No more work for him now, no more copying of MSS. There the happy husband, dressed in a flowered dressing-gown, stretched himself out at full length on the sofa and blew clouds of smoke all around him out of his long csibuk, stuffed full with the best Turkish tobacco.

Clementina was always scolding him for putting his legs upon the sofa. It was a nasty habit she said, and not only unbecoming but expensive, because it ruined the furniture. Clementina, in fact, was scolding him all day; and this was very natural, for any woman who has been condemned to obsequious servility for thirty whole years and has silently endured the caprices of her betters all that time, when she sets up as a lady on her own account will do her best to compensate herself for this interminable suppression of her natural instincts. But Mr. Margari used only to laugh when his wife began nagging at him. "*Alios jam vidi ego ventos, aliasque procellas,*" he would say. He was only too glad to have a home of his own at all.

"Don't worry, woman!" he would say with reference to the furniture, "when that's worn out, I'll buy some more. John Lapussa, Esq., will give me whatever I want."

"He may be fool enough to do so now," replied Clementina, "but just you wait till he has won his action against Madame Langai and has no further need of you, he won't care two pence for you then. I know Mr. John Lapussa."

"So do I," retorted Margari. "He has paid me hitherto to say what he tells me, he shall pay me hereafter for holding my tongue. John Lapussa, Esq., will have to take care that Margari has plenty to eat and decent clothes to put on, for, if Margari grows hungry, Margari will bite."

Mr. Margari spoke with an air of such impertinent assurance and blew about such clouds of smoke that Clementina began to respect him, and sat down on the sofa by his side, no doubt to protect her property. "If you hold his honour so completely in the palm of your hand," said she, "why don't you provide better for yourself and me? It is all very well for his honour to fork out now when you press him, but money goes and more is wanted. One of these days something will happen to him and he will die,—and you can't follow him to the moon."

This was indeed a hard nut for Margari to crack. One cannot squeeze much out of dead men. Such an impression did the remark make upon him that he took his feet off the sofa and sat bolt upright.

"Then what do you think I ought to do?" he asked his wife.

"Well, it is of no use his doling you out mere driblets; for the great services you have rendered him he ought to give you something more in proportion to your merits—a little estate in the country, for instance. There we could settle down comfortably."

"True, and he has lots of such little properties which are of no use to him at all. What do you say, for instance, to an estate of one hundred acres or so; it would be a mere flea-bite to him. But flea-bite or no flea-bite that's all one to me. I *wish* him to give it me and give it he must. I mean to pick and choose."

"And suppose he says no?"

"He'll never say that, or if he does, I shall say something to somebody and then it will be he who will be sorry and not I. Oh, he'll take jolly good care not to make Margari angry. His honour has much more need of Margari's friendship than Margari has of his honour's."

And we shall very soon see under what auspices Margari hoped to get the little country estate from Mr. John Lapussa as a reward for his faithful services.

Meanwhile the action brought by Madame Langai against Mr. John Lapussa was still in its initial stage. Both parties were inexhaustible in producing documents and raising points of law, but it seemed highly probable that Mr. John would win. Mr. John appeared almost daily before the magistrate, whom he called his dear friend and whom he frequently invited to dine, an invitation which, naturally, was never accepted. One day Mr. Monori, for that was the worthy magistrate's name, asked Mr. John whether he knew anything of a certain Margari who was soliciting the post of a clerk in the district court and gave as his reference the Lapussa family in whose service he had been for some years. Mr. John, with his innate niggardliness, at once seized this opportunity for disembarrassing himself of an importunate beggar by saddling the county with him. He exalted "the worthy, excellent man" to the skies, and especially praised his rectitude, his sobriety, his diligence!

"But is he trustworthy?" inquired the magistrate. "You see there are various little cash payments he will have to see to, is he clean handed?"

"As good as gold, I assure you. I could trust him with thousands. Why some of my own bills are in his keeping—" and with that he proceeded to say as many pretty things of Margari as if he were a horse dealer trying to palm off a blind nag on some ignorant bumpkin at a fair.

In his delight at having so successfully rid himself of such an incubus, he made his *valet-de-chambre* slip over to Margari to tell the worthy man to wait upon him on the morrow at 11 o'clock precisely, as he had a very pleasant piece of news to impart to him; for he meant to make Margari believe that it was through his, Mr. John Lapussa's special influence, that he had obtained the coveted appointment and so get him to renounce all further claims upon his old patron.

On the very same day Mr. John was surprised to receive a visit from the magistrate, Mr. Monori, and this certainly was a wonder, for the magistrate never made any but official visits.

"To what do I owe this extraordinary pleasure?" asked Mr. John, familiarly inviting the magistrate to sit down on a couch.

"I have come in the matter of this Margari," said Monori, holding himself very stiffly and fixing his eyes sharply on Mr. John. "Since our conversation of this morning, the circumstance has come to my knowledge that one of my colleagues in the county of Arad has succeeded in finding the long-lost Coloman Lapussa."

At these words Mr. John began to smooth out the ends of his mustache and chew them attentively.

"The young man confesses to having forged the bill, but asserts that it was Margari who led him to do so, and that the bill signed by him was originally for forty florins only, so that undoubtedly somebody else must have turned it into 40,000."

Mr. John coughed very much at these words.— no doubt the bit of mustache which he had bit off stuck in his throat.

"This is a very ticklish circumstance. I must confess, continued Monori, "for although the young man's offence has thereby been considerably lightened, yet the burden of the charge has now been shifted to other shoulders hitherto quite free from suspicion. No doubt, he being a minor, under strict control, did what he did as a mere schoolboy frolic, but this Margari and an unknown somebody else will find it not quite such a laughing matter."

Mr. John's mustache was by this time not enough for him, he began nibbling his nails as well.

"But what are you driving at?" he said. "How does all this concern me?"

"It concerns you, sir, in this way: you told me that Margari was your confidential agent, and therefore he must have destroyed the bill at your bidding."

"I only said that to help him to get a small official post. I am responsible for nobody. What have I to do with the characters of my servants, my lacqueys."

"But you assured me that your bills often passed through his hands."

Mr. John fancied that the best way out of this unpleasant *cul-de-sac* was by adopting a little energetic bluffing.

"What do you mean by cross-examining me in my own house?" he cried, with affected *hauteur*, springing from the sofa.

The magistrate rose at the same time.

"Pardon me, but I am here not as a visitor, but in my official capacity—as your judge."

And with that he coolly unbuttoned his *attila** and drew forth from the inside pocket a large sealed letter.

"You must swear to every one of the interrogatories administered to you by me."

"I? I'll swear to nothing," cried Mr. John. "I am a Quaker and therefore cannot take an oath."

"This document, sir, is a royal mandate and whoever refuses to obey it is liable to penalties."

"What penalties?"

"A fine of eighty florins."

"Eighty florins? There you are then, take them!" cried Mr. John flinging down the amount eagerly and thinking to himself that this mandate was indeed a juridical masterpiece, not being binding on a rich man—for what after all is eighty florins?

"Very good," said Mr. Monori, giving him a receipt for the amount, "I'll come again to-morrow."

"What for?"

"I shall again call upon you to answer my interrogatories upon oath."

"And if I won't swear?"

"Why then you'll have to pay the court fine *toties-quoties*. A *juratus tabulae regiae notarius* will call regularly every day and exact the fine

---
* A fur pelisse, worn on state occasions.

from you until such time as you make up your mind to take the oaths. Good-day."

After the magistrate had withdrawn Mr. John's fury reached its climax. First of all he poured forth his wrath upon the poor inkstand, with the ink from which Monori had written out the receipt. This he dashed to the ground. The lacquey who rushed in at the commotion to inquire if his honour had rung, he seized by the nape of the neck and flung out of the room. Then he rushed after the man and pommelled him for daring to go out before he had been told to go. Finally he dashed out and, for the lowest silver coin he could make up his mind to part with, hired a hackney coach to take him to his villa near the park, for thither he had resolved to fly.

On arriving there he recovered himself somewhat.

So Coloman had been discovered and had confessed about his own doings and Margari's. Well he must simply disavow Margari, that's all. But suppose Margari were to make a clean breast of it? Well he could repudiate the whole thing of course. But then that wretched royal mandate? He must either swear or pay the court fine every day. It would be best perhaps to fly, to leave the capital of the magistrate behind him and set out on his travels. Perhaps then they would forget all about it. But then there was the law-suit! And suppose it should be decided in the meantime and decided against him! It was an absurd dilemma! To remain here was dangerous and to go away was also dangerous. What a good job it would be if that cursed forged-bill business could disappear from the face of the earth. The bill ought to be withdrawn. But that was impossible because it was already in the magistrate's hands, and therefore could not be ignored. And then the oath required of him. Either he must confess that he was personally interested in the matter and then he would not be required to swear but would at the same time make himself an object of suspicion, or else he must go on paying this infernal toll money in order to be able to cross the nonjuratory bridge, so to speak. It was an absolutely desperating syllogism, and after tossing about sleeplessly all night in the midst of this vicious circle, Mr. John resolved in the morning to set off at once for the vineyards of Promontor,* tell his servants that he meant to remain there and enjoy himself, and immediately afterwards get into a post-chaise and drive to his Sarfeneki property. Nobody should know his real address but his lawyer, and there he would await developments, only emerging in case of the most urgent necessity.

So he hastily swallowed his chocolate, wrapped himself in his mantle and fancied that now he might safely fly; but he reckoned without his host, for, on the very doorstep, he came face to face with Margari!

---
* A village a few miles out of Pest.

"What do you want here, eh?" he inquired fiercely of the humble man he feared so much.

"You were so good as to make an appointment with me, your honour," said Margari cringingly.

"Yes, yes, I know, I know" (he was afraid to warn him of his danger, with all the servants listening to them), but I cannot spare the time now, come some other day. I cannot give you anything here."

"But your honour was good enough to say that you had some glad tidings to communicate."

"Another time, another time! I am very busy just now."

Mr. John would have shaken off Margari altogether, but Margari was not so easily got rid of. He had already ascertained from the coachman that Mr. John was off to Promontor and did not mean to return again in a hurry, so he resolved to take his measures accordingly. He rushed forward to open the carriage door, helped Mr. John to get into the coach, wished him a most pleasant journey, no end of enjoyment and other meaningless things, all of which made much the same agreeable impression upon Mr. John as if an ant had crept into his boot and he could not kill it because he was in company. Only when the carriage door was shut to and he saw Margari's face no more did he begin to breathe freely again.

Margari however attributed this reception, or rather, non-reception, to the capricious humours to which his honour was constantly liable without rhyme or reason (it is a peculiarity of self-made plutocrats as everybody knows); but he was not a bit offended,—he knew his place. His honour doesn't want to see Margari just now, very well, he shall not see him so he jumped up behind the carriage alongside the lacquey. But how surprised his honour will be when he gets to Promontor to see Margari open the carriage door for him? How he will bid him go to the devil and immediately after burst out laughing and give him a present! And what will the present be? Has it anything to do with the good news with which he meant to surprise him? And all the while, Mr. John, inside the carriage was hugging himself with the idea that he had rid himself of Margari for a time and devoutly wishing that the cholera, or some other equally rapid and effectual disease, might remove the old rascal off the face of the earth altogether.

When the carriage stopped at the picturesque vineyards of Promontor, Mr. John almost had a stroke when, on looking through the glass window, the first feature of the panorama that presented itself was the figure of Margari, hastening to open the door with obsequious familiarity.

"You here, Sirrah," he roared (he would have choked with rage on the spot if he had not said Sirrah). "How on earth did *you* get here?"

Margari instantly imagined that his honour's flashing eyes, convulsive mouth and distorted face were the outward signs of a jocose frame of mind, for there was always a sort of travesty of humour in Mr. John's features whenever he was angry. So, to his own confusion, it occurred to him to make a joke for the first time in his life.

"Crying your honour's pardon, I *flew*," said he.

And in fact the very next instant he was sent flying so impetuously that he did not stop till he plumped right into the trellis-work surrounding a bed of vines. Never in all his life before had Mr. John dispensed such a buffet. Margari fairly disappeared among the leaves of the friendly vine arbours.

It was now Mr. John's turn to be frightened at what he had done. He was frightened because every box on the ears he gave used regularly to cost him 200 florins, a very costly passion to indulge in. And besides he was particularly anxious just then to keep Margari in a good humour. A man may loathe a viper but he had better not tread on its tail if he cannot tread on its head. Horrified at his own outburst of rage, the moment he saw Margari disappear in the vine-arbours, he rushed after him, freed him with his own hands, picked him up, set him on his legs again and began to comfort him.

"Come, come, my dear friend! compose yourself. I did not mean to hurt you. You are not angry, are you. I hope you are not hurt? Where did you hit yourself?"

Margari, however, began whimpering like a

schoolboy, the more the other tried to quiet him, the more loudly he bellowed.

"Come, come! don't make such a noise! Come under the verandah and wipe the blood from your face!"

"But I am not a dog!" roared Margari. "I won't go under the verandah, I'll go into the street. I'll howl at the top of my voice. The whole town shall see me bleed."

"Margari, don't be a fool! I didn't mean to hurt you. I was too violent, I admit it. Look here! I'll give you money. How much do you want? Will 200 florins be enough?"

At the words "200 florins," Margari stopped roaring a bit, but he wanted to see the colour of the money, for he thought to himself that if he quieted down first he would get nothing at all. So he kept on whining and limped first on one leg and then on the other and plastered his whole face over with blood from the one little scratch he had got.

Mr. John hastened to wipe Margari's face with his own pockethandkerchief.

"Come, come my dear Margari. I have told you I did not mean to do it. Here are the two hundred florins I promised you. But now leave me alone. Go abroad with the money and enjoy yourself and I will give you some more later on."

"I most humbly thank you," lisped the buffeted wretch with a conciliatory voice and he kissed Mr. John's two hundred florined hand repeatedly, while the other did all in his power to hustle him out of the door; and so engrossed was he in the effort that he never observed that some one had been observing the scene the whole time. He therefore regularly collapsed when a voice which he instantly recognized, addressed him: "Good morning, sir!"

The Lernean Hydra was not more petrified at the sight of the head of Medusa than was Mr. John by the sight of the person who had just addressed him. It was the magistrate, Mr. Monori.

At first he feared he had come after him for his diurnal eighty florins, but something very much worse than that was in store for him.

"Pardon me," said the magistrate drawing nearer, "but by order of the High Court, I am here to arrest Margari, and ascertaining that you had taken him away with you, I was obliged to follow to prevent him from escaping altogether."

Two stout *pandurs** behind the magistrate gave additional emphasis to his words.

"Arrest me?" cried Margari, "why me? I am as honest as the day. I am neither a murderer nor yet a robber. Mr. John Lapussa can answer for me. I am his confidential agent!"—and he clung convulsively to the coat tail of his principal.

Mr. John plainly perceived that never in his life before had he been in such an awkward situation. They could accuse him now of having instigated Margari to make a bolt of it. Had not the magis-

* Hungarian police officers.

trate seen him give the wretched man money to run away with? His first care was to disengage Margari's hands from his coat tail and next to hold him at arm's length so that he should not clutch his collar. Then with pompous impertinence he pretended not to know him.

"What does the man want? Who is he? How did he come hither?" he exclaimed. "I know nothing about him. I boxed his ears for molesting me, and then I gave him 200 florins which is the usual legal fine for an assault of that kind, to prevent him bringing an action against me. We have nothing else in common. Take him away by all means. Put him in irons. Give him whatever punishment he has deserved. Yes," he continued, seizing the astounded Margari by the cravat, "you are a refined scoundrel. You persuaded my dear nephew Coloman to take that false step and then you yourself changed the forty florins into forty thousand. You wanted to ruin the young man's future and bring a slur upon the family. I know everything. His honour the magistrate told me all about it yesterday, and that is why I hand you over to the law for punishment." And with that he shook him so violently that he fell on his back again, this time into a bed of tomatoes, whereby his white linen pantaloons very speedily became stained with the national colours.*

The dialogue that thereupon ensued no short-

---
* Red, white and green.

hand reporter could have reproduced, for the pair of them began forthwith to rave and storm at one another with all their might, stamping, swearing, shaking their fists, and loading each other with abuse. When they had got as far as calling each other robber and scoundrel, the magistrate thought it high time to interfere, and at his command Margari was torn forcibly out of the tomato bed, led to a hackney coach and thrust inside; yet even then he put his head out of the window and shouted that he did not mean to sit in prison alone but would very soon have Mr. John Lapussa there also, as his companion. All the efforts of the two pandurs were powerless to silence him.

As for Mr. John, the magistrate simply said to him: "Sir, it is not good for a man to make use of nasty tools, for by so doing he only dirties his own hands."

Then he got into a second hackney coach and drove away after the first one.

Even Mr. John could see that it was now quite impossible for him under the circumstances to think of quitting Pest.

CHAPTER XVIII

THE UNDISCOVERABLE LADY

Squire Gerzson Satrakovics thought it best after that night at the *csárdá* to go back to Arad. This wondrous event, the clue to which he could not hit upon anyhow, must needs interest Hátszegi most of all. It would be a terrible thing to appear before him with the tidings that the lady who was intrusted to his care, had been lost on the way; yet, nevertheless, this was the first thing he must say, and after that they would consult together as to what was to be done to find her and where they were to look for her.

Never had Mr. Gerzson approached a bear's den with such beating of heart as he now approached Hátsegi's chambers. His breath almost failed him as he seized the handle of the street door and wished it might prove locked in order that it might take a longer time to open it.

And locked indeed the door proved to be, he had to ring. Thus he had, at any rate, a respite, for he must await the result of the ringing. And a long time he had to wait too, so long indeed that it was necessary to ring again. Even then there was no response. Then he rang a third time, and after that he went on ring-ring-ringing for a good half hour. At last the bellrope remained in his hand and he put it into his pocket that it might testify to the fact that he had been there. Then, for the first time, he noticed that the shutters were all up—the surest sign that nobody was at home.

Gerzson explained the matter to his own satisfaction by supposing that the whole household was at the races. It was the last day of the races and he reached the course just as the betting was at its height and everybody's attention was concentrated on the event of the moment. At such time the crowd has no eyes for men, everyone is occupied with the horses. Mr. Gerzson therefore had plenty of time to scrutinize all who were present, but look as he would he could not see Leonard anywhere.

At last he could stand the suspense no longer, and during the interval between two races, he descended from the grand-stand, in a corner of which he had ensconced himself in order to get a better view of the field, and mingled in the ring with his brother sportsmen awaiting resignedly for the expression of amazed and horrified inquiry which he expected to see in all faces the moment they perceived him.

But how taken aback was he when the first man who cast eyes on him gave vent to a loud: Ha! ha! ha! whereupon everybody else began laughing also and pointing their fingers at him and exclaiming: "Why here's Gerzson! Gerzson has come back again!"

"Have you all gone mad?" cried Gerzson, confused by this inexplicable hubbub.

He really fancied that he had fallen among a lot of lunatics, till at last Count Kengyelesy forced his way through the crowd towards him, put both his hands on his hips and began to quiz him: "Well, you are a pretty fellow!—you are a pretty squire of dames, I must say!

"But what's the matter? What has happened? Why do you laugh?"

"Listen to him!" cried the count, turning to the bystanders. "He actually has the impertinence to ask us why we laugh! Come, sir! where did you leave the Baroness Hátszegi?"

"I don't see what there is to laugh at at such a question?" replied Gerzson, in whose mind all sorts of dark forebodings began to arise.

"What have you done with the baroness? What have you done with our friend Leonard's wife, I say?" persisted the count.

"That is a perfect riddle to me," growled Gerzson in a low voice.

"Ha! ha! ha!" laughed the count, "it is a riddle to him what has become of his travelling companion."

"But can any of you tell me what has happened to her? Is she alive?"

The count clapped his hands together and flung his round hat upon the ground.

"Now, that is what I call a *leetle* too strong!

He asks: is she alive? Why, comrade, where have you been in hiding all this time?"

"A truce to jesting," cried Gerzson fiercely. "Tell me all you know about it, for it is no joking matter for me, I can assure you."

On perceiving that Gerzson was seriously angry, Kengyelesy drew nearer to him and enlightened him without any more beating about the bush: "Well then, my dear friend, let me tell you that you have behaved very badly. First of all you made all four of Hátszegi's horses lame; in the second place you compelled his poor wife to spend a night in a *csárdá* of the *puszta,* and in the third place you got so drunk that you began to quarrel with her and at last did not know whether you were boy or girl. The poor little woman has grown almost grey with terror, and after you had fallen to the ground in liquor she sent the coachman to town for fresh horses and, leaving you under the table, tried to make her way back to Arad."

"That is not true," interrupted Gerzson, his whole face purple with rage.

"What is not true?"

"Where is the baroness?"

"Stop, stop, my friend! Don't run away! You'll never catch her up, for, early this morning, she drove back to Hidvár in a postchaise with her husband."

"That can not be true. Did you see her?"

"I saw her through my own field glass. But we all saw her—did we not, gentlemen?"

Many of those present admitted that they had indeed seen the baroness.

"But my dear fellow," said the perturbed Gerzson, "this is no joke. On the contrary, my adventure with the baroness is somewhat tragical, and I'll trouble you to expend no more of your feeble witticisms on me."

Kengyelesy shrugged his shoulders. "I did not know you would take it so seriously, but so it is."

"From whom did you hear all this, from the baroness?"

"No—from Hátszegi."

An idea suddenly flashed through Gerzson's brain.

"Did you speak to the baroness herself?"

"No. I only saw her through the carriage window when they drove away."

"Was she veiled?"

"No, my friend. It was her very self I assure you."

"Thank you. And now, if you like, you can go on amusing yourself at my expense. Adieu!"

Only when he had got home and flung himself on the sofa in a state of stupor, did he begin to reflect a little calmly on what he had heard. There was so much about the affair that was startling and incomprehensible, true and untrue, probable, incredible, shameful and exasperating, that he could make neither head nor tail of it.

That the baroness *had* returned must be true, for they all maintained that she had come back while he was lying drunk. It is true that he had got drunk, but he had no recollection of having been quarrelsome and misbehaving himself. Strain his memory as he might, all he could call to mind was Henrietta, with her angelically gentle face, sitting before him at the table and telling him the legends of the Transylvanian Alps—all the rest was a blank.

Up he jumped at last and began pacing up and down the room. At last, after much reflection, his mind was made up, he had formed a plan.

"I'll be off. I'll be off immediately. I'll go straight to her. I am determined to learn from her own lips exactly what happened to me and how I came to make such a fool of myself. I will speak to her myself."

And immediately he ordered his coachman to put the horses to; but he told not a living soul whither he was going, even to the coachman he only mentioned the first stage.

At a little booth at the end of the town he bought four and twenty double rolls and a new wooden field flask. When they came to the River Maros, he descended to the water's edge, rinsed out his flask at least twice and then filled it with water, finally thrusting both the rolls and the flask into his travelling knapsack. After that he drew on his mantle, clambered up into the back part of the coach, stuck his pipe in his mouth and his pistol in his fist and never closed an eye till morning.

And it must be admitted that Mr. Gerzson's mode of travelling on this occasion was decidedly eccentric. On reaching a village he would tell his coachman where to go next but he never told him more than one stage in advance. Every morning he would consume one of his rolls and wash it down with the lukewarm brackish water of the Maros—and bitter enough he found the taste of it too. He never quitted the carriage for more than two or three minutes at a time, and he presented his pistols point blank at everyone who approached him with inquisitive questions.

Only twice during the night did he allow the horses an hour or two of rest—and then away over stock and stone again.

The coachman, who was unaccustomed to such queer ways, presently shook his head every time he received orders to go on further, but by dawn of day he had had about enough of the job.

"Your honour," said he, "are we going to stop at all? It would do the horses no harm if they had a little rest."

"What's that to you, you rascal, eh?" roared Mr. Gerzson, "I suppose you're sleepy, you lazy good-for-nothing? Off the box then, you hound, you! I'll drive the horses myself, you gallows-bird!"

The old fellow, who had been in the service of the family for twenty years and had never had so many insulting epithets thrown at his head before explained that he did not speak for himself but for the horses.

"If they perished on the spot, Sirrah, what business is it of yours? When one pursues the enemy in time of war, does one think of food or fodder?"—whence the coachman concluded that there was some one whom the squire meant to cut to pieces.

It was only when they came to the road leading to Hidvár that the coachman began to suspect that they were about to go in that direction. It was now the evening of the second day and both man and beast were tired to death. It was indispensable that they should stay the night here, for if they passed Hidvár they would have to go on the whole night before they reached the next stage—or come to grief on the road, which was much more probable.

"You will stop in front of the castle!" commanded Mr. Gerzson when they were crossing the castle bridge.

The coachman looked back and shook his head. He did not like it at all.

"Shan't we turn into the castle yard?" enquired he.

"No!" bellowed Squire Gerzson, so venomously that the "why not?" he was about to say, stuck in the poor coachman's throat like a fish-bone.

"Now listen to me," said Gerzson, when they

had fairly got across to the other side: "Keep your eyes open and try and take in what I am going to say to you. I don't know how long I may remain inside there—possibly some time. At any rate you must not loiter about here with the horses but go on to the priest and beg him, civilly, mind, to kindly accommodate my nags in his stable and give them two bushels of maize. As soon as I return I'll settle with him, but don't say anything about payment, or else you will offend him. Kiss his hand, for he is a priest and you are only a lazy vagabond. If you hear no news of me by to-morrow morning, put the horses into the carriage again and return to Arad where Count Kengyelesy will tell you what to do next."

Then he turned upon his heel and set off towards the castle.

It was already evening. In the upper story seven of the windows were lit up and the moon shone into the eighth. That was Henrietta's bedroom. Squire Gerzson knew it. He was quite at home in the castle.

At the hall entrance he encountered Leonard's huntsman, an impertinent, bony, jowly loafer whom he had never been able to endure. The fellow barred the way.

"Good evening your honour."

"Why should *you* wish *me* good evening, you stupid jackass! Do you suppose I have travelled five and twenty miles for the pleasure of wishing *you* good evening? Who's at home?"

"Nobody."

"Go along with you, you sodden-headed son of a dog. Nobody at home and seven windows in the upper story all alight!"

"It is true the rooms are lit up, but that is on account of her ladyship—they are sitting up with her."

"Then where's your master?"

"He has trotted into Klausenburg for the learned doctor."

"What is the matter with her ladyship?"

"I don't know. They say she is mad."

"You are mad yourself, you stupid beast. Who told you that?"

"I saw it, I heard it myself, and others also have seen that she is mad."

"Cannot I speak to her?"

"How can you? That's just the mischief of it, that she cannot be spoken to."

"You rascal, I tell you your master *is* at home. I am sure of it."

Long-legs shrugged his shoulders and began to whistle.

"Look ye here, my son," said Gerzson, scarcely able to contain himself, "the fist that you see in my pocket here is pulling the trigger of a revolver and I have a jolly good mind to send a bullet between your onion chawing teeth, so I should advise you not to try any of your tom-foolery on me. On this occasion I have not come to pay your master a visit but for other reasons. Speak the truth, sirrah! Is your master at home or is he not?"

"I have just told you that there is not a soul at home except her ladyship, and she is mad."

At that same moment Gerzson thought he heard a fiddle in the upper story.

"What, music here!" he cried.

The fellow laughed.

"Yes, they are trying to cure the sick baroness by playing to her."

"But I hear the sound of men's voices also as if there were guests here."

"Where? I hear nothing. It is only the dogs barking in the enclosure."

"You did not hear it, sirrah?"

"I heard nothing."

"Very well, my son, I see you have orders to make a fool of me; but it strikes me that both you and your master will have to get up pretty early to do that. You need not be so anxious to guard the door. I shall not try to force my way up to your master. I'll wager he will come and see me first. Wait a bit."

And with that Gerzson sat down on the step, tore a leaf out of his pocketbook and, placing it on his knee, wrote with his pencil the following words: "Sir, I declare you to be a miserable coward. If you want to know why, you will find me at the parson's, there I will tell you and after that we can arrange our little business between ourselves. "GERZSON SATRAKOVICS."

Mr. Gerzson had even taken the trouble to provide himself with sealing-wax and matches so he could seal his letter without any difficulty and the step served him as a table.

But suppose even this letter did not make Hátszegi come forth? Struck by this idea he tore open the note again and added this postscript: "If you do not give me proper satisfaction, I will wait for you at the gate of your own castle and shoot you down like a dog!!"

Surely *that* would be enough!

Again he sealed the letter and was about to hand it to the huntsman when it suddenly occurred to him that Hátszegi might chuck the note unopened into the fire. Now, therefore, he wrote on the outside of it, just below the address: "If you don't open this letter, I will have an exact copy of it posted upon the notice-board of the club at Arad."

"And now, you door-keeping Cerberus," said he, "take this and give it to your master, wherever he may be."

He wasted no more words upon the fellow, but went straight to the dwelling of the old priest who was awaiting him in his porch.

"I must beg your reverence for a night's lodging, I am afraid," said Squire Gerzson, cordially pressing the old clergyman's hand. "There is serious illness at the baron's house so I don't want to incommode them with my company. All I want is a place whereon to lay my head. My wants are few. You know me of old."

"Gladly will I share with your honour the little I have. God hath brought you hither. I am glad you did not stay at the castle. The company there is not fit for your honour."

"Then there is company there, eh? What sort of folks are they?"

"Folks I should not care about meeting. Drahowecz and Muntya, and Harastory, and Brinkó, and Bandán, and Kerakoricz, and . ."

"That will do," interrupted Mr. Gerzson, aghast at so many odd, strange names not one of which he had ever heard of before. "New comers, I suppose?"

"I was sure their names would be quite unfamiliar to your honour," remarked the priest smiling, and he led his guest into his narrow dwelling, looking cautiously round first of all to make sure that nobody was listening. Once inside he carefully barred the door, seated his guest at the carved wooden table, which was covered with a pretty covering made from foal-skin, and filled a dish with fresh maize pottage, adding thereto a ham bone and a jug of mead. Mr. Gerzson fell to, like a man, on the very first invitation; and each armed with a wooden spoon, attacked the maize pottage from different points till their assiduously tunnelling spoons met together in the centre of the large platter.

"A capital dish, your reverence, really capital."

"Very good for poor folks like we are, I admit. I know you don't have fare like this in Hungary."

"I suppose we don't know how to prepare it properly," said Gerzson.

And then the priest explained how hot the water must be when maize meal or sweet-broom meal has to be mixed with it, how the whole mess must be stirred with a spoon, how a little finely grated cheese has to be added to it, and how it had then all to be tied up in a cloth like a plum-pudding and have milk poured over it. And Squire Gerzson listened to him as attentively as if he had come all the way from Arad to Hidvár on purpose to learn the art of cooking maize pottage. And after that they pledged each other's health in long draughts from the mead jug.

"And now," said the priest when they had well supped, "I know that your honour spent all last night upon the road. You must be tired and instead of boring yourself by listening to my uninteresting gossip, it would be better, methinks, if we both went to bed."

"I shouldn't mind lying down at all, but alas! I have an appointment here with some one."

"May I ask with whom?"

"I have written the baron a letter and I await a reply."

"He will not send one: he is too much taken up with his pleasures just now."

"My letter contains things which a man durst not ignore."

"Was your letter an insulting one?"

"I don't wish to advertise its contents."

"Very good. But for all that you may as well lie down. The ways of the baron are incalculable. Even when he is angry he knows what he is about."

"Then we'll wait for him till morning."

"Meanwhile repose in peace. My humble dwelling is not very luxurious, but let your honour imagine that it is a hunting hut in the forest."

"But where then will your reverence sleep?"

"I'll go out to the bee-house. I can sleep there excellently well, I have a couch of linden leaves."

"Nay, but I also love to sleep on linden leaves, covered with my *bunda*.* I'll lie there to-night. I am accustomed to sleeping in the open air at night, and you are an old man"—he forgot that he was one himself—"I could never permit you to sacrifice your comfort for my sake."

The clergyman paused for an instant like one who is suddenly struck by a new and odd idea.

"You said just now that you had insulted Hátszegi, did you not?" he asked.

"Well—yes!—if you *must* know."

"Grossly?"

"Yes, and most deliberately."

"Very good, I only asked the question out of

---

* A sheepskin mantle.

curiosity. You shall have the choice of your resting place, where would you like to sleep?"

"I choose the bee-house."

"Good. It is true that the night air is not very good for me. I will sleep then in my usual resting place."

"And I will sleep among the bees. Their humming close beside a man's ears generally brings him dreams that a king would envy."

"Then good night, sir."

"Good night."

They parted at the little porch. Gerzson wrapped his *bunda* round his shoulders and went towards the bee-house, but the priest returned to his chamber, blew out the light, lay down fully dressed on his bed, took up his rosary and fell a-praying like one who does not expect to see the dawn of another day.

He knew his man; he knew what was coming.

Squire Gerzson, on the other hand, troubled himself not a jot about possible consequences. With the nonchalance of a true sportsman, he lit his pipe and, lest he should set anything on fire, he made up his mind not to sleep a wink till he had smoked his pipe right out.

In order that slumber might not come upon him unawares, he resolved to fix his eyes on the castle windows—as the best preservative against dropping off. He could see them quite plainly from the bee-house.

The illuminated windows were darkened one by

one. It seemed as if, contrary to the words of the clergyman, the revellers within there did not mean to await the rosy dawn glass in hand, but had lain down early.

For, indeed, it was still early. The village cocks had only just crowed for the first time. It could not be much beyond eleven.

After the lamps had been extinguished, the castle stood there in the semi-obscurity of night like a black, old-world ruin. It stood right in front of the moon which was now climbing up behind its bastions and where its light fell upon two opposite windows which met together in a corner room it shone through them both and lighted up the whole apartment. This room was the baroness's dormitory.

While Mr. Gerzson was luxuriating in the contemplation of the moonlight, he suddenly observed that the moonlight falling upon the windows was obscured for an instant, as if somebody were passing up and down the room. In a few moments this obscuration was repeated, and the same thing happened a third time, and a fourth, and many times more, just as if some one were passing up and down in that particular room in the middle of the night restlessly, incessantly.

Mr. Gerzson counted on his pulses the seconds which elapsed between each obscuration—sixteen seconds, consequently the room in which this person was to-and-froing it so late at night like a spectre, must be sixteen paces from one end to the other. So long as the other windows had been lit up, this person had not begun to walk but as soon as the whole castle was slumbering its restless course began.

Gerzson felt that if he looked much longer, he would become moonstruck himself.

Slowly divesting himself of his *bunda,* and after knocking the burning ashes out of his pipe, he noiselessly quitted the bee-house, traversed the garden and sprang over the fence at a single bound. Then he stole along in the shadow of the poplar avenue leading up to the castle till he stood beneath the moon-lit window, climbed, like a veritable lunatic on to the projecting stones of the old bastion, and gazed from thence, at closer quarters, at the regularly recurring shadow.

But not even now was he content, but began to break off little portions of the mouldering mortar and cautiously throw them at the window. When one of these little fragments of mortar rattled against the glass the whole window was quickly obscured by a shadow as if the night wanderer had rushed to it in order to look out. Gerzson felt absolutely certain that he must be observed for there he stood clinging fast on to the moulding. A few moments afterwards the shadow disappeared suddenly from the window and again the moonlight shone uninterruptedly through it.

Gerson determined to remain where he was, to see what would come of it.

In a short time the shadow reappeared in front of the moonlight, the window was silently and very slightly raised, and through the slit fluttered a rolled up piece of paper.

This missive fell from the moulding of the bastion down into the moat. Mr. Gerzson scrambled down after it, grabbed at it in the dark and sticking it into his pocket, returned to the dwelling of the priest.

Not wishing to arouse the clergyman, he went to his carriage which stood in the stable and lit the lamp in order to read the mysterious missive.

The letter was written on a piece of paper torn out of an album. He recognized Henrietta's handwriting, and the contents of the note were as follows: "Good kind Gerzson! I implore you, in the name of all that is sacred, to depart from hence this instant. Depart on foot by bye paths—the priest will guide you. If you do not wish me to lose my reason altogether, tarry here no longer. I am very unhappy, but still more unhappy I should be if you were to remain here. Avoid us—and forget me forever—your affectionate—respectful—friend who will ever mention you in her prayers—and whom you have treated as a daughter—HENRIETTA."

Gerzson's first feeling on reading this letter was one of relief—evidently Henrietta was not angry with him or she would not have alluded to herself as his daughter! There must therefore have been some other reason for her turning back other than the squabble between them which Hátszegi had so industriously circulated. Well, he would settle accounts with Hátszegi presently.

What he found especially hard to understand, however, was the mysterious warning contained in the letter.

"Well, my dear parson," he said to himself, "I very much regret having to arouse you from your slumbers, but there's nothing else to be done," and, unscrewing the coach lamp, he took it with him and went towards the house.

The hall door was closed, he had to shake it.

The parson was evidently still awake, his voice resounded from within the house: "All good spirits praise the Lord!"

"Amen! 'Tis I who am at the door. Let me in reverend father."

The priest immediately opened the door and, full of amazement, asked Mr. Gerzson what had happened.

"Read that!" said Gerzson handing him the letter and lighting him with the lamp.

"This is the baroness's writing," said the priest, who immediately recognized the script.

"What do you say to its contents?"

"I say that you must get away from this place immediately. I quite comprehend the meaning of the baroness's directions."

"What! fly from a man whom I have just called out?"

"No, you must fly from the man you have *not* called out."

"I don't understand."

"You will one day, but there is no time for parleying now. First of all, put on my garments, while I dress up in peasants' clothes."

"Why?"

"Why! Because I must be your guide through the mountains. I cannot trust another to do you that service. Do quickly what I tell you."

The priest gave his orders to Mr. Gerzson with imperious brevity, but that gentleman, even in his present situation, could not divest himself of his homely humour, and as he was donning the parson's long cassock and pressed the broad brimmed clerical hat down upon his head, he fell a laughing at the odd figure he cut.

"Deuce take it!" he cried. "I never imagined that I should ever be turned into a parson."

But the priest was angry at the untimely jest and turning savagely upon Squire Gerzson, said: "Sir, this is no time for jesting, we are both of us standing on the very threshold of death."

Gerzson was no coward, nor did he trouble himself very much about death, but the emphatic tone of the parson at least induced him, at last, to take the matter seriously.

"Then according to that you also are in danger on my account?"

"Ask no questions! I knew what would happen when I gave you a night's lodging."

Then he took out of a drawer a packet of letters and bade Gerzson put them in the pocket of his cassock as the coat he was wearing had no pockets.

"Why do you take these with you?"

"Because I fear to leave them here, and also because I believe I shall never return to this house any more. I have one request to make of you and that is that you will read these letters and keep the contents to yourself." Gerzson promised to do so.

It was just as the descending moon seemed to be resting on the summits of the mountains that the priest and his guest quitted the quiet little house by way of the garden. The night which covered the retreat of the fugitives was pitch dark. Nobody but one who had been accustomed to that district for years and knew all its ins and outs could have found a path through those wooded gorges.

By the morning light the fugitives perceived the little posting station on the high road. There the priest exchanged clothes with Gerzson and resumed his clerical attire.

"Nothing can detain us now," said the priest, "you can procure post horses here and return home, but I go in an opposite direction."

"Whither?"

"The world is wide. Do not trouble yourself about me. In a month's time we shall meet again."

"Where?"

"At this very place."

The priest hastily quitted Gerzson and returned towards the forest, while the latter went on to the little town, where he speedily got post horses.

When now he found himself sitting all safe and sound, in the carriage, it suddenly struck him how remarkably odd it was that he and the parson should have actually fled away from a non-existent danger. How they would laugh at him from one end of the kingdom to the other! Suppose Henrietta had been playing a practical joke upon him! But then, on the other hand, Henrietta was not of that sort—so he consoled himself.

But there was another thing which bothered him a good deal. The coachman had been left behind with the four horses and would not know what to make of the disappearance of his master and the priest. When, however, the post chaise stopped in front of his house at Arad who should he see coming to meet him through the gate but this very coachman whose astonishment at the meeting was even greater than his master's. And then, to the amazement of the postillion, master and servant fell upon each other's necks and embraced each other again and again.

"Come into the house," said Mr. Gerzson at last, "and tell me what befell you. I don't want you to bellow it out here before all the world."

"I hardly know how to put it, sir, but I will tell it you as best I can. After watering the horses, I lay down and went to sleep. A loud neighing suddenly awoke me and, looking around, I saw a great light. The parson's house was all in flames. Up I was in a jiffy and ran to the door to call your honour but I found the door was locked from the inside. I then ran to the windows and found that the shutters were nailed down over them. What horrified me most of all, however, was that nobody came from the castle to put the fire out. Then I began to roar for help and while I was roaring and running up and down looking for an axe with which to batter in the door—'burum! burum!' I heard two shots and the bullets whistled to the right and left about my ears. At that all my pluck went down to my heels; I rushed under the shelter of the barn, cut the tether ropes of the horses, swung myself up on to the saddle horse, driving the others before me, and trotted into Arad without once stopping to water them."

So he had reached home more quickly than Squire Gerzson himself.

"Well, my son," said Gerzson, "all that you have told me is gospel truth I have no doubt, but say not a word of it to anybody, or else . . ." (and here he uttered the threat which the ordinary Hungarian common folk fear most of all)—"or else the affair will come before the courts and you will have to give testimony on oath."

After that he was sure of the fellow's silence.

CHAPTER XIX

THE SHAKING HAND

WHOEVER in an evil hour encountered Fatia Negra had a shaking hand for the rest of his life.

Ever since that meeting at the *csárdá* Henrietta's hand also trembled to such an extent that it was only with the utmost difficulty that she could sign her own name.

What happened to her after that meeting? Whom did she recognize in Fatia Negra? How did she get home?—all these things remained eternal secrets. The lady was never able to tell it to anybody. Perchance she herself regarded it as a dream.

The poor lady used now to pray all day. For hours at a time she would kneel before the altar of the castle chapel returning thence to her perpetual walking to and fro, to and fro, kneeling down to pray again when she was tired out. And so she went on from morning to evening, nay, till late into the night, sometimes till midnight, sometimes till the dawn of the next day, up and down, up and down, between four walls, and then on her knees again a-praying.

She never appeared in the dining-room; her meals were sent to her room. She scarcely touched them, it was difficult to understand how she kept body and soul together.

She only quitted her chamber to go to chapel. At such times she would frequently meet domestics or strangers in the castle corridors, but she looks at nobody and says not a word. She does not notice that they are there, that they are amazed at her, that they greet her. No one has heard her speak for a long time.

And therefore they think her mad. At first only the domestics whispered this among themselves, then the villagers—and in a month's time it was notorious through Transylvania that the youthful Baroness Hátszegi was out of her mind.

Early one morning, as Henrietta was returning from chapel, there suddenly appeared before her a ragged woman who must have been hidden in some niche as the servants had not seen her or driven her out.

"Stop one moment, my lady," whispered the woman and Henrietta seemed to hear in that whisper the voice of an old acquaintance, though she did not recognize the face. It was half masked in a cloth and the little she could see of it was disfigured by wounds and scars like the face of one who had been badly injured by fire. Henrietta was horrified at the sight of her, she looked so dreadful.

"Don't be frightened, my lady," said the woman falling down on her knees before her and seizing

Henrietta's dress to prevent her from escaping, "I am Anicza."

Henrietta fixed her eyes upon the woman full of stupid amazement, and vainly sought in her face for some trace of the ideal loveliness which only the other day, so it seemed, had made her so charming. She began to fancy that the woman was under some evil spell and that if anyone could but repeat the talismanic word, her former loveliness would be restored to her.

"You cannot recognize me your ladyship for my face was burnt to death in the Lucsia Cavern. Oh, if it had only always been what it is now. I am much better as I am now. God has punished me because I let my soul be lost for the sake of my fair face. I am not vain now as I used to be. Yes, God has smitten all of us on account of our sins, as your ladyship already knows; but none has he smitten so hard as me. I denounced all my kinsfolk and acquaintances to the tribunal to be avenged on one man who had deceived me,— all of them were taken except him and he escaped. And now I am a beggar, an accursed creature whom everyone drives from his door, but what care I?—I never feel hungry. They took away all my father's property—heaven only knows how much there was, more than twenty thousand ducats, I think, and it would have been mine for I am his only child. I was summoned before the court, they said they would reward me for denouncing the society, they said they would give me a thousand ducats. Ha, ha, ha! a thousand ducats for making myself the wretched creature I am! But I did not come here to frighten your ladyship, I came here to humbly beg a favour. Gracious lady, the magistrates told me that a mixed commission will be appointed to try the forgers and that his lordship, the baron, will be the president of this commission; on him depends the life and death of everyone concerned.

Henrietta felt obliged to lean against the wall.

"My lady, I do not expect impossibilities, I cannot wish that the guilty should remain unpunished —justice is justice! But the leader of the whole gang was Fatia Negra, he planned everything, the others only carried out his orders. And now there is a lot of false witnesses ready to swear that my father was the ring-leader and throw all the blame upon him, but it was Fatia Negra and nobody else as God knows."

Every time the peasant woman mentioned Fatia Negra's name a spasmodic twitch convulsed Henrietta's pale features.

"Gracious lady," continued Anicza, "I implore you by the tender mercies of God not to abandon me. Grant me my petition! Either let them kill me or lock me up with the others. I implore you, my lady, to speak or write to your husband (if these things must be in writing) on my behalf. Do not let me perish. God will not be angry with you for protecting me."

Henrietta was now even less able to speak than

before. But though she could not express herself in words, she placed one hand on the girl's head and raised the other tremulous hand to heaven, as one who takes a solemn oath before God. Then she tore herself away from Anicza, who had stooped to kiss the hem of her garment, and hastened back to her own room. On reaching the threshold of the house she looked back and saw that the girl had sunk down in the dust and was gratefully kissing the very traces of the footsteps of the departing lady.

On reaching her room Henrietta paced up and down it for a long time, wringing her hands as she went and moaning loudly: "My God! my God!" Then she flung herself down on her couch, writhing like one in mortal agony.

But soon she strengthened her heart and sat down at the writing-table. What had become of that beautiful handwriting of hers which had resembled copper plate? Scarcely legible letters now issued from her trembling hand, dumb witnesses of the terror of her heart, and yet write she must for it was her petition to her husband. Ah! that she should be forced to write to him.

Her letter was as follows:

"DREAD SIR: Tremulously and submissively I approach you. In the name of an unhappy creature I appeal to your compassion. You will be the judge of a lot of wretched men. Be merciful to them. By the grace of heaven I implore you, condemn them not! In the name of God, I implore you not to sign their death warrants. By the terrors of eternity I implore you do not ruin these men, for they are most innocent. N. N."

She durst not subscribe her own name.

And now she waited, she watched for the moment when Leonard quitted his room and, slipping in, laid the petition on the couch where he would be sure to find it. Nobody observed her.

The same day she encountered him, she had in fact sought for such an encounter. It was in the great armoury. Leonard, as soon as he perceived his wife, began humming some mad operatic tune, an opera bouffé air and bawled through the door to the dog-keeper to unleash the hounds.

The pale lady nevertheless approached him, with tottering but determined footsteps, and folding both her trembling hands as if in prayer, stood mutely in front of the door through which Leonard would have to pass, like some dumb spirit from another world. But Leonard merely shrugged his shoulders and passed her by, whistling all the time.

Again, on the following day, the timid petition lay on Leonard's table, written in the same tremulous characters. Henrietta had written it again, and again had crept into his chamber and in whatever part of the house the magnate might now be found, he everywhere encountered this pale tremulous figure who pressing her hands together and without uttering a word gazed at him beseechingly, imploringly—only they two knew why.

On the third day Leonard again found the petition and again encountered Henrietta.

This time he spoke to her.

"My dear Henrietta, have you read ' The Mysteries of Paris?'

Henrietta, as usual, only stared at the speaker with frightened eyes and said nothing.

"How did you like the description of Bicêtre? A horrible place, eh? I have noticed that you have been behaving in rather a peculiar way lately. In fact, the whole district has been talking about it and saying that you are a little crazy. I have been asked all sorts of questions about it too.—Hitherto I have always told everybody that it is not true.—But if once I should say that it *is* true, then, you will be most certainly shut up in a mad house. Regulate your conduct accordingly."

CHAPTER XX

THE FIGHT FOR THE GOLD

OF LATE Mr. Gerzson Satrakovics had invented for himself a peculiar sort of pastime.

He had renounced bear hounds and grey hounds and all other kinds of dogs, he did not care a jot when partridge shooting began, but he hung up his gun on a nail and began regularly visiting one after another the session courts of the counties of Arad, Biehar and Temes, in all of which he was a justice of the peace, and moving resolutions.

The object of these resolutions was to induce the three counties to endeavour with their united strength, and in conjunction with the Transylvanian counties of Hunyad, Fehér and Zarand, to extirpate the robber bands that had so long been terrorizing the whole district. He compiled lists of the atrocities perpetrated in the various localities and connected them all with the name of one particular robber, the notorious "Fatia Negra." He produced convincing proofs of the existence of a combination extending from the depths of the dungeons to the summits of the mountains which was held together by the magic influence of this one man and he left no stone unturned to bring him to book.

He, naturally, became quite a laughing stock

for his pains, and his acquaintances could not for the life of them understand what had come to the man.

"Why, old fellow!" said Count Kengyelesy to him one day, after he had been indulging in an unusually fiery philippic at Quarter Sessions, "why, old fellow, what sort of venom have you swallowed that makes you perorate so savagely against this worthy Fatia Negra. If anybody has cause to complain against him it is I, for he relieved me of 1,000 ducats on the high road, and so cleverly did the rascal manage it, that I cannot find it in my heart to bear him any ill-will. But what have you got to do with him I should like to know? What is all this cock and bull story you keep on spouting out concerning organized robber bands and mysterious chieftains? Is it your ambition, my friend, to become public prosecutor?"

"Yes, it is, and public prosecutor I will be, too. I want six counties to place their armed constabulary at my beck and call, and if they do, I'll wager that I'll so purify all these Alpine regions that the robbers will not have a single lurking hole left."

"Rubbish! Don't make a fool of yourself. Besides, they say that Fatia Negra has flown to America."

"Newspaper lies. He is here, I know he is."

"And suppose he is, what harm can he do? This band has been cut off to the very last man. They have all been sentenced heavily, the older men to twenty years penal servitude, the younger men to penal servitude for life. I had it from Hátszegi himself who was the president of the mixed commission that tried them, and signed the judgment himself. The whole fraternity is now sitting in chains in the trenches of Gyula Fehérvár and we have seen the last of it."

"What guarantee have you of that?"

"What guarantee?—why the security of the whole region ever since. Why, everyone there can now sleep with open doors and if you yourself were to lie dead drunk in the public thoroughfare you would not have your money stolen from your pocket any more."

Squire Gerzson protested vehemently against the assumption that he was in the habit of sprawling tipsily on the king's high road.

"I'll tell you," said he, "why everything is so secure just now. The confiscated gold of Fatia Negra is still at Gyula Fehérvár, as a forfeit to the crown, and, sooner or later, must be sent to Vienna. Fatia Negra is *not* dead, his robber band has *not* been captured and does *not* sit in irons at Gyula Fehérvár, and the present tranquillity and imagined security suit their plans nicely. The band now pretends to have vanished, but just you wait till the gold is sent under convoy from Gyula Fehérvár to Vienna—and you will see some fun."

"How do you know that?"

"I know it sir, because I know that this man, this brazen faced, iron-fisted man is not such a chicken-hearted creature as to allow a half-million or so to be snatched from him without stirring every nerve and muscle to try and win it back again. For I know that hitherto he has always triumphed over the power of the law and has always escaped from the most dangerous ambushes."

"Well, all I can say is that I do not understand what you have to do with this worthy man."

* * * * * * *

The falsely coined gold pieces deposited at Gyula Fehérvár, had, after the trial was over, to be sent to Hungary to be recoined. The precious consignment filled two post-wagons and was of the estimated value of a million and a half. Four and twenty Uhlans were told off to escort it. This was a more than sufficient protection for the most costly treasure at ordinary times. Moreover, in Hungary, cavalry has always inspired the mob with terror. During the disturbances at the time of the cholera outbreak, two squadrons of Hussars were easily able to quell the whole riot. It was impossible to calculate how many robbers and peasants the four and twenty Uhlans were capable of coping with. So, at least, the county magistrates believed.

The soldiers were commanded by a lieutenant, the post-wagons were under the charge of an official accountant and a comptroller. All the postillions were provided with pistols and it was strictly ordered that the wagons were not to travel on the high-road after six o'clock. There was no lack of precaution, anyhow!

Now when the post wagons had reached the celebrated Bridge of Piski,* lo, there and then, face to face, four and twenty horsemen came, riding towards them from the opposite side of the bridge and the five and twentieth was Fatia Negra.

All the four and twenty had black crape wound round their faces, their clothes had the lining turned outwards and they were well provided with swords, csákánys† and muskets. Fatia Negra himself rode a vigorous black stallion and held in his hand a broad, naked sword.

The horse of the Uhlan lieutenant took fright at the sight of the black faces and began to rear, it was as much as his rider could do to prevent him from springing over the parapet of the bridge.

Fatia Negra and his band halted in the centre of the bridge and did not budge from the spot.

The lieutenant was a brave soldier, who never lost his presence of mind; he tightened the reins of his plunging horse and turning towards Black-Mask, exclaimed: "Who are you, what do you want, and why do you block up the bridge?"

A deep, thundrous manly voice replied to him from afar: "I am Fatia Negra. The treasure which you have with you is mine,—it has been stolen from me. I now want to have it back

---

* It was here that a small band of Hungarians under Czsez and Kureny held a whole Austrian army at bay on Feb. 9, 1849.—*Tr.*
† Hooked axes.

again. I have brought hither a man to every man of yours, we are as strong as you. I meet you openly in the light of day. Give me back my gold or you shall have a taste of my iron."

The lieutenant, who was one of the best swordsmen and one of the bravest heroes in the regiment, did not think twice about accepting the challenge, but put spurs to his steed and fell upon the adventurer who awaited him in the middle of the bridge.

He encountered a terrible antagonist. Fatia Negra warded every blow and countered instantly; the young officer was thrown into confusion by the superior dexterity of his opponent, and it was only a soldier's sense of honour that induced him to continue an attack which was bound to end fatally for himself: practised fencers always know at once whether they can vanquish their antagonist or not. At the same time it was really surprising that Fatia Negra did not immediately take advantage of his strength and skill. He seemed to be sparing his enemy, nay, he even retreated before him step by step.

Meanwhile the *melée* on the bridge had become general. The lancers hastened to the assistance of their leader, the black masks slashed away at them with their csákánys, and soon there were very few among the combatants who had not received a lance thrust or a csákány blow. The adventurers were forced by the lancers to the opposite end of the bridge, when the miller, who lived in the mill beside the bridge, thrust his head out of the window and shouted: "Take care, soldiers! the beams of the bridge have been sawn through!"

Was this the fact? Was it the plan of the adventurers to entice the horses on to the bridge in order that it might break down beneath their weight?—or was the miller also an accomplice and only shouted this because the soldiers were gaining the upperhand? In either case the warning cry had a magical effect upon the pursuers, for they immediately turned back in alarm and strove to reach their own end of the bridge again.

And now they perceived what a two fold trap the cunning adventurers had set for them, for whilst the lancers had been fighting with the mounted robbers, a large band of footpads armed with firearms had surrounded the post wagons in their rear, disarmed the postillions and were now engaged in attempting to overturn the wagons into the ditch by the roadside.

The lancers dashed towards the wagons and freed them in a moment from the hands of the mob which, on their appearance, dispersed among the brushwood by the roadside from whence they began firing.

Not far from the bridge was a *csárdá,* and there the cavalry and the post-wagons sought a refuge. And indeed they needed it. The number of the footpads armed with guns was about a couple of hundred; they enfiladed the whole road and, more than that, it was easy to perceive that some of the tall roadside poplars had been sawn through beforehand so that they might be made to fall down and thus make it impossible for the post wagons across the road behind the backs of the soldiers, to force their way through.

The soldiers had, indeed, no reason to fear that the rabble, nine-tenths of which had no professional knowledge of the art of war, would boldly storm the *csárdá,* for in such a case the soldiers would know how to defend themselves vigourously, well provided as they were with carbines; but they were well aware of one thing, to wit, that if they allowed themselves to be surprised after nightfall they were lost, for the robbers could then set fire to the house over their heads and burn them alive.

For their lives they cared nothing; it is a soldier's business to die; but how to save the enormous sum of money intrusted to them—that was the problem. Four and twenty horsemen in a solid mass might, with a desperate effort, cut their way through a mob, despite every obstacle, but to take the heavy wagons along with them was impossible, for the road in front was barred by the mob; the bridge and the road behind by the felled poplars.

Fortunately, the officer in command had read the history of Napoleon's Russian campaign and he recollected how the guard on one occasion had saved the military chest from the Cossacks when the wagon, from want of horses, had to be left behind. He now applied his knowledge practically.

The ducats were taken out of the post-wagons and distributed among the soldiers; knapsacks, cartridge-boxes, belts and shakos were filled with the treasure; not a cent was left in the wagons, yet they nailed down the chests inside them carefully that it might take all the longer to break them open. Then they mounted the postilions and the civilians on the spare horses, hastily threw open the gates and the whole band rushed into the courtyard.

A sharp volley poured in upon them from every side; some of them were wounded, but none mortally, for their assailants either fired from afar or aimed badly. And this was well, for every dead man among them would have been worth 100,000 guldens.

Fatia Negra and his horsemen stood close at hand with their loaded muskets pointed in their hands, but they did not fire.

"Let the lancers run if they like!" cried Fatia Negra. "Give all your attention to the wagons!"

The cavalry soon escaped from the mob of sharpshooters, leaped over the barriers and began galloping rapidly back to Széb safe and sound. And they had need to haste, for it was easy to foresee that as soon as the cry of victory behind their backs had changed into a cry of fury, it would be a sign that Fatia Negra's band was rushing after them.

And, indeed, scarce a quarter of an hour had elapsed, when they could perceive clouds of dust whirling up behind them which proved that the audacious adventurers, after discovering the fraud, were actually in pursuit.

What unheard of audacity! In broad daylight, on the King's highway, within the borders of a highly civilized, well-organized state, a troop of adventurers dares to attack an equal number of trained soldiers. Gold must have turned the heads of the men who had the audacity to do such a thing! Yet they did it.

The soldiers saw the cloud of dust behind their backs gradually draw nearer, the neutral ground between gradually diminished, the fellows were capitally mounted, there could be no doubt of that.

The lieutenant ordered his men to halt and face the foolhardy bandits. He arranged them two deep and spread them out so that they extended right across the road. He himself stood in the centre a little in advance of the rest; the civilians were in the rear.

Presently single shapes were discernible through the approaching cloud of dust. The robbers were galloping along in no regular order with intervals of from ten to twenty yards between each one of them.

More than a thousand yards in front of his comrades galloped Fatia Negra. His splendid English thoroughbred, as if it would outstrip the blast which whirled the dust aloft, flew along with him and seemed to share the blind fury of his master who waved his flashing sword above his horse's head and bellowed at his opponents from afar like a wild beast.

"We'll seize the fellow before his companions come up," said the lieutenant to his men. "Cut him down from his horse and capture him alive."

"Hurrah!" roared the lonely horseman, now only a yard off. "Hurrah!"—the next moment he was in the midst of them.

And now began a contest which, had it been recorded in the chronicles of the Crusades, would have been regarded as an act of heroism that only awaited immortality from a poet great enough to sing it. Fatia Negra, alone and surrounded, fought single-handed in the midst of the hostile band. His light sword flashing in his hand like lightning, never stayed to parry but attacked incessantly. Handless swords and headless shakos flew around him in the air and withersoever his horse turned its head, an empty space gaped before him, every antagonist retreating before him. So close was the *melée* that the soldiers stood in each other's way and could not use their firearms for fear of shooting their comrades. The lieutenant was the only man who did not avoid him. Like a true soldier who considers wounds an honour, he did not trouble himself to recollect that his adversary was superior to him both in strength and skill, but strove incessantly to urge his horse towards him. Twice he struck the fellow but he did not seem to feel the blow. Once he dealt him a skilful thrust in the side, but the sword bent nearly double without entering his body. "Ha, ha, ha!" laughed Fatia Negra—he must have put on a coat of mail beneath his jacket—and the same instant he countered so savagely that if the lieutenant had not dodged his head, he must have lost it. As it was the sword pierced through his shako and out poured the gold pieces by thousands on to the highroad.

At the sight of the shower of gold pieces, Fatia Negra roared like a demon. What he had done hitherto was a mere joke—now the battle began in grim earnest.

"Down with your heads, down with your headpieces!" he thundered, and with the fury of a lion he flung himself on his opponents, everyone of whom wore on his head the dangerous magnet which irresistibly attracted his flashing sword.

He himself was invulnerable. Neither sword nor lance could penetrate his shirt of mail. And meanwhile his companions were rapidly galloping up. Now another shako flew into the air and the horse's hoofs trampled the falling ducats in the mud.

"Shoot down his horse!" cried the voice of the post-office functionary from the rear, and the same instant three pistol shots resounded. At the third, which struck him full in the chest, the animal reared high in the air. Fatia Negra, perceiving the danger, and before the horse had time to fall and crush him, leaped from the saddle on to the ground.

And now he attacked the enemy on foot. He was blind now. He saw nothing before him but blood and ducats—he was drunk with both.

All at once he observed that he was alone, and, fighting the air—he no longer felt the contact of swords, or skulls or human bodies. After the officer had been wounded, the post-office functionary took the command and concluded it advisable not to await the arrival of the whole robber band. It was his duty to save the money. He ordered the soldiers to turn back and make the best of their way to Szászvár, the money that had been already spilt was given up for lost. It was of no use for mere men to attempt to grapple with such a devil incarnate as Fatia Negra.

"After them, after them!—Give me a horse!" roared Fatia Negra to his comrades as they came galloping up, whereupon they all leaped from their nags, not so much indeed for the sake of giving him a mount as for the sake of grabbing the scattered heaps of ducats.

"Let that alone; it won't run away" cried the adventurer. "The bulk of it is galloping in front of us—follow me!"

And at that, without waiting their decision, he seized one of the horses, swung himself into the saddle and dashed after the lancers. Nobody followed him. The robbers were wise enough to perceive that if they left lying here these thousands of ducats, actually won, in order to run after ten times as many which they had still to catch, (not to mention the broken heads which they were sure to get into the bargain), the loafing members of the confraternity who were following behind them on foot, would pocket the booty nicely at their ease, so they stayed where they were, with the comfortable persuasion that Fatia Negra would be sure to turn back when he perceived he was alone.

He, however, never gave them a thought, but putting spurs to his horse, pursued the soldiers. In vain. He had no longer a blood horse beneath him and was unable to overtake the bearers of the lost treasure. Nor did they halt again to give him anything to do. Looking back from time to time, they saw how a single horseman was galloping after them, with his sword blade firmly gripped between his teeth, and a shuddering recollection of the old nursery tales of nether-world monsters came over them.

The solitary horseman pursued them right up to the toll-house of Szászvár, and even when he gave up the pursuit the toll-man saw him for a long time trotting round about the outskirts of the town shaking his fist and shouting imprecations. Once or twice he drew near enough to fire his pistols through the doors and windows of the toll-house, and so great was the spell of terror surrounding the person of the terrible adventurer that nobody ventured outside the city wall to try and capture him; nay, the burgesses even remained under arms in the streets all night guarding the principal entrances for fear lest Fatia Negra and his band might take it into their heads to formally besiege the place, and, had it only depended upon his will to do so, he would assuredly have made the attempt.

But it never came to that. On returning to the place of combat Fatia Negra found his horsemen still searching in the mud and darkness for the lost ducats, and made an attempt to reorganize his band, which did, indeed, do a little maurauding on its own account; but when the news reached him, through one of his paid spies, that four hundred infantry with a cannon had reached Szászvár from Szeb—the very word "a connon" had such an effect upon the robbers that they scattered in every direction as if a tempest had dispersed them. Next morning there was not a trace of them anywhere.

CHAPTER XXI

THE HUNTED BEAST

SUCH a piece of audacity could not be overlooked.

That a robber horseman should in the middle of the nineteenth century and within the confines of a civilized state take it into his head to attack, in broad daylight, post wagons defended by a strong escort of regular soldiers—was a thing unheard of.

The news spread like lightning through the six confederated counties and everyone seized his sword and musket. So old Gerzson Satrakovics whom everybody had laughed at, was right after all. It was universally agreed that a stop must be put to this sort of thing once for all. There was no waiting now for the meetings of Quarter Sessions. The lord-lieutenants of the counties proclaimed the *statarium*,* called out the *banderia*† and gathered together the county *pandurs*‡ and the militia, in order by their combined efforts, to extirpate the evil without having recourse to the assistance of the military—a measure always repugnant to the freedom-loving Magyars.

---
* A decree authorizing summary procedure.
† Mounted gentry.
‡ Police.

Squire Gzerson was elected the leader of this vast hunt, whose area extended over hundreds of square miles, by all the six counties concerned—it was generally felt that this was but due to him for the neglect of his warnings—and Mr. Gerzson proved on this occasion that if he was not a great strategist, at any rate he was a great beater up of game. His plan was to occupy all the mountain roads and passes leading out of the six counties with armed bands of militia, while at the same time he himself advanced slowly along the highroads with his gentlemen-volunteers joining hands together from place to place. Between various groups of the volunteers were regular lines of *pandurs* who had to thoroughly scour all the forests they came to. The encircling network of this gigantic army of beaters grew narrower and narrower day by day and was to converge towards a fixed point which Squire Gerzson said he would more definitely indicate later on.

Moreover there was a flying column admitted to the full confidence of its leader, whose duty it was to appear suddenly and unexpectedly in all parts of the closely environed region, in order to head off anything like a definite plan of defence on the part of the adventurers and track them down more easily. The leadership of this special corps was entrusted to young Szilard Vamhidy, upon whose ingenuity, determination and ability Squire Gerzson professed to place the utmost reliance.

As soon as he had received this important charge, Szilard took horse and set off at the head of his four and twenty *pandurs*. First of all he went in the direction of the Alps of Bihár and along a narrow mountain path and through a melancholy, uncanny, region with not a living plant by the wayside and not a morsel of moss on the naked rock. No sound is to be heard there but the eternal sighing of the wind, and in the dizzy depths below the traveller sees nothing but dense, dreary forests crowding one upon another with the Alpine eagles circling and screaming above them.

It was just the place for a hunted band of robbers to turn upon their pursuers for a last life and death struggle,—here where even the bodies of the slain would never be found. For not once in two years does a wanderer chance to come this way, and long before that time the wolves and the vultures will have dispersed the bones of the fallen.

Yet this time the robber bands did not fall in with their pursuers, a sufficient proof that Szilard's plan was skilfully laid and unanticipated. For had Fatia Negra had any idea of his design, it is absolutely inconceivable that he would not have laid in wait for him on this spectre-haunted path, where ten resolute men could have held a whole army at bay.

For hours Szilard's long troop of horsemen pursued their way along without meeting a soul. Late in the afternoon they came upon the first shepherd's hut. The herdsman himself was out in the forest with his flocks; there was nobody at home but a lame dog which barked at them.

In the evening they met a mounted countryman carrying maize to be ground at the mill, him they took along with them as guide.

After that they travelled all night long, passing through Skeritora and Nyigsa, till they came to the cataract of Vidra, which they reached at dawn of day.

The houses of these Alpine villages are so far apart that next neighbours cannot even see each other's dwellings, as there is at least half a league between them. This circumstance and the night-season favoured Szilard's plans. They could surround each house, one by one, without the inhabitants of the other houses being aware of what had happened in the first ones.—A fruitless labour for they found nothing of a suspicious nature.

Tired out, the band, early in the morning, reached the house beneath the waterfall; here they felt the need of halting. Szilard put some questions to the guide and then dismissed him, commanding him to return to Skeritora.

When the guide had mounted, the *pandur* sergeant observed to Szilard: "I fancy, your honour, that that rascal does not mean to return to Skeritora, but as soon as he is out of sight will turn back and give the alarm beforehand in all the districts on our line of march."

"I fancy so too."

THE HUNTED BEAST 379

"But then every suspected person will get wind of the whole affair and have time to bolt."

"That is just what I want. The trouble is at present that they lie so still."

And with that he ordered half of his *pandurs* to lie down and sleep and the other half to remain awake and so relieve each other every three hours. So the *pandurs* rested till midday and then the sergeant began to urge Szilard to set off again or else they would arrive too late.

"It is too early yet," replied Szilard, and he spent a good half of the afternoon there doing nothing. Only then did he take horse again, complaining to everyone how much yesterday's ride had taken it out of him, and asking everybody he met on the road, coming or going, where the next village lay?—how to get to it?—and in what direction the highroad lay?

The old *pandurs* naturally began murmuring among themselves. "Oh!" said they, "if he keeps on blurting out his whole line of route like this, we shall only have the empty nests of the robbers to thresh out for our trouble."

"And this chap thinks, forsooth, that he will capture Fatia Negra!" growled the veteran sergeant.

But no sooner did they get beyond the fenced fields than Szilard suddenly turned his horse's head and leading the way to the other side of the mountain-stream, cut his way through the forest, ordering his comrades to hurry after him as speedily as possible. What he was aiming at, nobody had the least idea. If he meant to lose his way in the forest he was setting about the best way to do it.

Suddenly he ordered his followers to dismount and lead their horses by their bridles up to the top of the mountain. The old sergeant now guessed what he was after, but did not approve of it.

"There is no path for a horse up this mountain," said he.

"Silence, sir! I know what I am about. Follow me!"

And so, for a good half hour, cursing their leader bitterly beneath their breaths, they painfully struggled after him up the dangerous path and then, suddenly, a marvellous sight met their gaze. An immense cavern gaped open before them through which, as through a tunnel, they could reach the valley on the other side. This was the so-called "Roman Gate." Many believe that the Romans dug this passage through the mountain, but this marvellous piece of workmanship has been carried out on too vast a scale for anybody else but Nature to be its architect; it is possible, however, that the Romans may have used this passage for their campaigns.

And now the *pandurs* understood the plan of their young leader and were ready to follow him blindly through fire and water.

In another half hour they had passed through the "Roman Gate" and reached the valley beyond, and by next morning Vamhidy had lit down like a thunderbolt from the sky where nobody expected him.

By the evening he had run down eight persons who were under very strong suspicion. After dusk the same day he sent the following letter to Gerzson by one of his men: "I feel certain I hold the thread of the whole conspiracy in my hands. We are on their track."

At nightfall he encamped in a lonely mill, which he chose because, in case of necessity, it could easily be defended. He had reasons for thinking that he might be attacked in the night.

The mill was built over a rushing mountain-stream so that the stream shot through and under the building, over the wheels. In front, three sluices confined within the basin the collected flood of water which was here very deep. A broad, thick board, laid across three stout piles, formed the bridge which connected the foot-path sloping down from the forest, with the foot-path on the opposite side.

Towards evening his pickets came and told Vamhidy that a blind beggar wanted to speak to him and in secret, so that nobody could hear.

Szilard ordered the blind man to be led in. He seemed to be a muscular, athletic fellow with broad shoulders and a huge body—what a pity he was blind.

"Domnule, are we quite alone?" inquired the blind man when he stood before Vamhidy.

"We are quite by ourselves; what is it you want, my good fellow?"

"Thank you, sir, for calling me a good fellow, for I *was* good for something once upon a time, and will be so again. I am the famous Juon Tare whose eyes were burnt out in the Lucsia Cavern when they wanted to catch Fatia Negra, and the monster set the whole cavern on fire. I want the head of Fatia Negra. I am after that head now and when I get it all my woe will cease. Do you want that head Domnule?—I can tell you where it is."

"Well?"

"Have you pluck enough not to be afraid of him, Domnule?"

"I am afraid of nothing."

"And yet many brave men fall back at the sight of that black face, which never changes, which is just like steel and which they fancy neither sword nor bullet can hurt; but my nails have torn his body and I have seen his blood flow."

"Say where he is!"

"Close at hand."

"In which direction?"

"Ah! Domnule!" sighed Juon Tare, "how can I answer that, I who can see neither heaven nor earth?"

"Then how do you know that he is hard by?"

"Ah, Domnule, I can recognize him by his voice, and if I do not hear him speak, I can recognize the sound of his footsteps when I hear him draw nigh. Nobody else has his trick of walking. Sometimes he goes as softly as a spectre so that only the ears of a blind man can detect his footfall and at other times he tramps as if the whole earth beneath him were hollow and it resounds at every step. Oh, I have often heard him approaching when he was still far, far away."

"But do you know anything certain about him?"

"I will tell you everything, Domnule, beginning at the beginning. You see that I am blind, a blind beggar, for begging is my trade. So long as my wife was alive, I had no need to turn beggar, for she worked for me and kept me. But she died. After that I would gladly have died of hunger, but she left me a little son, a child but two years old and I go a begging for him. Above the brook here on the King's highway is a stone bridge built by the county. Early in the morning my little son is wont to lead me hither and then returns to the village, little mite as he is the wife of the scrivener looks after him, and in the evening he comes and fetches me home again. Whatever is given me by charitable wayfarers I share with my poor hostess, who is poorer than any beggar. Yesterday something happened. It was this. I was sitting outside there at the end of the bridge and as I had not heard a human voice about me for a long time and it was extremely hot, slumber weighed heavily upon me. I struggled hard against it but it was too much for me. I was afraid that if I fell across the road a cart might go over me. So I laid myself down under the arch of the bridge. I knew the place well for I had often sheltered there from the storm. Suddenly I was awakened by those familiar footsteps. They passed across the bridge over my head. I will take my oath that it was he. He stood still in the middle of the bridge. Shortly afterwards I heard the sound of many more footsteps coming, some from the left and some from the right. Men were coming in all directions towards the bridge and there in the middle of it they stood; I counted them—there were four and twenty of them."

Szilard now began to listen attentively.

"Then he spoke. Oh, even if I had had the light of both my eyes, I could not have seen him so plainly before me as I saw him in my blindness when I heard him speak. It was indeed he, at the very first word I recognized him; but when I tell you what he said, then you also will recognize him Domnule. Those four and twenty men are a sworn confederacy. It was a secret plot they were hatching at that place, where nobody could surprise them, as it is girt about with woods on every side. He called his companions here to tell them of the measures that were being taken against them. He told them they had no need to fear all that the six counties were doing but that the little band which was zig-zagging through the whole district was greatly to be feared. It was the cause of all the mischief and must be put out of the way. But his comrades made no reply. They grumbled and muttered among themselves and at last they said that this would be a difficult thing to do. They all said they would not tackle the *pandurs* because they were better shots than any robber and were used to hunting and all its wiles. In vain were all the assurances of Fatia Negra; they said they meant to hide away as best they could. 'Then hide and be d—d to you,' said their leader, 'I will tackle them single-handed. I'll seek them out and show you that they too are but mortal men.' Those were his last words to them; they scattered again, to the right and left, and I heard their departing footsteps over my head. But believe me, sir, Fatia Negra will try to do what he said."

"What! come and attack us?—alone, against so many?"

"You do not believe what I say, sir, but so it will be."

"Nay, my good fellow, but are you quite certain you did not dream it all?"

"Domnule, in the first moment of my amazement that is what I fancied myself. How can a blind man know whether he is awake or dreaming. . I therefore drew forth my pocket-knife and with the point of it I cut a cross in my left arm. Look, sir, there it is!"

Juon tucked up the wide shirt sleeve from his herculean arm and Szilard was astonished to see the half healed and cross-like scar—it had been a deep gash.

"So now, sir," pursued Juon, "you can see that I am not dreaming. Watch well, for Fatia Negra will come. Not to-night for he awaits you on the road by which you came. But to-morrow he will know that you have dodged him by going through the 'Roman Gate' and to-morrow night you can safely reckon upon him."

Szilard charged Juon not to say a word to anybody about what he had told him and promised him a reward if what he had said really came to pass.

That night nothing happened, and till the afternoon of the next day he lingered idly at the mill. Towards midday they heard in the forest a loud barking of dogs; the miller said it was no doubt the lord of the manor hunting bears.

"He chooses a very inopportune time," growled Vamhidy, "he will scare *my* game away."

The hunters were not long in issuing from the forest, they seemed to have lost the track of the bear.

Vamhidy sent word to the gentlemen that he would be much obliged to them if they would postpone their amusement to some more convenient season as business of a graver sort was going on here. Word was at once brought back that the company was quite ready to do as he said. The dogs were quickly leashed again, the beaters recalled by signals and the whole hunt came straight towards the mill. A few moments later Vamhidy recognized in the leader of the hunt—Leonard Hátszegi.

It was an unwelcome surprise on both sides, but Hátszegi was the first to recover himself, and he greeted him with as radiant a countenance as if he had never had any cause of quarrel with him.

"We both of us seem to be on a hunting expedition your honour!" said he.

"Mine is an official pursuit."

"And mine pure pastime. Had I known you would have taken this road, I should certainly not have engaged in such a mal-apropos diversion. But it is over now, we are all going back. My bear may run—how about yours?"

"No sign of him yet."

"Well, I could regale you with no end of interesting anecdotes concerning the hunted adventurer, for I have had more than one famous *rencontre* with him myself. If it were only worth your while to pay us a visit at Hidvár I could promise you the heartiest reception—not only on my own part but also on the part of my wife."

"I am much obliged to your lordship," replied Vamhidy coolly, "but I am bound by instructions from which I cannot depart. It is not pleasure that brings me hither. Besides I have got a sure clue at last which I must follow up and I know not whither it may lead me."

"Bravo! So you are on his track at last, eh!

Take care my friend it is not a false clue. These rascals are very crafty."

"It is a real clue that I have discovered. You must know that before the confiscated gold captured in the Lucsia Cavern was sent to Vienna, every coin of it was marked with a little cross, a very simple official precaution, but it has proved very useful to us. Now I have come upon these marked ducats among the people here. They themselves, I believe, are innocent and can give the name of the persons from whom they received them; and so, by tracing the various intermediaries, we shall come at last, upon the original dispensers of these ducats. I can imagine how Fatia Negra will laugh when he hears that the soldiers of six counties are hunting for him in the depths of the forests and tapping every rotten tree-stump in search of him while he is sitting comfortably in some large theatre and eyeing the ballet-dancers through his opera glass; but he will be very much surprised when, one fine day, without any preliminary siege-operations we shall tap at his own door and enquire: 'Is Fatia Negra at home?'"

Hátszegi laughed heartily.

"Not a bad idea, upon my honour! I myself am inclined to think that the worthy highwayman will be sooner found in a coffee house than in a forest. I only regret that I did not mark my own coins so that I might recognize them again."

And so laughing and whistling, he returned to

his party which appeared to consist of mere dependents and gave them his orders.

"Unpack the horses and get lunch ready," said he, "we will not go any further."

Then he turned again to Vamhidy.

"Since we are obliged to capitulate to superior force, would you be so good as to pick out with me a nice, round, shadowy spot in the forest where we may encamp and share with each other our provisions which have thus become the spoils of war?"

"Thank you, my lord," replied Vamhidy coldly, "but I have already had my lunch."

His lunch, by the way, had consisted of a maize cake baked in the ashes.

"Then won't you allow your men to drink my health in a glass of wine, since they are actually on my domains?"

"My *pandurs* are not allowed to drink; they have to remain sober. They must not leave the mill without my leave and your lordship must not camp out here although the mill is your property. For just now I am 'verbiro,'* here with the right to open and close every door as I may think fit."

"Then I shall know how to respect your authority. All the same, I do not withdraw my offer. My castle and every house and shanty on my estate is at your disposal and if you should not find me at home at Hidvár, as I have to be off early to-

* A magistrate with the power of life and death in his hands.

morrow morning to Szeb, my wife will be delighted to see you."

And with that he threw his gun across his shoulder and tripped away with well bred nonchalance across the field, and, calling to his party to follow him, disappeared in the depths of the forest from which he had just emerged.

* * * * * * *

And now it was evening and the heavens were full of stars and Szilard began to gaze at the stars and as he did so he forgot all about the official burdens that weighed so heavily upon his shoulders, all about Fatia Negra and the robbers. He fancied that his eyes encountered among the stars the eyes of "another" whom slumber and happiness had deserted just as they had deserted him.

How close to each other chance had brought them once more! He had only to accept her husband's invitation in order to meet her face to face. What would they not have to say to one another?

The night was quite still, the whole region was dumb save for the gurgling of the water rushing through the sluices. The *pandurs* were snoring in the living room, for they were allowed to sleep till two o'clock. Only Vamhidy kept watch with a single *pandur* who was guarding the prisoners in the cellar.

"The Lord God bless thee!" a hushed voice suddenly resounded from among the brown bushes and Szilard distinguished by the light of the rising moon a tall dark shape approaching the mill path. It was blind Juon.

"How did you know anyone was here?" enquired Szilard suspiciously.

"I heard you sigh, sir, once or twice and I knew you were awake for I warned you beforehand to watch—to-night he will be upon you."

"Who?"

"Who? Why Fatia Negra."

"So you think he will be bold enough?"

"I know that he is already on the way."

"And where were you just now?"

"I was working in the mill-ditch."

"At night! What were you doing there?"

"I have removed the supporting beam underneath the bridge leading across the reservoir! It was a hard bit of work but I had the strength to do it."

"Why did you do that?"

"Because he will come from the opposite side and immediately he steps on the middle of the bridge the plank will give way beneath him and he will fall into the water like a mouse in a trap."

"What is the good of that, he will only swim out again."

"Yes, but his pistols will then be full of water and he will be unable to use them against you."

Szilard began to perceive that he had a most determined ally with all sorts of ideas in his head that had never occurred to himself.

"But surely, my poor, fellow, you do not imagine that anybody will be mad enough to face so many armed men alone."

"I don't know, sir, but I also do not know whether you yourself may not be alone among so many armed men, for I hear snoring among the very guard you told off to watch the cellar."

Szilard was startled. He immediately hastened to the place indicated and there, sure enough, he saw the sentry stretched at full length across the cellar door. He angrily hastened to arouse him and seized the sleeper by the arm; but all his efforts were powerless to awake the fellow,—he might just as well have been dead.

"Try to wake the others, sir," said Juon.

The pandurs lay in long rows stretched out upon the straw in the meal magazine.

Szilard spoke to them, first gently, then loudly, and at last angrily, calling them by name, one after the other; but not one of them awoke. He tore the sleepers away from their places, but they were not aware of it; as soon as he let them go they rolled back again into their former positions.

"What has happened?" cried the confounded Szilard.

"There must be a traitor among them, sir, a hireling of Fatia Negra; he has his hirelings everywhere, in forests, in palaces, in dungeons, in barracks, everywhere. And this traitor has mingled thorn-apple juice in the drink of his comrades and they will now sleep on for a night and a day. The traitor himself is pretending to sleep along with his fellows but he is only awaiting the arrival of Fatia Negra and then up he will get and release the captives. It was an artful dodge, your honour!"

Szilard felt a tremor running through all his limbs.

"You see, sir, you are here alone, but Fatia Negra is never alone. But so far no great harm has been done. We will make him to be alone also. We cannot find out just now which of the four and twenty is a traitor. But we will bind the whole four and twenty hand and foot, and then the traitor also will be helpless."

Szilard began to perceive that this blind man was right in everything. His words must be listened to, for the danger was close at hand, there was no time for hesitation. So he quickly routed up all the halters in the mill and they set to work.

The blind giant laid the pandurs one by one across his knee and placing their hands behind their backs crosswise held them towards Szilard, who bound them fast. Three and twenty of them felt nothing of all this and the four and twentieth who did feel it thought it just as well to go on feigning slumber, for had it been discovered that he was awake one grip of those enormous fists would have made of him a sleeper indeed—for ever more.

"Is your sword sharp, sir?" enquired the blind man when this piece of work was done.

"Yes, and I have pistols likewise."

"Test them, sir, for I suspect they have been tampered with."

"What?"

"If ever, sir, you have pursued some wild beast, a bear or a buffalo, for instance, you know the rule surely: never rely upon any weapon which has not been freshly loaded by your own hand. Let us take the loading out of your pistols. It won't do to fire them off for we are lying in wait for big game and at such times one must keep very quiet."

Szilard hearkened to the warning and drew the loading out of both his well charged pistols. It is usual when the powder is taken out to blow down the barrel and as he did so now he remarked that something was wrong. The ramrod encountered some soft substance which he drew forth. Juon smelt it and pronounced it to be the wax of wild bees.

"You see, sir, you will not be able to discharge this pistol, for the touch holes are so plugged up that it will take you some hours to thoroughly clean them."

"At any rate I have still the firearms of my pandurs."

"Let us examine them also, sir!"

They did so forthwith and found that they too had been utterly ruined. And all this must have been done while Szilard had been sitting outside and his men had been sleeping!

"Then your sword is sharp, sir, eh?" enquired

the blind man, "for I hear the footsteps of Fatia Negra."

The sensitive ears of the blind man "scented" so to speak the well known footfalls while they were still approaching on the distant forest paths.

The young man felt an involuntary shudder run through his body as the moment drew near when he would have to face the hunted foe. The magical mysteriousness which enveloped his pursuer; the marvellous audacity which ensured the success of all his projects; his gigantic bodily strength—all these things were sufficient to make any man's heart beat more quickly at the prospect of encountering Black-Mask in a life and death struggle at a lonely place.

But Szilard was resolved to see the business through. The strong will peculiar to men of his nature broke down his fear. He had no business to tremble, it was not permitted to him to fear. He who has a sword in his hand is never alone—a sword is also a man.

The blind man trembled in his stead. He feared for him. When Szilard returned with his naked sword, the blind man passed his finger along its edge from end to end to test its sharpness.

"A good sword, a very good sword, Domnule. Fear him not, but when he scrambles out of the water, rush upon him and strike at his neck. Do not aim at his body for this accursed one wears a coat of mail so that no weapon can pierce him. If he comes to close quarters, do not defend yourself but slash away at him, you may perhaps be wounded, but if you stand on the defensive, he will kill you. If he gets too much for you, call out and I will rush in and strangle him with my naked hands. Oh, what would I not give now for the sight of my two eyes."

And the blind man began to weep bitterly.

"That man killed my wife and blinded me and now when I hear him approach, when I hear him coming towards me all alone I cannot see him. I cannot rush in and close with him. Be valiant, Domnule, and God be with you. May the soul of my Mariora direct the edge of your sword and darken his eyes. Hearken!—is not that he approaching!"

And it was actually he. The tall elegant figure was descending the moonlight rocks with a light, elastic tread, dressed from head to foot in a black atlas mantle. Szilard saw him drawing nearer and nearer, step by step, to the mill behind a pillar of whose verandah he himself was concealed expectant.

At the very moment when he perceived this figure, his former terror gave way before a strange, resolute fury which now filled his heart, a feeling familiar only to those whose blood is set boiling whenever they are suddenly confronted by a pressing danger. He feared the man no longer, he burned to encounter him.

Blind Juon stood beside him and pressed his hand. They both of them began to listen intently, nature itself was as still as if the wind also would listen. Nothing was audible but the dull measured tramp of the approaching footsteps.

The black shape now footed the bridge; with a confident gait he approached the middle of it, another step and the bridge gave way beneath him and with an involuntary cry the man in black plunged into the water.

"Now, sir, rush in!" whispered Juon to Szilard. But the latter could not help thinking at that moment that it was an act of cowardice to attack a man when he could not defend himself, even though that man was a robber, so he allowed him to scramble out onto the other side.

The black mantle had fallen from the shoulders of Fatia Negra into the water and there he now stood before Szilard with his wet clothes clinging closely to his body like a statue of Antinous, a shape of athletic beauty.

In his girdle were a couple of pistols, in all probability rendered useless by the water and a long Arab yataghan almost as long as an ordinary sword but without the usual cruciform hilt.

Szilard barred the way.

For an instant Fatia Negra was taken aback by his antagonist's unexpected wariness and courage, but the next moment his drawn yataghan flashed in his hand and the second flash was the clash of the contending weapons.

And now happened what happens hundreds and thousands of times in actual life. At the very first onset Fatia Negra, the notorious, the practised, the invincible swordsman was disarmed by a young civilian who had never, perhaps, held a naked sword in his hand before and possessed no advantage over his opponent save the courage of an honest man as opposed to the effrontery of a malefactor—a marvel indeed!

Both of them had lunged at the same time, neither of them had parried, Szilard's sword cut through his adversary's wrist and at the same instant Fatia Negra's yataghan fell from his hand.

The wounded robber set up a howl like a wild beast and Juon, lurking beneath the verandah of the mill responded with another howl of joy that sounded like an echo. The blind man had recognised that Fatia Negra was in danger and at once rushed out upon him.

The disarmed adventurer lost his presence of mind along with his sword. His right hand suddenly sank helpless to his side and his stout heart was seized with a sort of paralysis. He perceived that this was the man sent by fate to announce to him that his last hour was at hand. He turned and fled toward the forest.

Szilard rushed after him.

Take care," screamed blind Juon. But none heeded him. Fatia Negra flew away before his enemy. At first he left him far behind, but gradually the continuous loss of blood began to weaken him and it also occurred to him that even if he succeeded in distancing his adversary, he would still leave a trail of blood behind him. To complete his confusion the moon made the whole region as light as day. He was forced to sit down on a tree stump to tie up his wounded hand; at least he would stop the flow of blood and make the trail more difficult to follow.

While with the help of his left hand and his teeth he was binding up his useless right hand, his pursuer overtook him.

"Fatia Negra—surrender!"

The only reply the adventurer gave was to try to fire his pistols and finding them only flash in the pan he hurled then one after the other at his enemy's head. Szilard then had practical experience of the rumor that Fatia Negra could throw very well even with his left hand,—had he not leaped aside at the nick of time the pistols would have dashed his brains out.

Then up Fatia Negra started to his feet again and fled away still further. The pursuer and the pursued now sped along with pretty equal energy, though the loss of blood continued to weaken the robber. Yet he made one desperate effort to scale the steep side of the mountain. An ordinary man could rarely breast such an ascent, yet he tried it. But he soon found that even thus he could not shake off his enemy. He remained indeed some hundreds of paces behind but he could not dodge out of his sight in the now open glade.

On the brow of the hill the adventurer stopped to pant and surveyed the undulating thickly wooded hills stretching away on every side of him. He drew a silver whistle from his bosom and gave with it three penetrating signals which re-echoed from among the distant mountains. But it was only an echo, only the note of the whistle that he heard, he waited in vain for anything else. All his accomplices had evidently hidden away.

And again the pursuer overtook him. He waited till he was only two paces off and then he seized a stone weighing half a hundred weight and hurled it at him—the tree trunk behind which Szilard had taken refuge bent beneath the blow. Then Fatia Negra fled down towards the valley.

It was a desperate way for him to take, for down hill his adversary could cover the ground as quickly as he could; the distance between them was never more than ten paces, the wound the robber had received began to enervate his whole body, and he was not long in finding out that the hurling of missiles is a very profitless mode of warfare when you have only one hand at your disposal.

Panting hard he fled on further seeking refuge. And now he took to zigzagging through the wood in the hope of dodging his pursuer if only for an instant as a flying fox is wont to do when he is already nearing his hole whose entrance he does not wish to betray to his pursuer.

A little further on a stout quickset hedge barred their way. Fatia Negra burst through it and Szilard followed in the gap that he had made.

THE HUNTED BEAST

Suddenly a hunting lodge came in view—at least the antlers on the top of the porch and above the windows suggested that that was what it was intended for.

One of the windows looking out upon the forest stood open. Fatia Negra suddenly stopped short, waited till his adversary was close up to him and then shaking his fist at him sprang through the open window.

Vamhidy did not hesitate a moment about following the adventurer into the house. He forced his way through the window and found himself in a dark corridor at the extreme end of which the footsteps of the hunted adventurer were still resounding. And after him he ran straightway.

CHAPTER XXII

THE SIGHT OF TERROR

"My dear Henrietta," Leonard had said to his wife the day before, as he shook the dust of the chase off his clothes, "very shortly some guests will arrive at Hidvár and possibly they may be numerous. May I ask you to make ready for their reception?"

Henrietta signified by a motion of her head that she understood.

"It is possible you may have to perform the duties of hostess without my assistance, for I have to be off at once to Szeb and don't expect to be back for a couple of days. It is possible that the gentlemen in question may arrive during my absence which I should very much regret. Nevertheless you may depend upon my hastening home as quickly as I can to meet them here."

All this did not seem to interest Henrietta very much. Leonard noticed it.

"Let the gentry, my dear, occupy the room overlooking the park, the servants had better have the six rooms generally given to hunting parties on the ground floor, with the four and twenty beds."

At these directions the lady looked at her lord with an expression of surprised inquiry.

"I see," resumed her husband, "you are asking yourself what sort of company that can be for whose master one room suffices while the servants require six. I will tell you. It is the armed corps from Arad which is charged with the capture of Fatia Negra and his associates. As they will pass by this way I don't see how they can avoid calling at Hidvár. In fact I have invited the magistrate who commands the corps to make Hidvár the centre of his operations and if he is a sensible man he will accept my invitation. The name of my guest I have not yet mentioned," continued Leonard with easy levity, "it is Szilard Vamhidy, a justice of the peace of the county of Arad—really a very nice young man."

Henrietta became as white as a statue.

"You will greatly oblige me, my dear Henrietta, if you will do your best to make our guest feel quite at home in our house. But you are a sensible woman, so I have no need to press the point. Let me kiss your hand—*au revoir!*"

Henrietta watched him go out, watched him get into his carriage and bowl off and then began to weep and hide her head among the cushions that nobody might hear her.

They are pursuing Fatia Negra! . . . Szilard Vamhidy is pursuing Fatia Negra!

He will come hither, he will enter this very castle. Leonard himself has invited him!

He will certainly come to see his former love once more. The thought was terrible!

But it must not, it should not happen.

Leonard himself had invited Vamhidy to his castle. This man relied too much on the terror of a poor timid woman, he built too much on that nimbus of terror which made him so horribly unassailable in her eyes. What! first to invite the former lover of his wife to be his guest and then show his indifference by choosing that very time to absent himself from the house for some days!

But on one thing she was resolved—Vamhidy should not find her at Hidvár. She would fly. She would leave her husband's house. Where should she go? Who would receive her? What would become of her? She did not know, she gave the matter no thought, but one thing was certain: Szilard and she might meet together in the grave but they should never encounter each other beneath the shadow of the halls of Hidvár.

There was nobody she could confide in. All the servants were her husband's paid spies and her own jailors. The priest had disappeared altogether from Hidvár. In her despair an old memory rose up before her. She called to mind that during the earlier days of her stay at Hidvár when she had explored the whole region under the delusion that she could make the wretched happy, she had often passed a little house which had always riveted her attention. It was a little hunting hut in the midst of the forest built entirely of wood and planed smoothly outside like a little polished cabinet. In front of it stood broad spreading fruit trees, crowded with flowers in spring, crowded with fruit in autumn, wild vines and moss grew all over its roofs.

In the midst of the listening woods this little house had such an inviting exterior that the very first time she saw it, Henrietta could not resist the temptation of entering it.

The door of the little house stood open before her, being only on the latch. She had stepped in: there was nobody inside. In the first room there was furniture of some hard wood; close to the wall stood a carved side-board with painted earthenware on it, on a table was a pitcher of a similar ware full of fresh pure water. The door of another room to the right was also open and in that room also she found nobody. There stood a bed with a bear skin for a coverlet, other bear skins spread on the floor served instead of carpets and on the walls were bright lynx, and wildcat skins.

From this room there was a door leading into a third room and here also she found nobody. The walls of this room were covered with weapons—guns, pistols and curiously shaped swords and daggers, in rows and crossed, hanging on nails and leaning against the walls. On the oaken table stood stuffed beasts and birds, under the table was a stuffed fox fastened to a chair; a pair of wild boars' heads with powerful tusks were over the door, but there was no sign of any living beast.

Henrietta fancied that the master of this little house must be away but not far off and she made up her mind to wait till he returned home. Yet one hour after another passed away and Henrietta was at last obliged to go on further lest she should have to pass the night there and, only when she was already some distance away, was she struck by the peculiar circumstance that all round the hut grass was growing thickly and that no path led up to it.

In a few weeks' time curiosity drew her again in the same direction. Alone, without any escort, she stood before the forest dwelling, fastened her horse to the fence and passed through the door.

Everything was just as she had seen it on the first occasion. In the first room on the table was the earthenware pitcher full of water; in the second room was the bed covered with a bear skin and in the third room were all the guns and other weapons just as she had seen them before.

Again she waited for a long time for some of the dwellers of this little house to draw near, and again she waited in vain; even by eventide not a human being had approached the hut.

These hut dwellers must be curious folks she thought, they leave everything unlocked, evil disposed people might steal everything.

On the way back she met some charcoal burners and asked them about the lonely little house in the midst of the forest. Three of the four pretended not to understand: they did not remember ever seeing such a house they said. The fourth, however, told the lady in reply that in that house dwelt "Dracu."*

This only made Henrietta more than ever curious. She asked the priest about it and even he was inclined to be evasive. He evidently either knew nothing about it or was casting about in his mind for some plausible explanation. At last he said that rumour had it that a huntsman's family had either been murdered or had committed suicide there, and, ever since, nobody dwelling in the district could be persuaded to cross its threshold, let alone steal anything out of it; they would not even take shelter there during a storm, for they believed that an evil spirit dwelt there.

Henrietta, however, did not believe in these invisible evil spirits. The evil spirits she was acquainted with all went about in dress clothes and surtouts. The atmosphere of mystery and enchantment which made the little house uninhabitable only stimulated her fancy. She determined to discover whether it was really uninhabited or not.

Accordingly, when she entered the house for the third time, she plucked a wild rose and threw one of its buds into the pitcher of water on the table, a second on the bear skin coverlet of the bed and a third, fourth and fifth she stuck into the barrels of the muskets hanging up in the armour room.

When now, she visited the lonely house for the fourth time, she looked for the rose buds and

---
* The Devil.

could not find one of them in the places where she had put them. Consequently there must needs be someone who slept in the bed, drank the fresh water from the pitcher and used the firearms.

Her thirst for knowledge now induced her to enquire of her husband concerning this little dwelling and he, then and there, elucidated the mystery.

It was quite true that a lonely inhabitant of this house had once been murdered there, that the common people believed it to be haunted, and that consequently not one of them would cross its threshold at any price either by day or by night. An old landed proprietor from the mining town of X., who owned a small strip of forest in those parts and was at the same time an enthusiastic huntsman, had taken advantage of this popular superstition to buy this little house, for a mere song. He used it as a hunting box. He could not afford to keep a huntsman of his own to look after it and knowing that if he locked it up, thieves would most probably break into it and steal everything, he left the doors wide open and everyone instantly avoided it as uncanny. The reason Henrietta never met him was that this old gentleman was a government official, who had to live most of his time in the town of Klausenburg, but whenever he was not hunting here he was out in the forests all night till dawn when he turned into the little house for a nap and was off again before the afternoon; and so Henrietta who regularly visited the hut in the afternoon, naturally never encountered him.

Leonard even named the old gentleman's name and then Henrietta remembered meeting him at the *soirées* at Klausenburg. Leonard, however, warned his wife never to mention the matter in the presence of the old gentleman in question, if she should ever meet him, for he had sundry relations with poachers and other people of that sort. The fact was, his own strip of forest was not very large and therefore he very frequently trespassed on Leonard's property in pursuit of game. The old gentleman was, therefore, very desirous to keep his passion for the chase a secret, especially as his relations with Leonard were none of the best.

After that Henrietta had visited the little forest house no more. This prosaic explanation had robbed it in her eyes of all its mysterious interest, nor did she think it becoming to enter a house whose owner was not on very good terms with her husband. Only now did the recollection of the little forest dwelling recur to her, and in the terror of her soul she began to regard the little moss-covered hut whose doors stood open, night and day, as a possible asylum. It was the only place where she could take refuge, the only place where she had no need to fear spies, where nobody would look for her, where she might remain in hiding and from whence she might either return home or wander further out into the world according as fate was kind or unkind to her.

At night there would be nobody in the little house, for the enthusiastic old hunter would be stalking the forest. It was also possible that his official duties might keep him away for days together. But even if she were to meet him, why should she be afraid of the eccentric old man? Would she not rather find in him a natural protector who would conduct her out of the mountains to Klausenburg or Banfi-Hunyad, from whence she would make her way to Pest and there seek a refuge in her aunt's house?

She did not think twice about it, but accepted the idea as a heaven-sent inspiration which it was her duty to follow. She put on a shawl as if she were only going to take a walk in the moonlight and descended into the park accompanied by the gardener's daughter whom she had bribed to help her to escape. The girl succeeded in hoodwinking the men servants by dressing herself up in a mantle of her mistress's, pretending she would have supper out in the park as the night was so fine and warm, so that by the time the fraud was discovered and the alarm given, Henrietta had had a start of several hours and although the men, fearful of the anger of their master when he should return and find his wife flown, searched in every direction with lighted torches they were unable to discover a trace of the missing lady.

Terror lends strength to the most feeble. Ordinarily Henrietta was so weak that it was as much as she could do to promenade through the park. But to-day after a two hours' run over stones and through briars and bushes, at midnight, she still did not feel weary. From the top of a hill she looked back. She could still see the tower of the castle of Hidvár in the valley, but it looked blue through the mist in the distance and then she hastened down into the valley whose steep overhanging sides hid her even from the moonlight.

The night was noiseless, the forest dark. Now and again a humming night beetle circled round and round her and obstinately pursued her as if he also was a spy sent after her. The poor thing's heart throbbed violently. What if she had lost her way? What if she fell into the hands of the robbers whom they were now actually pursuing through the woods? Yet still greater was her terror of Hidvár and a hundred times more homelike was the dreadful forest with its giant trees speaking in their sleep than the tapestried walls of the Castle of Hidvár.

Suddenly a glade opened up before her which seemed to greet her as an old acquaintance.

Yes, indeed, there were the wild roses which she had so often plucked to adorn her hat. The hunting-box could not be far off now. It conceals itself to the right of the rose bushes beneath a lofty birch.

A few moments later she found herself outside its door.

As she laid her hand on the latch, a thought of terror transfixed her. What if the door should be shut?

But she had only to press the latch in order to put all her fears to flight. The door this time also was not fastened.

Standing on the threshold she enquired with a trembling voice: "Is anybody in?"

No answer.

Then she closed the door behind her and opened the door of the second room. There also nobody responded to her enquiry. The third room was also open as usual, nay even one of its windows was opened towards the orchard. Moreover, everything was in its proper place just as she had always found it—the weapons, the bear skin coverlet and the water pitcher.

It occurred to Henrietta to close the door from the inside so that nobody might come upon her unawares while she slept. But then the thought also struck her that it was not right to lock the old gentleman out of his own house especially as he might turn up in the early morning tired out and half frozen. So she ultimately decided to stay up for him in order to tell him, as soon as he arrived, that she meant to obtain a separation from her husband, whose conduct she could no longer endure. Till then she would try hard not to go to sleep. But she was tired to death from her long run through the forest and was obliged at last to throw herself on the bear skin coverlet to rest; and gradually sleep overcame all her anguish, all her terror.

She might have slept for about a half an hour, a restless, phantom-haunted sleep at best, when she suddenly awoke.

It seemed to her as if she had heard a distant cry. Perhaps she had only imagined she had heard it in her slumbers, and perhaps what she had dreamt was so awful and what she fancied she had heard was so terrible, that it had awakened her.

She began to listen attentively. After midnight every light sound seems so loud.

She fancied in the great stillness that she could hear rapidly approaching footsteps.

Again a cry! like the cry of a hunted beast, like the cry of a wounded wolf!

She was not dreaming now, she could hear it plainly. She saw where she was. The moonlight was streaming through the window, she could see to the end of all three rooms.

Suddenly at the window overlooking the garden whence the moonbeams streamed in, a black shape appeared which obscured the moonlight for an instant.

This shape leaped through the window and, panting hard, rushed through the two rooms into the third where the arms stood.

Henrietta saw it fly past her bed, she heard its panting sobs and—recognized it.

It was Fatia Negra! this was Fatia Negra's house!

And this was not all.

Close upon the traces of Fatia Negra rushed another phantom with a drawn sword in its hand, but its face was towards her and she recognized in it—Szilard Vamhidy.

And yet she did not lose her consciousness at this double sight of terror, though it would have been much better for her if she had.

Fatia Negra plunged into the armoury and plucked down a pistol from the wall.

Szilard paused on the threshold.

"Halt!" cried Fatia Negra with a voice like a scream—"this is my house and your tomb."

Szilard did not condescend to reply but drew a step nearer.

"Sir, but one word more," said Fatia Negra in a fainter voice and so hoarsely as to be scarcely audible, "you have wounded me, you have run me down; but your life is now in my hands and I could kill you this instant if I had a mind to. Let us bargain a bit: I won't kill you if you will not pursue me any further. You return and say you could not catch me. I swear to you that to-morrow I will send you twenty thousand ducats."

With contemptuous coldness Szilard replied: "Surrender, I will not bargain."

"You won't bargain, you crushed worm you! The mouth of my pistol is on a level with your forehead. I have only to press my finger and your head would be shattered—and yet you dare to have it out with me? Do you want to save your head?"

"I mean to have yours," said Szilard and he drew a step nearer to the adventurer.

"My head, eh? Ha, ha, ha! You would have it would you, and have it here! Take it then!"

At that moment a piercing shriek startled the two deadly antagonists and in the adjoining room a white figure fell prone upon the floor.

The next moment there was a loud report and Fatia Negra fell back lifeless on the bear skin carpet.

At the very moment when he had laughed aloud and cried: "Take it then!" he had suddenly put the mouth of the pistol into his own mouth and fired it off. The heavy charge blew his head to bits, Szilard felt a warm red rain showering down upon him.

So Fatia Negra, after all, did not give up his head, the pistol shot had annihilated it.

And nobody ever knew who Fatia Negra really was.

CHAPTER XXIII

THE ACCOMMODATION

It was now the seventh time that Mr. John Lapussa had informed Mr. Sipos that he wanted to see him and for the seventh time word was sent back that the lawyer could not come. Why could he not come? They could not say. Finally a message was delivered to the effect that the lawyer could not come either that day, or the next, or indeed on any other day in the whole year. In a word Mr. Sipos declined to have anything more to do with the Lapussa family or its affairs. Their transactions were not at all to his taste.

So, as Mr. Sipos would not appear at the summons of Mr. John Lapussa, Mr. John Lapussa must needs call upon Mr. Sipos.

He was wearing mourning in his hat and tried hard to lend his face a funereal appearance also.

"Have you heard the news?" he asked.

Mr. Sipos had heard nothing.

"Don't you see the mourning in my hat? Alas! my poor niece, unhappy Henrietta!"

"Well, what has happened?"

"Hátszegi has been drowned in the Maros."

"Impossible, he was a first-rate swimmer."

"His horse ran away with him, he had lost all control over it. When he saw that the horse was determined to plunge into the river from the high bank, he tried to spring out of the saddle, but his spur unfortunately caught in the stirrups and the horse dragged him down with it into the water. There in the full stream, with his head downwards and his legs in the air, he vainly attempted to extricate himself. The frantic horse swam with him to the opposite shore, dragging the poor wretch after it, and before the opposite bank was reached, his head was so shattered that it was impossible to recognize his features. It is now a week since they buried him in the family vault at Hidvár. Poor Henrietta! So young to be left a widow! And to have lost so handsome, so beloved a husband through so sad a death! Really lamentable!"

"I wonder what the rascal is after now," thought Mr. Sipos.

"My heart really is breaking for her! If only there were not these unhappy money differences between us. I am not a tiger. My heart is not made of stone. Perhaps you don't believe me! Let me tell you that I have half resolved, despite the old gentleman's will, to transfer to my niece, Henrietta, the Kerekedar property."

"Because its expenses are greater than its revenue, I presume?"

"None of your poor witticisms, sir. I am ready to make any sacrifices to oblige my relatives. The world misjudges me. They call me greedy and avaricious; if only they could look into my heart!"

"What you have done hitherto, sir, does not testify to any great regard for your relatives. For instance, look at the case of my client, young Coloman—for you know that Vamhidy has instructed me to act for him. What intrigues, what tricks were employed to fasten upon him the suspicion of forgery! Nobody knows that better than you, sir. And let me tell you that although my young client is nothing but a strolling player, I shall spare no pains to thoroughly vindicate his good name and you, with all your wealth and property, will be unable to affect the issue one jot."

Mr. John pondered for a moment. "Look here," said he at last, "let us pitch the whole confounded suit into the fire. I have a compromise to propose. I candidly confess I am in a bit of a hole. That bill business is now before the courts and when it comes on for trial, it will cause a horrible scandal and people have condemned me beforehand. I only wish I had never mixed myself up in it."

"Suppose I help you out of the difficulty!"

"In that case you may dictate your own conditions and I will consent to them beforehand."

"There is only one way to save you. Henrietta must say that the bill is not forged, but is really signed by her and she must then pay and cancel it, then every foundation of a charge against you vanishes."

"A sublime idea," cried Mr. John springing

from his seat. "And now let me hear your conditions."

"My only condition is, complete satisfaction to be made to the children of your second sister."

"What! surrender a whole third of the property to them without any deduction?"

"We will accept nothing less."

"What must I do first then?"

"First you must pay the baroness forty thousand florins."

"Forty thousand florins! Why?"

"In order that she may meet the bill as soon as she has acknowledged her signature."

"Well, and what next?"

"You must sign deeds whereby you undertake to surrender to the children of your late sister the estates of Zôldhalom and Orökvar bequeathed to them by your father."

"Why, they are the best paying properties of all."

"Then pay them the value of the estates in cash."

"That would seriously inconvenience me."

"Then make over your houses in Vienna and Pest."

"I cannot find it in my heart to part with them."

"Then propose some other expedient."

"Very well, I will. Give me till to-morrow to think it over."

And with that Mr. John put on his hat and took his leave.

The following day the lawyer awaited him in vain; then he waited for him a whole fortnight, but Mr. John never came near him. Then he went to the courts to find out what was being done and there he learnt, to his astonishment, that the declaration of the Baroness Hátszegi acknowledging the genuineness of her signature to the bill had already arrived.

What had happened was this: As soon as Mr. John had got Sipos's opinion gratis, he quickly traveled post to Hidvár and had a chat with his niece over the business. The poor lady was so utterly crushed by her misfortunes that she could scarce fix her mind steadily on anything and was a mere tool in his hands. She accepted the properties offered to her by her uncle—what did it matter to her now how much or how little they brought in!—and gave an acknowledgment in writing that the signature to the bill was her own.

Mr. Sipos was therefore not very much surprised when one day he received a commission from the baroness's agent to pay over the forty thousand florins in question to a financial agent at Pest. So Mr. John made a rattling good profit out of the transaction and Henrietta in return for her generosity had to pay up in cash as Mr. Sipos had shrewdly anticipated she would have to do all along. But it was all one to Henrietta.

CHAPTER XXIV

CONCLUSION

MEANWHILE the long drawn out process between Mr. John and his sister Madame Lángai continued its course. There was no thought of a compromise between the parties. Madame Lángai expended so much of her private means in the action that nearly the whole of the property left her by her husband went in costs. She could now neither keep her coach nor live in a large house. She cooped herself up in a couple of small rooms, visited nobody and wore dresses that had been out of fashion for at least four years—and all to be able to carry on the action!

It was ten years before the suit came to an end.

Mr. John lost it and a fearful blow it was to him, for he had to pay out a million to his sister without any further delay. It is true he had as much again left for himself, but to be the possessor of only a single million is nevertheless a fearful thought to anyone who has hitherto been the possessor of two millions.

The poor plutocrat! How deeply it disturbed him to be obliged to pay his only sister her due portion! How the constant thought that he was now only half as rich as he had been before gnawed his life away! Poor, poor plutocrat!

Szilard had a brilliant career—a career extending far beyond the horizon of this simple story. He never married. Count Kengyelesy quizzed him often enough and was continually asking him why he did not try his luck again with his former ideal now that she had become a widow. All such questions, however, he used to evade in a corresponding tone of jocularity. But once when Kengyelesy inquired seriously why he never approached Baroness Hátszegi and at the same time reproached him for his want of feeling in so obstinately keeping out of the poor lady's way, Szilard replied: "I am not one of those who can be thrown away to-day and picked up again to-morrow."

After that the count never mentioned Henrietta's name in Szilard's presence again—and who knows whether there was not some impediment between these two from which no sacrament could absolve them. Who knows whether it might not after all have been as well for Vamhidy to avoid any meeting whatever with—the widow of the late Baron Hátszegi?

Yet it was she who was, in any case, the most wretched of them all. Although only six and twenty she could already be called an old woman. She was the victim of her shattered nerves night and day. The least noise made her tremble. The opening of a door was sufficient to make her start up. When she was only four and twenty she had already given up plucking out her grey hairs, there were so many of them. She found no relaxation in the society of her fellows and therefore avoided all social gatherings. Most of her time she spent at home, sitting all by herself in the remotest chamber of the house, half of whose wall was by this time overgrown by the asclepia which Szilard had given her ages ago—or so it seemed to her. This was the only one of her acquaintances which had not forsaken her, and luckily for her it was tenacious of life, for if that too had perished, with whom could poor Henrietta have held converse?

So there was at least one creature in the world to whom this possessor of millions could still confide her reminiscences and her sorrows. Poor rich lady, all the poorer because of her great wealth! Poor plutocrat!

THE END

www.ingramcontent.com/pod-product-compliance
Lightning Source LLC
Chambersburg PA
CBHW051740300426
44115CB00007B/639